Exploring Women's Past

EXPLORING WOMEN'S PAST

ESSAYS IN SOCIAL HISTORY

Patricia Crawford (Ed.)
Margaret Anderson
Raelene Davidson
Patricia Jalland
Margaret Ker

George Allen & Unwin
Sydney   London   Boston

First published 1983 by Sisters Publishing Ltd.
This edition published 1984

George Allen & Unwin Australia Pty Ltd
8 Napier Street, North Sydney NSW 2060 Australia

George Allen & Unwin (Publishers) Ltd
18 Park Lane, Hemel Hempstead Herts HP2 4TE England

Allen & Unwin Inc.
Fifty Cross Street, Winchester Mass 01890 USA

National Library of Australia
Cataloguing-in-Publication entry:
Exploring women's past.
   1984 ed.
   Previous ed.: Carlton South, Vic.: Sisters
   Publishing, 1983.
   Bibliography.
   Includes index.
   ISBN 0 86861 604 4.

   1. Feminism — History — Addresses, essays, lectures.
   2. Women — Social conditions — Addresses, essays,
   lectures. 3. Women's rights — Addresses, essays,
   lectures. I. Crawford, Patricia, 1941- .
305.4'2

Typeset by Fingers Typesetting, Box Hill
Printed and bound by Globe Press Pty Ltd, Melbourne

Contents

Acknowledgements

We are grateful to the following for financial assistance towards the publication of this book: the History Department of the University of Western Australia; the Minmara-gun-gun Committee; St. Catherine's College, University of Western Australia; the Australian Federation of University Women (W.A.) Inc.; Zonta Club of South Perth.

We would all like to thank the women who have come to our seminars and discussed the book with us, especially Pen Hetherington and Michele Kosky. Our thanks too to those who have typed our work: Dianne Hollis, Erlinda Lawson, Pamela Low and Barbara Williamson.

Preface

This second edition offers me the opportunity to explain how we came to write this book in the first place.

In the late 1970s at the University of Western Australia several of us were researching and teaching the history of women. Although we were working on different places at different times, we were all talking about similar problems of interpretation: how both to uncover the information about women's lives in the past, and to place their experiences in a social context. Furthermore, as feminists, we wanted to share our discoveries about women's past with the wider community of women in Australia. Michele Kosky, who was a student at the time, suggested to the Melbourne publishers, Sisters, that they should commission a book about our work. *Exploring Women's Past* appeared in 1982 as Sisters' first venture into history.

We have all tried to make our research intelligible to people who do not usually read history, and in the two early chapters about women in medieval and early modern times we have attempted broad overviews of the subject. Because the book is based on our research, it has found an audience among undergraduates as well as general readers, and the last three chapters in particular communicate the results of detailed studies. We hope that the book continues to appeal to both sets of readers, and to open up for discussion some of the important questions about women's past.

The original group has scattered. Margaret Ker is busy with two small daughters. Pat Jalland is writing three books on women in late nineteenth-century England. Raelene Davidson's doctoral research is on working-class women in the clothing and boot trades in twentieth-century Victoria. I am writing a monograph with another early modern historian about women in seventeenth-century England. Margaret Anderson is at the Museum of Migration and Settlement in Adelaide, where she continues her studies of families in nineteenth-century Australia.

Patricia Crawford
August 1984

Introduction

In this collection we have departed from the traditional way of
writing history by crossing boundaries of time and of space in order
to explore the questions which interest us. The essays range from
Europe in the medieval period to Western Australia in the early
twentieth century. A longer perspective enables us to make comparisons and contrasts, to see long-term patterns in women's lives. Inevitably, as we approach the present, an overview becomes more difficult, trends harder to discern. Research in more recent periods is
therefore more specialized: potentially, it is richer, for the sources
are more numerous and more readily available. Indeed, it is possible,
as Raelene Davidson's chapter shows, to create source material by
asking questions of women themselves. Specialized studies will help
us to understand the ways in which women's lives are changing now.

The first chapter is about women in Europe between 600 and 1500.
Margaret Ker argues that women were more involved in the decision-
making process in medieval society than in more recent times. By
interpreting for us the voices of women in that society, she shows
that there were avenues through which they could achieve a degree
of autonomy both within and outside the confines of their family.
A woman who chose not to marry could enter a convent where she
might gain a measure of power and authority. The idea that nuns
had a degree of independence unknown to later women is one which
interested nineteenth-century feminists, although it is not a popular
idea among feminists today. Nevertheless, by drawing attention to
the 'brides of Christ', Ker reminds us that the history of women in
society has not been one of progress and improvement in all areas.
She also discusses the activities of some of the 'poor mortals' in

medieval society: by a brief account of the roles of women in the market-place and in peasant agricultural communities, she provides a useful basis for one of the book's comparative themes, the work of women.

My own chapter explores the variables affecting the lives of women in England between 1500 and 1750. In pre-industrial society, the family was a working economic unit. Not until the factories developed in the late eighteenth century did work and home become separate. Child-bearing and rearing dominated women's married lives, for no reliable means of family limitation were available. This was a society in which Christian values dominated. The sixteenth-century Reformation abolished the medieval nunneries. No longer were women able to voice religious ideas of central significance to their society through the accepted medium of the institutional church. Those in Protestant England who had spiritual truths to express were forced into religious sects or into prophecy. As prophets women were, by definition, marginal people to their society – even mad.

Margaret Anderson's chapter about women in nineteenth-century Western Australia shows how women's lives were shaped both by their child-bearing and by an ideology about good women. Lacking any reliable means of contraception, most women had large families of eight to ten children and thus spent the bulk of their adult lives, as in earlier societies, pregnant, lactating and child-rearing. Anderson describes the ideology which placed women in a domestic role for which, it was argued, both God and Nature had intended her, and argues that these beliefs contributed to the violence against many women in Western Australia.

The same ideas which placed wives and mothers on a pedestal in the nineteenth century made the unmarried woman a rejected, negative figure. Patricia Jalland explores the implications of this through case studies of the lives of some spinsters of British political families in the late nineteenth century. These women were restricted by the social class of their families of origin. Unlike the unmarried women of the working class who were forced to earn their own livings, their families had sufficient means to make independent work socially unacceptable. Yet, as Jalland shows, the women's responses to this situation varied. While some acquiesced in the socially ac-ceptable role of 'dutiful daughters', caring for aged parents, others rebelled in ways which were often self-destructive. A few women managed to take advantage of their social situation to establish independent lives.

Just as ideology affected the lives of women married and single, so it affected prostitutes. In nineteenth-century Britain and Australia these women were censured as immoral and deviant. Raelene Davidson's chapter shows that prostitution was an economic opportunity for women in Western Australia. Myths about prostitutes influenced colonial legislators in the 1890s and thereafter. They refused to recognize that economic necessity could put women on the streets, arguing that most of the prostitutes were not Australian but from overseas. Davidson does more than examine male ideology on this issue, for she discovered that even though women had little choice in becoming prostitutes, many of them regarded it as a reasonable way of earning a living and had positive self-images.

Questions and problems present themselves to us in writing about women, a relatively new area of historical research. Traditional techniques do not always work, as contributors to a recent collection, *Doing Feminist Research,* have shown. Ann Oakley, for example, found that the standard method for interviewing women in as impersonal a way as possible, yielded neither the best results nor those she sought. Raelene Davidson, interviewing prostitutes, came to a similar conclusion. The one-to-one interview was a less fruitful and comfortable situation: far more revealing and enjoyable was a group interview, in which women who excelled as raconteurs told their stories, as they had done in similar situations before. As we try to discover women's past, we need to develop new tools of investigation.

Since we have tried to do more than simply add the history of women to traditional accounts of society, we need a transformed methodology in order to give weight to their lives. One important example of our difficulty is that of relating women to the class structures as they are currently defined by historians. If class is defined by a relationship to the means of production, do women take their status from their families of origin and their husbands? Where do single women fit? If housework is seen as an inevitable area of activity for women, for nearly all women do take responsibility for households, then are they one *class* of unpaid labour? We want a new approach to the classic distinction between paid and unpaid work, household and factory work. Perhaps we require a new approach to questions of class. The current discussion in the feminist movement above the compatibility of Marxist and patriarchal theory is about the need for some new formulations: the idea that men are oppressed by capitalism, women by men, seems less than satisfactory.

Massive changes have taken place in European civilization since the period with which we began this collection, and European society has spread to other countries. The rate of change in the last two centuries has been far greater than in the pre-industrial period. Industrialization, the development of capitalism, huge increases in world population, and technology have altered the material basis of society. But although societies changed rapidly, many ideas did not shift. Beliefs about the inferiority, subordination and weakness of women were so built into the ideologies of societies and into institutions of law, government and religion that they survived other changes even if they seemed less and less appropriate. The ideal of woman as 'helpmeet for man' is less relevant today when women are not spending their lives in economic dependence on men and rearing large numbers of children: but still it lingers on. Technological change has revolutionized housework, but it may not have been an unqualified liberating force in women's lives. So long as housekeeping is deemed to be the proper province of women, change in technology affects the *ways* in which they clean, wash and cook for their families, but does not necessarily free them from household tasks. Standards of cleanliness or of culinary expertise may rise so that women are still busied at domestic tasks. In the same way, technology now offers women the opportunity to control their fertility. Fewer years of women's lives may be spent in child-bearing but women's maternal role remains a barrier to their occupying different jobs in the community. Child-care is still generally deemed to be the responsibility of women, and the advice literature now places great emphasis upon the quality of mothering. Thus, while a woman today may spend fewer years in reproduction, she may spend a longer time in caring for the emotional needs of her family.

Part of the task of writing about women's past is to formulate questions which will provide useful answers. If we are to understand the status of women, we need to pose new questions, not just ask about where women fit in relation to the male-dominated world. We can explore ways in which women exercised power in the past and ways in which they challenged the dominant ideology. But we also need to understand the experiences of the majority of women, and this means that we need to understand why it was that many women did not see themselves as oppressed any more than many women do today. We need to investigate the process of socialization by which girls learnt what it was to be a woman, and to understand the families and education which combined to teach girls their roles so effectively that they internalized the values of the male-dominated society. We hope that the suggestions for further reading will help people to follow up some of these issues.

There is much to be done, not just in finding out about the lives of women in the past, but in rethinking methodologies. We are all still working on the issues we have raised in this book: on questions of class and consciousness, of the meaning of marriage and family to women, and of ways in which women in the past perceived themselves. Exploring women's past is a challenge for women now.

1

Margaret Ker

Brides of Christ and of Poor Mortals: Women in Medieval Society

(i) *Introduction*

What did it mean to be a woman in medieval western European
society? The historian's initial response to this question is that we
do not know. So few women who lived in western Europe between
600 and 1500 have left us any detailed records of how they saw themselves in relation to the society into which they were born, grew to
adulthood, grew old and died, that when we first seek to hear
the voices of our sisters in this period of history we are rewarded
only with silence, or with sounds so distorted by the basic restrictions of the surviving evidence, and by the vast distances of time
and space that we despair of our ability ever to interpret them in
a meaningful way.

Yet it is the contention of this chapter that our sisters are far from
silent, that they speak to us of the same range of basic concerns that
we experience in modern industrialized society, and that we can, and
indeed must, learn from their victories, often surprising, and from
their defeats, often familiar, if we want to understand, let alone alter,
the situation in which we find ourselves in the late twentieth century.
We must avoid the basic myth prevalent in capitalist society that the
development of western European society has been the story of
continual progress in material, intellectual and spiritual (however
interpreted) terms, of continuing growth in power-sharing, for we
are, especially if committed to ideas of social change, in constant
danger of adopting an implicitly patronizing attitude towards our
ancestors. It is time that consciousness-raising moved into an
historical perspective extending as far back into the past as is
practicable and relevant. In a western European context this seems
to go back at least as far as 600. If we do not go back this far we

shall have an imperfect understanding of the traditional pre-industrial society which was swept away in the eighteenth and nineteenth centuries, leaving, it will be argued, a disproportionately large legacy of ideas relating to women which have been absorbed, usually quite anachronistically and often in distorted form, into the cultural patterns of industrialized society. Insofar as this absorption was in any sense consciously willed by the male-dominated power structure of the new society, it can be argued firstly that the assumptions of pre-industrial culture were so widespread that their basis was not even understood, let alone questioned, by those in power, and in addition that all arguments based on a recognition of the historically-conditioned nature of restrictions on women have been suppressed, more or less ruthlessly, by those able to do so. We have been offered blinkers by our male intellectuals; we have been encouraged to look back only to remind ourselves that our struggle over time has supposedly paid dividends, that we have won battles – how hard it becomes to escape even in terminology from the values of a male-dominated society!

Our historical frames of reference are also affected. Our only escape from the traditional types of history dealing with the possession and exercise of power has been, in the past decade, to turn to look at those groups in society which did not possess or exercise power. One of the most fundamental lessons we can learn as we listen to our medieval sisters is perhaps that the most meaningful way of understanding and moulding the society in which we live is in terms not of power but of responsibility, first for defining social objectives and second for implementing them.

In this chapter I will address myself not to the vague question with which I opened (what did it mean to be a woman . . .?), but to a more precise and I think more appropriate one, to what extent were women in this period able to decide on and control their own destiny and the destiny of their society? Starting from the premise that the destiny of that society was viewed in terms very different from those we would commonly use today, I shall argue firstly that women were (relative to men) more involved in the decision-making process than in more recent times, and secondly that the degree of involvement decreased markedly over the period 600 to 1500, in both absolute and relative terms. That is, whilst women exercised responsibility in socially important spheres (especially religion) in the early part of the period, they exercised less in those same areas by 1500. In addition there were by 1500 new spheres of social activity (such as representative government and intellectual and mercantile activity) which totally or partially excluded women right from the start, sometimes, it has to be understood, for plausible practical reasons. Some of these stemmed from biology, but many stemmed from practical realities such as the tendency for military skills (based, admittedly, on training) to be confined to men, a tendency which made it almost impossible for a woman to cope with the life of a student or of a merchant or civil servant required to travel.

That these practical realities were backed up by a whole set of theoretical assumptions (often relics of still earlier cultures) must be admitted but not overemphasized. I shall be arguing that the importance of many of these theories about women has been overstressed simply because of the nature of the evidence readily available to traditional historians, many of whom have shown a total disregard for the first lesson of the student of primary sources: the injunction, 'thou shalt not' is clear evidence of prior community acceptance that 'thou shalt'. Put another way, social deviance is produced by the definer, not the deviant.

How was the destiny of society conceived of in the medieval period? The first point to note is that it was accepted that social change was neither possible nor desirable except in terms of the correction of flaws that had arisen through negligence, that is, a return to original perfection. It will be seen at once that this basic notion was likely, in contrast to the now prevailing one of social evolution, to favour women, for maintaining or restoring perfection has far more to do with responsibility than power. Anyone told they have a responsibility to change the world is likely to ask searching questions about their power to do so (and, as a point of interest, most Christian thinking of the late twentieth century on social justice provides very little in the way of answers). Anyone, on the other hand, told they have a responsibility to maintain a particular social order will ask a different set of questions, mainly centring round the definition of their particular personal responsibility (that is, how does the individual's life contribute to this maintenance?). And to this question everyone who accepted the basic tenets of Christianity (which were also the basic tenets of social theory) knew the answer: one avoided sin.

This answer begged, of course, the question of what constituted sin, and cynics might argue that the group in society with the responsibility for defining sin was the wielder of power in that society. Such an argument is oversimplistic, and ignores the degree to which the medieval Church at least (if not its successors) depended on the support of its customers for its very existence, let alone its power. The argument could more plausibly be turned on its head: defects in society must, however incomprehensible they might be at first sight, be the result of, indeed the punishment for, sin. This was applied to everything from major epidemics of plague through evil rulers to deformed babies, infertility, miscarriage and the failure of crops (not casually grouped together, for the unifying link is the failure of a natural process, that process being seen as a reward).

If, on this logic, the sin was not apparent to the sufferer then he had recourse to the experts to tell him literally where he had gone wrong. Hence, in the adverse conditions of the late medieval period, the alarming proliferation of varieties of sin, and at the same time the increasing disillusionment with the definers of sin, the clergy. Partly, no doubt, this arose because the 'sinner' despaired of his ability to avoid sin (and thus tended to feel resentment towards the definer of sin), but it also arose because the sinner continued to experience what he saw as punishment, without being given a plausible and feasible way of avoiding that punishment. If despair is a kind of corruption, then the absolute responsibility which the late medieval individual increasingly bore not only for his own salvation but for the salvation of the whole society was as corrupting as any absolute power could have been. But the failure of the medieval social vision proved, as we shall see, disastrous for women, for the role they could play in a society defined in terms of power was far more limited, especially when practical realities were reinforced by anachronistic ideas.

It will be assumed, for the purpose of the following discussion, that the prevailing social myth of medieval society, that is, that individual and social salvation (defined as the achieving and/or maintenance of the perfection which God willed for the individual and society) could be attained by the avoidance or correction of sin (defined as individual disobedience to God's will), was accepted at all social levels. This is a large assumption, and some attempt has to be made to justify it. In particular it might well be objected that, until at least 1200, our primary sources are almost exclusively produced by the clergy, for the laity were by and large illiterate. Even after 1200 the clergy, who comprised, as far as we can guess, a maximum of 2 per cent[1] of the total population, still produced the bulk of the written evidence, though increasingly they were writing for a partially lay audience. The argument that this imposes a fundamental and inescapable bias on the evidence at our disposal is a very plausible one, particularly for anyone studying the role of women in medieval society, for the clergy were, as is well known, in theory both celibate and chaste in the western Church (whereas in the eastern Church married men may be ordained as parish priests though monastic clergy and the higher clergy have to be celibate). This has led, far too easily, to the assumption that all clerical writing is likely to be highly anti-feminist in tone, an assumption reinforced by a common confusion between celibacy and chastity. Some discussion of these points seems to be necessary before we can begin to look with reasonable confidence at the way women contributed to the formulation and implementation of the medieval social myth.

First, a clarification of the difference between celibacy and chastity seems to be necessary. Celibacy means abstinence from marriage, chastity abstinence from sexual intercourse: in both cases the abstinence is generally assumed to be a deliberate decision rather than a lack of opportunity. The fact that Christian teaching has tended to condemn sexual intercourse outside marriage has undoubtedly been the primary reason for the equation of celibacy and chastity, but it does not alter the fact that there are two somewhat different ideals involved and that the implications of the two as regards the position of women are quite distinct.

Furthermore, it is interesting to note that in certain circumstances perfectly respectable Christian teaching has countenanced celibacy without chastity and chastity without celibacy. There are several instances of this in the Middle Ages. University academics (drawn for most of the period from the clergy) were expected to be celibate; they were not in practice expected to be chaste, in the sense that their unchastity was no more likely to interfere with their career than any other sin.[2] The same was probably true of the parish clergy; certainly their contracting of a common law marriage (by living with a woman) was listed separately, in diocesan visitation records, from their casual fornication (though the lists are fairly.lengthy on both counts)[3] and many bishops found it prudent to make the best of a bad job by issuing licences to the clergy to cohabit with the women formally termed their concubines.

Celibacy (as opposed to chastity) was important in a society where property holding was hereditary. The first concerted campaign for the strict enforcement of clerical celibacy in western Europe, in the late eleventh century (just after, significantly, the eastern and western Churches had drifted irrevocably apart after a diplomatic incident in 1054) came at precisely the time when property holding was becoming unconditionally hereditary in secular society. The theoretical justification was slightly more broadly based: marriage involved responsibilities in this world which were incompatible with the cleric's other responsibilities (whether as monk, priest, bishop or academic). Fornication was a very different matter since it involved no responsibility at all, but was to be condemned, like other sins, as a failure in personal perfection.

If celibacy did not automatically involve chastity, it is also true that chastity did not, and does not, automatically involve celibacy. Indeed all Christian denominations formerly preached chastity as the only acceptable form of birth control, either on a temporary or permanent basis as desired. The Catholic Church still does so, with or without the back-up of so-called natural methods of birth control, which are merely designed to make chastity as little of a burden as possible. In the medieval context, one finds examples both of proposed marriage contracts with a condition of chastity[4] and, more commonly, the acceptance of chastity (without a dissolution of the marriage bond) when one or both marriage partners became a monk or nun.[5]

The implications of all this as regards the position of women is that a celibate clergy is likely to undervalue the positive worth of marriage (though it is by no means certain that they will do so, as most clerical celibates are the products of marriage, often of consciously Christian marriage), and a chaste clergy is likely to undervalue the positive worth of sexuality and of women, or, perhaps more usually, to be afraid of both. Meetings of Alcoholics Anonymous are likely to convey a rather selective view of alcohol, but we have little difficulty in seeing this in its correct context, and can see this view as distinct from the view of a temperance society (though theoretically there might be an overlap in membership).

Some Christian writers, both from the early period of the Church (St Paul) or the medieval period (St Bernard of Clairvaux) did perhaps tend to assume that the strains associated with their own sexuality were generally shared, and this does make some of their statements apparently misogynistic, but it is hard to label all their writings as such and one would more accurately accuse them of having a depressingly low opinion of all human nature. St Bernard, for instance, is credited with the somewhat dramatic statement that 'to be always with a woman and not to have intercourse with her is more difficult than to raise the dead',[6] but it is quite reasonable to point out that this is more indicative of his opinion of his own nature than of the nature of women. Later we shall examine the importance of such views as regards the role of women within the monastic clergy.

The undervaluing by the clergy of the importance of marriage was far more important for the majority of women than any clerical misogyny based on suppressed sexuality, and this too will be discussed at some length subsequently. Here the point needs only to be made that very substantial changes occurred in the prevailing view of marriage over the medieval period, with the twelfth century appearing to be the time of most rapid social change. It is probably true to say that in no other area of social teaching has Christian doctrine undergone such marked change as that of marriage, and the point is worth noting because it is one of the most useful illustrations on a wider level of the theme of Richard Southern's brilliant interpretation of the history of the medieval church *(Western Society and the Church in the Middle Ages),* namely that in this period (as in others) the development of the Church was a reflection of and a response to social change on a wider level. This argument needs to be borne in mind as the most fundamental objection to the notion that evidence produced by the clergy can and must be dismissed as representative only of clerical views (which are assumed to be different from those of the rest of society).

On the other hand, in studying the history of women in the Middle Ages, it is equally if not more important to exercise extreme caution in using available evidence by examining carefully the purpose for which it was written. The statement by St Bernard quoted above, for instance, comes from a letter to fellow monks advising them against setting up a 'double monastery' where monks and nuns lived in the same religious community. It tells us absolutely nothing directly of what St Bernard thought about women in general, or about the Virgin Mary, his mother, the value of nuns, the position of women in lay society or the value of celibacy and/or chastity for parish clergy. On the first three points we have other evidence, in his devotion to the Virgin Mary, his obvious sorrow for the early death of his mother (which immediately preceded his becoming a monk) and his moving and supportive letters to nuns. We do not know what he thought about lay marriage or the parish clergy and we are not entitled to imply that we do, though we can presumably extrapolate from what we do know, as already mentioned, to the hypothesis that he thought women in general capable of achieving salvation and thus God's favour.

Unfortunately, to return to the original point, the need to treat our clerically-produced evidence with care does leave us rather short, for the medieval period, of evidence that throws light on the lifestyles of the vast majority of women. It is partly for this reason that a great deal of this chapter will deal with women within the clergy: their lives are, at least until 1200, the best documented. But it is also true that the lives of these very women may turn out to be more relevant to our present situation than those of the remaining 98 per cent of the population with whose lives we more readily identify. The latter I shall therefore discuss more briefly in subsequent sections, primarily to provide an overview and an indication of the present state of our knowledge.

If we take note of the points made above regarding the difference between celibacy and chastity the argument becomes more plausible. Traditionally the only way to safeguard one's autonomy as a woman may well have been celibacy; some women still think so, and chastity does not necessarily come into the picture in either case. On different occasions I have advanced to two friends the argument above, namely that feminists could usefully trace their 'spiritual' ancestry back to medieval nuns. Both appeared equally sceptical of the argument. One is a (married) feminist, the other a (celibate) cleric. I hope that in what follows, the case will be sufficiently convincing to overcome such scepticism.

(ii) Voices from the cloister

The voices that come to us from the cloister are on first impressions the hardest for us to hear and interpret in a meaningful way, though they are the most directly available to us. There are a few biographies of cloistered women, often virtually autobiographical because they are based on the author's close personal acquaintance with the subject (such as the twelfth century hermit and eventually formal nun Christina of Markyate).[7] There are a few letters (notably those of Heloise in the twelfth century, though these present a whole set of serious problems).[8] There are what might be called biographical fragments, based, like full biographies, on personal acquaintance. There are administrative records of nunneries,[9] and histories of such establishments (which also tend to figure in more general histories, written by clerics and reflecting their special interests). Sometimes the buildings themselves survive as visual evidence (allowing us for instance to draw comparisons with male monastic establishments and thus compare lifestyles).[10] If none of this sounds particularly promising, it is better than medieval historians tend to expect in trying to study most topics, certainly before about 1200. But it is evidence of a lifestyle so incomprehensible to most of us that we may well underrate its interest.

It is not easy for us to achieve empathy with women who in childhood or adolescence (or in middle age, perhaps as widows) apparently left the world, more or less voluntarily (clearly less voluntarily in the case of children, though social pressures on older recruits were often equally overwhelming), to devote themselves to a life of communal and individual prayer and study (not, it must be stressed, to lives of social work, teaching or nursing, all areas in which nuns are found today). We are apt to draw two very misleading conclusions from this: Firstly that women were 'forced' into nunneries, more or less directly, and would therefore have been made completely miserable had they resisted the pressures and remained in the outside world, secondly that they were probably fairly miserable and unfulfilled as nuns too: in sum that their lot was deplorable, unenviable and a typical crude example of male oppression (the first two conclusions being of course uncomfortably similar to some media images of feminists).

We would however find it much easier to achieve empathy with women who, in a society with strictly limited career opportunities for both men and women, chose voluntarily in adolescence or middle age to enter a career which enabled them to live reasonably comfortably in congenial company, to pursue their various interests and use their various talents – whether intellectual, social, artistic or administrative. We would empathise too with those who were placed in such a career structure by their parents and who were determined to make the best of their opportunities; with women who accepted the discipline of their community but not the discipline imposed on them by an increasingly male-dominated superstructure which claimed to have rights over their community – though such discipline was relatively rarely imposed, largely because the independence and administrative capability of the community was recognized and in some cases clearly feared. And such, on balance, seems to be the more accurate image of medieval nuns.

Where did nuns fit into the overall organization of the medieval clergy, and from which social groups and on what scale were they recruited? Medieval social thinkers from as early as the ninth century seem conventionally to have divided society into three groups: those who pray, those who fight and those who work. Each group had reciprocal obligations towards the other two: that is, those who prayed did so for the whole society, and those who fought were responsible for defending not only their own class (the military aristocracy) but also the clergy and agricultural workers, who stood in urgent need of military protection especially down to about 1050 when repeated waves of barbarian invaders ravaged western Europe. Such invasions highlighted the peculiar vulnerability of monasteries as repositories of works of art and precious metals and, as in all historical periods, the equal vulnerability of agriculture. Agricultural workers in their turn supported clergy and aristocracy, being in most cases tied to large estates (manors) belonging to either a monastery or lay aristocrat.

The characterization of the clergy as 'those who pray' reminds us that the function of most clerics (or at least those viewed as most important) until about 1200 was rather different from the general function of the clergy in most denominations of western Christianity today. There were two branches of the clergy, secular and regular. Secular clergy were so called because they lived in the world, providing pastoral care for the laity, specifically because as priests they administered the sacraments through which divine grace was bestowed on the recipient. Whether they provided pastoral care in a wider sense is debatable, for until at least 1200 the secular clergy were far inferior to the regular clergy in education and prestige. Parish priests were, judging by the records[11] (which were admittedly usually designed to record inadequacies), frequently barely literate (that is, they could hardly get through the liturgy of the Mass in Latin, apparently because they had to rely on memory because they could not read). They were often accused of all kinds of scandalous sins (presumably remarked upon because they set such a bad example to parishioners, though parishioners themselves may have been quite fond of a priest who joined them in the tavern and seduced other villagers' daughters, or wives).[12] The parish clergy were often not even celibate except in the strictest sense (their common law marriages being unrecognized sacramentally) and certainly not chaste: in sum, the parish priest was often barely distinguishable from his parishioners in habit or background (he might well be the illegitimate son of a liaison between the aristocratic patron of the church and a peasant woman). As long as the Church was unable or unwilling to raise the standards of the parish clergy, it was hardly a serious restriction on female career opportunities that women were ineligible for ordination as priests. After about 1200 the situation changed significantly, as we shall see.

In the early medieval period, to be a member of the regular clergy was to belong to the most prestigious group in society, the group who were recognized as doing most to secure the progress of society towards its ultimate goal of individual and corporate salvation. The regular clergy were so called because they lived according to a rule (Latin *regula*), in monastic communities physically isolated from the world. The general acceptance of their responsibilities for communal salvation is one of the ironies of ecclesiastical history, and excellent confirmation of Southern's thesis to which I referred above, namely that the history of medieval western Christianity involves ecclesiastical response to wider social developments.

St Benedict of Nursia, who lived in the late fifth and early sixth centuries, is generally viewed as the founder of western monasticism, since the rule he drew up for his own monks was followed, in some form or another, by most medieval monastic communities whether male or female. He himself gave assistance and advice to St Scholastica, his sister, and her community of nuns. There can be little doubt that the primary aim of St Benedict and his contemporary followers was to save their own souls by retreat from the collapsing ruins of the Roman Empire into small isolated communities who lived austere but stable lives based on spiritual and material self-sufficiency (that is, prayer and manual labour). The very strong emphasis on community spirit under the direction of the democratically-elected abbot was almost implicitly a rejection of the possibility of aid on any level from the outside world, a world whose chances of survival, let alone salvation, seemed fairly slim.

But western European society did survive the first wave of barbarian invasions and began to emerge into a series of very small decentralized political units run by newly powerful military leaders, often recent converts to Christianity who looked with awe and admiration at the havens of tranquility and ancient learning which Benedictine monasteries had become. What better way for these rulers, often converted late in life and with a legacy of sin which they despaired of shaking off entirely, to find favour with the God to whom they believed themselves responsible not only for their own souls but those of their families and their subjects, than by founding new monasteries and by endowing them or older monasteries with land, gifts and other support? What better way of paying particular attention to the family's spiritual welfare than by giving one's son or daughter to such an establishment? Nor should we assume that the son or daughter was likely to be anything but grateful for such a career opportunity, especially since they were more than likely to rise at above average speed to the top of the administrative ladder in such an establishment (a rise which their administrative ability, whether inherited or not, seems in most cases to have merited).

As a result, then, of enthusiastic public support from the newly Christian laity, western monasticism took on a function which its founder can hardly have envisaged and might well not have welcomed. Monastic establishments acted as the guardians of culture in both a literal and metaphorical sense (and before 1100 learning consisted mainly of studying and understanding ancient learning, rather than of independent intellectual inquiry or advancing the frontiers of knowledge). The laity, illiterate as they were, admired with largely uncomprehending enthusiasm such a function; but they did understand far better the regular clergy's other function, that of intercession with God. It was not only the preoccupations of a violent and relatively uncivilized world that made the laity so keen to employ the full-time expert in prayer, of course. The ways of the Almighty were as mysterious to the average early medieval noble as the ways of the taxation system to the average late twentieth century taxpayer, and in both cases the obvious solution is to employ an expert, especially since, in both cases, the cost of hiring that expert can be offset against what one owes the respective authority (an idea frequently expressed by medieval artists who depicted aristocratic patrons arriving in the divine presence carrying models of the ecclesiastical buildings they had endowed). 'Do-it-yourself' prayer was at best risky, though a thirteenth century aristocrat did express the opinion that the experts might be pricing themselves out of the market and even misrepresenting the demands of the taxing authority. On his deathbed William Marshal, who had risen from relative obscurity as the seventh son of a minor noble to be regent of England, and who had paid his debts to God not only by endowing monasteries but also by going on crusade, expressed the opinion that:

> The clergy are too hard on us. They shave us far too closely. I have captured five hundred knights and have appropriated their armour, horses and entire equipment. If for this reason the kingdom of God is closed to me, I can do nothing about it, for I cannot return my booty. I can do no more for God than to give myself to him, repenting all my sins. Unless the clergy desire my damnation, they must ask no more. But their teaching is false, else no-one could be saved.[13]

But if by 1220 such doubts, and such confidence, were seriously undermining the prestige of the regular clergy, it is unlikely that they were common in earlier periods (though it is worth noting that William Marshal's biography is probably the earliest biography of a non-royal layman to have survived). In 910 for example an earlier William, the Duke of Aquitaine, founded the famous monastery of Cluny for the following reasons:

Plainly God has supplied rich men with an avenue to eternal reward if they rightly employ their transitory possessions. Wherefore I, William, by the grace of God duke and count, earnestly considering how I may further my salvation while there is yet time, have deemed it expedient, in fact eminently necessary, that I should devote some of my temporal goods to the profit of my soul . . . Be it known, then, to all who live in the unity of the faith of Christ, that for the love of our Lord and Saviour Jesus Christ, I transfer from my lordship to the holy apostles Peter and Paul the town of Cluny . . . together with all that pertains thereunto: villas, chapels, serfs male and female, vines, fields, meadows, woods, waters and their outlets, mills, incomes and revenues, lands tilled and untilled in their entirety. I William and my wife Ingelborga give all these to the said apostles, first for the love of God and then for the soul of my lord Odo the King, of my father and mother, for me and my wife, for our bodies and souls. A regular monastery shall be constructed at Cluny, the monks to follow the Rule of St Benedict. They shall there ardently pursue celestial converse and sedulously offer prayers and petitions to the Lord both for me and for all.[14]

The regular clergy, then, were supported by the laity because they provided an expert service in prayer, a tangible collection of holiness, and a refuge for the patron's children and possibly in the long run for the patron's widow or the patron himself, who might retire into the monastery at the end of his life to prepare for death. Aristocratic widows often made very capable abbesses,[15] using their administrative experience from the outside world. In all of this women were on equal terms with men. Daughters were apparently no more likely to be placed in nunneries than sons were in monasteries, though they may have been placed there for slightly different reasons. The evidence suggests that (unlike the situation in the Roman Catholic Church today) there were more monks than nuns throughout the medieval period, though this may partly reflect the wider basis of recruitment for monks. Whereas St Benedict had explicitly welcomed recruits from any social class and given strict instructions that they were all to be treated equally, medieval monasticism tended to become socially exclusive and nunneries in particular became very aristocratic in basis and lifestyle. Most peasants were excluded simply because they were bound to lords who were unlikely to release them.

There is some evidence that women were viewed as more efficient in intercession than were men. This partly reflected other values in society. The way to advance in the lay world (as William Marshal for instance discovered) was to find a noble or royal patroness who would advance one's cause through her influence with her husband or son. In the spiritual world the intercession of the Virgin Mary was valued more highly than that of any other saint, and much of the literature concerning her tends to portray her relationship with Christ very much in terms of a rather domineering mother wielding great power over her divine son, an idea not unfamiliar to any modern Catholic schoolchild who sings the hymn containing the lines: 'Remind thy son that he has paid/ The price of our iniquity'. Small wonder then that with these images in mind Peter Abelard could write to his wife Heloise, after both had entered monastic establishments as a result of Abelard's castration by the hired thugs of Heloise's enraged uncle, begging for her prayers and the prayers of her fellow nuns, and reminding her that she is now his superior in that she is a 'bride of Christ'.[16] The whole of Abelard's correspondence with Heloise, fascinating and problematical as it is in so many respects, can be read usefully by anyone who wishes to understand the vital role played by women in medieval monasticism. But because of Heloise's initial reluctance to enter a nunnery (she accuses Abelard of having forced her to do so because he did not trust her,[17] and this masks the fact that a husband was obliged to make adequate provision for his wife before he himself could become a monk), it is not in her letters that we get most information on this. Her own career however, tragic though it was, and the obvious esteem in which she was held by contemporaries, is evidence of the equality which women enjoyed within the regular clergy as it developed until about 1150.

Nevertheless it became apparent even before the developments of the twelfth century that the position of women within western monasticism was a vulnerable one. The main reason for this was probably that they were never the initiators of developments within monasticism – at least, not of those developments which were to prove significant in the long run. This is partly because long term importance depended on lay support, and lay society, especially lay aristocratic society, was in the last resort male-dominated, however much its ideals may have been moulded and shared by women. In particular female monastic establishments were especially vulnerable to the consequences of barbarian invasion, and they were also vulnerable to the increased centralization of monastic organization even before 1150, a trend that was accelerated after 1150 to a degree which very clearly downgraded the importance of nunneries and the opportunities they presented for independent action by communities of women.

In the early centuries of Benedictine monasticism, down to at least 800, it was not uncommon for women to be in charge of double monastic establishments, which were particularly popular in Anglo-Saxon England[18] and which appear to have run into none of the disciplinary problems we might expect, problems which certainly did arise when the idea was revived in the twelfth century. Double monasteries consisted of communities of monks and nuns living in separate quarters but linked for administrative purposes. Part of the rationale for this (apart from simple convenience) was perhaps that such a community was less vulnerable to attack than an all-female community. Part reflected what was always a weakness in the attempt to run nunneries as autonomous units, namely that nuns needed priests to administer the sacraments. In the early centuries it was rare for monks to be ordained as priests, but a few members of any male monastic community would be so ordained and thus the community could be spiritually self-sufficient.

The double monasteries of Anglo-Saxon England were by any standards very impressive institutions enjoying both prestige and power in society, and there is no evidence that such prestige and power was in any way compromised by a woman's exercising supreme control. On the contrary, it was, as we shall see, a society which was perfectly accustomed to the exercise of administrative power by women, though in royal circles such women in theory exercised power on behalf of their husbands, or sons.[19] Some notable abbesses had already proved their administrative competence in the lay world.

After about 800, it became apparent that lay influence on monasticism had its dangers. Falling moral standards in monastic life, reflecting to some extent the dissolution and re-forming of political elites in the vacuum left by the collapse of the Carolingian Empire which had bound large parts of north-west Europe into some kind of political unity, led to moves in various areas of western Europe to initiate monastic reform by reasserting monastic independence. In an age of political chaos and renewed military threats by barbarians, women were perhaps not in a position to participate in such innovation. The reform movements[20] led by the Burgundian monastery of Cluny (founded 910) and various monastic houses in Lorraine rarely involved nunneries, and the movement itself threatened the prestige of older nunneries by implication, for it involved freeing houses from local control (by the aristocracy and ultimately by the local bishop) and placing them under the direct control of the pope. In the short term, since the papacy was at the nadir of its power in the tenth century, this made the new or newly-reformed houses virtually independent (just as the earliest Benedictine houses had been), but in the long term the increasing power of the papacy asserted itself.

From our point of view, the important thing is that neither short nor long term developments favoured female monasticism. Of course the older houses, both male and female, continued to exist (providing they were not destroyed by barbarian attack, as many in England were), but they were no longer in the forefront of developments, which meant that they no longer received such enthusiastic patronage from the laity, whether in the form of recruits or endowment.

In the last decades of the eleventh century disillusionment with old-style monasticism was increasingly apparent amongst both clergy and laity.[21] This was not so much because of decline and corruption as because of changed social circumstances. Lay society was becoming far more settled and prosperous and the idea that a monastery should be a haven of peace and splendour in a violent and uncivilized world no longer made sense to many. What was needed was a monastic lifestyle that in its turn provided a sharp contrast to the new realities of lay life, and this lifestyle was adopted first by individuals and subsequently by the new religious orders that were founded at the end of the eleventh and beginning of the twelfth centuries. Rejection of the world now involved a life of austerity and poverty, a denial of all the pleasures of the world, which had come to be seen as barriers to the pursuit of holiness. First individuals, both male and female, left lay society or older monastic houses to live alone or in small groups in remote areas, often previously unsettled or uncultivated, which meant that the new settlers had to be economically as well as spiritually self-sufficient. Then, as these individuals coalesced into groups, new orders such as the Cistercians were founded.

The Cistercians are particularly interesting to study for the light they throw on the changing status of women within monasticism. The most influential Cistercian of the early twelfth century was Bernard, abbot of the Cistercian monastery of Clairvaux in southeast France. We have already encountered his views on the dangers of women within monasticism, and the history of attempts by communities of nuns to attach themselves to the Cistercian order (not just because it was administratively convenient and a guarantee of stability, but also because such communities genuinely admired the Cistercian lifestyle) is a long and illuminating one.[22]

At first sight the flat refusal of the Cistercian hierarchy to admit female communities to the Cistercian organization, especially when coupled with St Bernard's apparently misogynistic views, appears to indicate a dramatic setback to the prestige of female monasticism. Such a view is misleading. It has to be borne in mind that the Cistercians succeeded beyond their wildest imaginings in attracting public support and that their phenomenal success in terms of recruits and foundations in the twelfth century presented many dangers, of which they were only too well aware. In fact the early Cistercian administrators fought a constant battle to preserve the purity of their ideal, which was threatened not only by floods of recruits, some of whom were inevitably unable, once their initial enthusiasm had waned, to live up to the rigours of Cistercian discipline, but also by the overgenerosity of lay patrons in terms of gifts. Small wonder that some of St Bernard's pleas for austerity seem decidedly lacking in charity:[23] his desperation may be compared to that of parents resisting the enthusiasm of doting grandparents.

The resistance of Bernard and his fellow Cistercians to the entry of female communities is essentially to be seen as part of this desperation: the organization was under strain enough without adding to its problems. No doubt too the Cistercian administrators were concerned with the constant battle to maintain individual moral purity amongst their flock: a battle that was possibly harder for the Cistercians than for the older orders which had relied heavily on child recruits who perhaps had less idea of what they were missing in terms of any secular pleasures. Cistercian recruits were adolescents or adults, giving up forms of social contact of all kinds to isolate themselves from the world amongst new companions.[24] It is no accident then that the cult of the Virgin Mary owed its sudden upsurge in popularity in the twelfth century largely to the efforts of St Bernard and his fellow Cistercians. She was to them a symbol of home comforts foregone in a noble cause in a way perhaps reminiscent of the Allied troops' devotion to Betty Grable. There is a vast difference between a sex symbol and a sex object, a point which has to be borne in mind because much male devotion to the Virgin Mary, especially in the late Middle Ages (together with much female devotion to Christ), has an element of physical involvement in it that is disturbing to modern sensibilities.

No doubt too St Bernard took the view that the Cistercian lifestyle was intrinsically unsuitable for women, and no late twentieth century woman needs to be reminded that this type of well-meaning chivalry and patronizing has probably done more harm to women than many far more blatant examples of oppression. Still, St Bernard had a point: the early Cistercians lived extremely hard lives centring not only round private and communal prayer (as with the older orders), but round manual labour in previously uncultivated areas in order simply to survive. Cistercian houses were not endowed, as older ones were, with already operating estates, and they deliberately sought physical isolation in areas previously considered unsuitable for settlement. Such a lifestyle was certainly very different from that to which aristocratic young ladies were accustomed; but it was by all accounts a considerable shock to many aristocratic young men too, and the fact remains that the women who wished to join the Cistercian order knew perfectly well what it involved, and were presumably attracted to the order by its austerity.

The Cistercian hierarchy was probably genuinely puzzled by such persistence, but their puzzlement turned to horror, and perhaps more overt hostility, when they discovered the initiatives taken by the self-styled Cistercian nunneries, which not only preserved their autonomy from the local bishops but also resorted on occasions to the quite unheard-of expedient of acting as their own priests to preserve their autonomy from any male interference.[25] In the long run the Cistercian order had to admit female communities, though by the time it did so in the thirteenth century the order had in any case declined considerably from its former austerity.

Other new orders of the twelfth century dealt with the pressure for female involvement differently, in many cases by reviving, temporarily at any rate, the idea of the double house. One example of this is the small English order of the Gilbertines, founded by a former parish priest, Gilbert of Sempringham.[26] Gilbert was in the best sense a man of the world, a great success as a parish priest and a competent and practical administrator who was not without an ability to produce the dramatic gesture when necessary. He was a man who inspired great affection throughout his life and who had the good sense to welcome this at face value rather than to question its moral purity or suspect its potential dangers. On one occasion, however, when as an old man he discovered to his horror that a nun entertained affection for him that even he had to admit was impure, he resorted to the practical solution of stripping completely naked so that the ludicrous nature of the physical attraction should become apparent.[27]

For all St Gilbert's practicality, Gilbertine double houses ran into problems and eventually disappeared. One such incident throws light on several aspects of female monastic life and the tensions imposed from within the community as well as from outside.[28] It concerns a nun in the double community at Watton in Yorkshire, a community which was renowned for its piety and austerity (the nuns performed their own manual labour as well as engaging in public and private prayer). Its reputation was threatened by the activities of a nun who (unusually for the new orders: she was perhaps an orphan) had joined the community at the age of four. She had apparently never shown any aptitude for religious life, and eventually she and one of the male members of the community became lovers. By the time this was discovered she was already pregnant. The man fled, but was found by other monks on the basis of information supplied by the nun, and brought back. He was handed over to the nuns, who had already shown their fury at the disgrace brought upon the community by the nun by fettering her and feeding her on bread and water. They brought her into the presence of her lover, handed her a knife, and forced her to castrate him. One of the nuns then grabbed the testicles and thrust them into the mouth of the pregnant nun.

The narrator of the story, Aelred of Rievaulx, a Cistercian abbot who was writing to an anonymous friend, expressed approval of the nuns' piety and zeal, though not of their act. Certainly the episode suggests that the ideal of chastity was so enthusiastically supported by the nuns of Watton that in order to preserve or restore it they went to lengths certainly not demanded by the male members of the community even if they tacitly condoned it (they had after all brought the fugitive monk back and handed him over to the nuns for discipline). It should be noted that castration was a recognised judicial punishment as well as apparently being one resorted to unofficially, so we cannot attribute Aelred's qualms to his sex.

For Aelred it was what happened subsequently that gave the story its real significance, however. When the nun was on the point of giving birth she saw a vision of the Archbishop of York, who advised her to say certain prayers and psalms. He subsequently returned with two beautiful women and took away the newborn baby. The incredulous nuns could find no trace either of the birth or of the baby, and having consulted Gilbert, who called in Aelred to check their story, they apparently forgave their sister and received her back into the community whose reputation had been saved by Christ's obvious forgiveness of the sinner. Aelred, presumably feeling that Christ could hardly be expected to come to the rescue every time monastic virtue proved unequal to temptation, thought that the story confirmed the wisdom of the Cistercian resolve not to be led into temptation in the first place.

Interestingly it seems to have been generally assumed that men were if anything more easily led astray than women (a view partly dependent on the image of Eve as the temptress) and down to 1200 the monastic ideal centred very much on the avoidance of temptation by retreat from the world into a community that acted as a spiritual version of Weight-Watchers (or Alcoholics Anonymous). Such an idea found favour with the laity, who traditionally believed themselves (or perhaps had been led to believe themselves) to be incapable of avoiding temptation in the world. By 1200 this whole view had however come to be seriously questioned. Two developments, both with important implications for women, had contributed to this.

One, the crusading movement, will be studied subsequently in connection with its importance for aristocratic women. Here the point to note is that when in 1095 Pope Urban II invited western Christians (he probably only envisaged the aristocracy but in fact all classes of society responded) to go off to the Holy Land to save it from the Moslems, he initiated a whole new phase in lay involvement in the attaining of salvation (individual and communal) and thus in actively and directly moulding social action. The reward promised for involvement in the crusade amounted in common understanding to a guarantee of salvation (what precisely Urban II meant to offer and was theologically entitled to offer is a matter of considerable historical controversy),[29] and for many people at least it was an offer too good to refuse. Not only was the guarantee a far surer one than the older method of endowing monasteries (about which, as we have seen, there was decreasing enthusiasm) but the terms were far easier to a society running out of military outlets (and land) at home and settling into a pattern of consumption that militated against over-generosity towards experts in prayer unless they were particuarly outstanding. Crusades established the principle of spiritual 'self help', and the possibility of salvation through 'worldly' activities.

The principle was reinforced by intellectual developments in the twelfth century, developments which centred in the newly-emergent universities which came to displace the monasteries as centres of learning (and which excluded women, whose opportunities for learning thus remained static at a time when men's increased dramatically). University learning, unlike monastic learning, was innovative (and this worried St Bernard just as much as other forms of temptation) and speculative. It involved important developments in many areas of knowledge, but for our purposes the most important, apart from medicine,[30] was the theology of sacraments.

Sacraments involve the bestowing of divine grace on an individual, and whilst there was from the first a substantial divergence of opinion (later reflected in Reformation debates) on the degree of initiative necessary on the part of the recipient, even the most minimal degree of initiative involved a newly stressed degree of self-help on a direct and continuing basis. To mention a few of the more relevant aspects of sacramental theology to emerge at this time, the twelfth century move to restrict the laity to communion in one kind, that is, only the host (transubstantiated bread) not the chalice (of transubstantiated wine) reflected not only stricter definitions of transubstantiation but probably also a greater likelihood that the laity would want to receive communion at all, as opposed to simply hearing mass (though receiving communion remained the exception rather than the rule).[31]

Similarly confession[32] (the sacrament of penance) developed from an occasional event (in the very early Middle Ages strictly a once-only event for any individual) to a sacrament to which the laity as well as clergy were supposed to resort whenever they had committed mortal sin. From the point of view of a still largely uneducated laity this begged the question of what constituted mortal sin, so in 1215 it was laid down that the laity were to go to confession at least once a year, which enabled the clergy to keep track of their parishioners and to instruct them on an individual basis (also, in theory, to root out heresy). Confession depended increasingly in the later medieval period on the penitent's awareness, aided by the confessor (priest) but also by his own private study, of precisely where and when he had offended God. Endowing religious establishments provided at best a back-up insurance policy.

Finally it was in the twelfth century that marriage was fully defined as a sacrament. In a sense this lessened the superiority of the clergy, which had previously been evidenced either by the obvious holiness of the regular clergy (in theory), or by the ordination of the priest (i.e. the sacrament of holy order). By stressing the sacramental nature of marriage (to which the priest is merely a witness) the Church advanced the status of the laity considerably; but the development also, quite deliberately, gave the laity new responsibility in the quest for salvation. In sum, the potential spiritual significance of worldly concerns was stressed.

Developments within the clergy after 1200, then, reflected not only purely secular developments but also a redefinition of the spiritual responsibilities of clergy and laity. The clergy could no longer justify themselves as passive possessors of expertise in holiness; increasingly they both expected to, and were expected by the laity to, play an active part in the world rather than fleeing from it. We are still, of course, a very long way from the clerical activists of twentieth century Latin America or Asia, but there was a very clear demand for improvement in pastoral care in the late Middle Ages and this led not only to a new emphasis on the importance of the secular clergy (though it must be added that reform of the secular clergy proceeded, in spite of numerous initiatives, very slowly indeed), but also to the formation of new religious orders more involved in pastoral care. Both developments seriously disadvantaged women. It came to be far more important, in terms of areas of responsibility open to women, that they were excluded from the priesthood, and the fact that, as we shall see, the family became increasingly important in religious terms provided (and has continued to provide, many would say) very inadequate compensation for such a loss to anyone who defines the purpose of life in terms of Christian spirituality.

As regards the new religious orders, it is true that, as with the Cistercians and other new orders of the twelfth century, there were practical reasons for women's lack of participation. But again one doubts their ultimate validity, and constantly encounters well-meaning and disastrous male estimates of female weakness.

The new religious orders abandoned the contemplative life of monks based, at least in the opinion of the laity, on the notion of spiritual service to the whole community, in favour of an active life of service to the community in the world. St Francis and St Dominic founded orders of friars[33] who were (initially) supported by small-scale, day-to-day almsgiving by urban populations amongst whom they lived and worked as preachers and (to some extent) social workers. Both attracted women supporters, and in the case of St Francis in particular these were a source of difficulty. St Clare, an early supporter of St Francis and quite probably a significant influence on him as he crystallized his ideas, clearly wished to emulate his life in its simplicity and devotion to community service. Admittedly it was not by any stretch of the imagination a life to which an aristocratic young woman could adapt as easily as could an ex-soldier from a merchant family. Nevertheless the adoption by St Clare and her followers (the Poor Clares) of a lifestyle closely modelled on that of the older, enclosed, orders can hardly be considered inevitable given that from early in the thirteenth century onwards women elsewhere in Europe, in areas as highly urbanized as central Italy, were following a lifestyle apparently close to what Clare originally had in mind.

The area then known as Flanders (now in northern France, Belgium and West Germany) gave rise, for reasons of which historians are still unsure, to the *beguine* movement.[34] *Beguines* were women who lived a strict life of piety and poverty either alone or in groups, engaging in charitable works as well as feats of devotion which are, with their overtones of hysteria, less attractive to us. Because the *beguines* were not amenable to ecclesiastical discipline, since they were not members of religious orders, they frequently fell foul of the authorities, who were, perhaps understandably, nervous of the potential for mass hysteria. But many orthodox churchmen admired them greatly, and *beguines* (the term is inevitably a somewhat vague one) were to be found in this area for the rest of the Middle Ages.

Interestingly, they appear to some extent to reflect a local surplus of women in the population, though some had actually been married and had rejected marriage in favour of a life of non-institutionalized piety. Even earlier in the Middle Ages one finds women of this type, the best known being Christina of Markyate[35] in the twelfth century. Christina had been married off by parental arrangement, although she made it clear to her family that she preferred the religious life. In a bid to silence her objections her parents had, as they thought, arranged for her to get drunk on her wedding night. But when her husband eagerly entered the bedroom he found a perfectly sober Christina, who suggested that they should live together chastely for several years and then enter religious establishments (married couples could, as we have seen, do this by agreement). Burhred was not keen on the idea, so Christina fled from him and took refuge with a hermit named Roger. Later after Roger's death other women joined her, and eventually a nunnery was formally established. Christina obviously valued male companionship, for she formed a close friendship with the abbot of St Albans, Geoffrey, in spite of some contemporary disapproval. Nor does she appear to have a personal dislike of her husband; it was merely that from early youth she had dedicated herself to chastity as part of her service of God. This point is worth stressing because male historians are apt to portray nuns as having a near-hysterical aversion to men, and thus to marriage. We are of course familiar with this kind of slur on feminism.

Thus we can say that the voices from the cloister speak to us of the increasing relative disadvantaging of women within the clergy in the period 600 to 1500. Though this process was clearly not aided by the existence of elements of anti-feminism, the main factors were social ones over which male clergy had at best limited control. The downgrading of women's importance in the clergy was not generally speaking deliberate or even conscious, but it was very real, and our evidence suggests that it was clearly perceived, resented and resisted by women themselves. Heloise, for all her dependence on Abelard for advice on how to run her nunnery (three of the letters which survive from their correspondence have this as their theme, though it is possible that Heloise resorted to the topic as the only one on which Abelard would agree to continue to correspond)[36], voices very clearly the growing feeling that monasticism had never been entirely geared to female involvement. In seeking Abelard's advice on matters such as diet and clothing (for instance on the underwear that menstruating nuns might wear, a matter with which the Benedictine Rule understandably did not deal),[37] she reflected the fact that it was no longer acceptable to adapt the Rule on the basis of personal initiative: it was to be followed as literally as possible, and this inevitably created difficulties.

Brides of Christ the nuns might be, but a bitter irony that emerges in one of Abelard's letters is that, precisely because transubstantiation involved the changing of bread and wine into the body and blood of Christ, nuns were not to be permitted to handle the altar vessels, or even the altar cloth except when they had to wash it.[38] It was all very well for Abelard to try to console Heloise for her loss of an

32

earthly husband by reminding her that 'you were previously the wife of a poor mortal and are now raised to the bed of the King of kings',[39] but he did not apparently think through the metaphor very carefully.

6

(iii) Voices from the castle

Nuns comprised at most 2 per cent of the female population of medieval western Europe; women of the aristocracy perhaps another 2 per cent. What we know about aristocratic women we almost always know because of their role as wives, mothers or daughters: that is, the role an aristocratic woman could play in her society was almost entirely dependent on whose wife, mother or daughter she happened to be, and in none of these spheres did she in practice have any choice. It does however need to be borne in mind that men were equally unable, in many cases, to choose their wives, or to escape from the limitations of their parentage or of their ability to produce heirs. One either submitted to the communal discipline of the family or to the communal discipline of the quasi-family of the monastery or nunnery (headed by the explicitly paternal or maternal figure of the abbot or abbess).

Individualism, if it existed at all,[40] was a luxury reserved for the poor, precisely because, to return to our opening theme, the poor were least burdened with responsibilities; to put it another way they had nothing to lose. For every reluctant bride like Christina of Markyate we could probably find a reluctant male layman: Louis IX of France[41] or Edward the Confessor of England, both better suited to the life of a monk yet forced, with varying degrees of success, to fulfil their lay responsibilities. Only a few were lucky enough to escape from such a situation: St Francis and St Thomas Aquinas only at the price of strong parental disapproval, Peter Abelard only because he was able to surrender his inheritance as the elder son of a Breton noble to a younger brother.[42] The interests of the family unit took precedence over all else.

There is no reason to suppose that women resented this restriction imposed by society any more than men did; if we wanted to make any kind of generalization at all on the basis of the fragmentary surviving evidence we would have to admit that they seemed to revel in it to a greater extent than men did. From the early medieval period there are frequent examples[43] of extremely pushy mothers going to any lengths to advance the interests of their sons (including arranging the murders of rivals). Insofar as day-to-day aristocratic life (as opposed to social theory) revolved more around power than responsibility, women were often in a better position to play the power game than men were, for they were recognized as exercising enormous influence and patronage and were better placed to conduct domestic intrigue. If there were female victims of the game they were likely to be daughters-in-law. In the thirteenth century for instance Louis IX of France[44] was so thoroughly under the thumb of his mother, the formidable Blanche of Castile, who virtually ran the kingdom for him until her death, that Louis had to sneak down the backstairs even to visit his wife Margaret (and sneak back up them again very smartly if Blanche approached). Small wonder that Margaret chose to join Louis on crusade in Egypt even though she was heavily pregnant at the time of her journey and gave birth to her baby en route after making one of her small entourage promise to kill her rather than allow her to fall into enemy hands. No doubt anything was better than staying at home with Blanche.

Aristocratic women proved themselves capable of directing life, despite its restrictions, to their own advantage. The crusading movement is a prime example of this. Some women felt it to be to their advantage to accompany their husbands: Eleanor of Aquitaine accompanied her first husband Louis VII of France in the middle of the twelfth century, though her conduct in Constantinople was so scandalous that Louis had the marriage annulled on their return home even though this meant the loss to the French kingdom (best envisaged at this time as a kind of family business) of Eleanor's territory of Aquitaine, which she had inherited from her father and took with her in her second marriage, to Henry II of England. In this marriage, incidentally, Henry did in one sense exercise the upper hand. He virtually imprisoned Eleanor for part of her life, but this was partly in response to her own intrigues against Henry through their four sons.

On the other hand, many women found it to their advantage to stay at home whilst their husbands were away,[45] for this left them in charge, often for years at a time, of large and complex estates in the administration of which they could, if they so wished, play an active role. This was in addition to their normal responsibilities in running the household itself, a task involving considerable administrative skill. The interesting point is that women were expected to be capable of doing all this: the frivolous and incompetent aristocratic woman is noted as the exception, not as proof of male preconceptions. The crusading movement, which lasted throughout the twelfth century, proved in the short term at least as advantageous to women as did World War I, though in both cases the long term gains were more suspect and may well have been counterbalanced by a significant backlash.

The ability of women to exercise power within the structure of royal and noble courts is the more surprising because this structure was based on the link between landholding and political power and landholding was in turn based on military power. The 'system' which we call feudalism[46] (thus systematizing it far more than the evidence warrants!) depended on the basic notion that in a premonetary economy geared to war a warrior was to be rewarded for past service and supported in present and future service by a grant of land. Such a grant did of course presume that the estate could be run in the warrior's absence (which probably meant that he had to be married), and from the point of view of convenience it probably meant also that in normal circumstances a warrior was expected to produce an heir to take over the land and the obligation of military service. In other words, feudalism depended on the family: the earlier system whereby warriors were supported in the lord's household made celibacy almost as essential for warriors as for monks, and was inconvenient for lords if they in turn were married and running a fully fledged household (rather than what amounted to a barracks). But precisely because landholding was dependent on military service, which women could not provide, women were theoretically bound to exercise power through their husband or son who did provide the military service. Hence the origins of restrictions on the holding of property by women, restrictions which continued for centuries after they had become entirely anachronistic.

After about 1300, various trends emerged which in the long run proved detrimental to women. For the remainder of the medieval period we could say that the aristocracy tended to lose some of its power yet retain most of its responsibility, and that the strains caused by this discrepancy probably fell heavily on women, who thus, as in later periods, tended to be the main victims of economic crisis.

From the late twelfth century, government was increasingly in the hands of university trained bureaucrats,[47] rather than aristocrats, clerics or members of the royal family (notably in the early Middle Ages as we have seen the queen or queen mother). The aristocracy was increasingly restricted to a life of conspicuous consumption[48] either at court or on country estates: even war became more a matter for professional, mercenary soldiers. This lifestyle had to be maintained despite falling profits from landholding resulting from the widespread demographic and economic crisis of the period after 1300, and we may assume that the burden of maintaining the standard of living fell most heavily on the wife as the person in charge of household management and finance. Life for the late medieval aristocratic family was more comfortable in the material sense, with improved standards of accommodation and domestic furniture,[49] but it was increasingly parasitic and thus less fulfilling. It is from this period that we hear, for instance, the voice of the dying Duchess of Brunswick, responding to her confessor's astonishment at her confidence of salvation:

> Beloved father, why should I not now go to heaven? I have lived here in this castle like an anchoress in a cell. What delights or pleasures have I enjoyed here, save that I have made shift to show a happy face to my servants and gentlewomen? I have a hard husband (as you know) who has scarce any care or inclination towards women. Have I not been in this castle even as it were in a cell?[50]

The duchess, in finding in her religion her consolation, such as it was, for the hardships and frustrations of life, probably conformed to a pattern common in the medieval and early modern period. From the days of the conversion of Europe it seems to have been expected that women should set the religious tone of the household and superintend the religious education of their children and the religious practice of the household.[51] It was not that male faith was assumed to be any less real, but rather that a woman's constant presence in the household made her better able to undertake the responsibility on a continuing basis, relatively undistracted as she was by the sordid cares of the military and political world. The household represented a position midway between the wickedness of the world and the complete tranquility of the monastery. Most aristocratic households probably had their own chaplain (and chapel) and did not have to rely on the inadequate services of the local parish priest.

When we recall that religious belief encompassed the total world view in the early medieval period, we realize that a woman's religious responsibilities as wife and mother were of great and general significance. The stress on the sacramental nature of marriage to which I have already referred heightened this significance. The trend had, however, a negative side, in the apparently mounting stress on the potential for sin within the family and within the marriage bed in particular. An important recent work, Thomas Tentler's *Sin and Confession on the Eve of the Reformation,* devotes a fascinating chapter to 'Sex and the Married Penitent'[52] which illustrates this well. He himself warns that he does not wish to imply that the material on which he bases his book (manuals of advice on confessional practice, directed to both clergy and laity) was overwhelmingly preoccupied with the dangers of sexuality. But the fact remains that this was probably the area in which the average aristocratic lady had most opportunity to commit sin (simply because her overall opportunities were so limited), and we have to remember that the late medieval crisis created a widespread belief that God was punishing humankind for its sins, a belief that inevitably led to lay anxiety to be made aware of sin. The large number of aristocratic women who supported the Reformation enthusiastically and who moulded pious Protestant households may well reflect the fact that here, as in the more general field, was where the late medieval crisis had been felt. Ultimately the Catholic way of shouldering the responsibility had become too burdensome, and aristocratic women had despaired of their ability to please God by their piety and devotion. Luther's proclaiming of the reality of salvation 'by faith alone' may have proved particularly attractive to such women. At any rate the prevailing myth that it was Protestantism which elevated the household by imbuing it with religious significance needs to be debunked once and for all.[53]

It goes almost without saying that a society which was based on hereditary landholding placed great importance on a woman's role as childbearer. But it is very difficult to know how women viewed this role. The undeniable fact that for both men and women children were a means of exercising power in society does not in any way have as a necessary corollary an assumption that either men or women were lacking in parental affection. The likelihood is that women were more affectionate towards their children simply because they saw more of them. The father of William Marshal for instance used his young son as a hostage in an agreement he broke, and when reminded that he had endangered his son's life remarked with a calmness bordering on callousness that he had 'anvil and tongs with which to forge another'.[54] But William was his seventh son and he probably knew very well that King Stephen, who held his son, was too generous and mild a man to put the boy to death. There was little sentiment in any medieval love, but it is hard to know whether this is a necessary component of affection. What we can say is that men and women devoted themselves to doing the best, as they saw it, for their children, in a society where the individual's wishes were never as highly regarded as the good of the family.

(iv)   Voices from the fields

At least 95 per cent of the population of medieval Europe until at least 1300 was engaged in agriculture or pastoralism; after 1300 the urbanization of some areas of western Europe probably made very little difference to the overall picture.

Inevitably we know relatively little[55] about this vast majority of the population, for they were illiterate and hence historically inarticulate, and their lifestyle was so foreign to the literate minority that we cannot expect them to tell us a great deal about the reality of being a medieval peasant. On the other hand the records that do survive concerning the peasantry have some definite advantages to counterbalance their obvious limitations. In the main they are administrative records describing the ways in which those in power dealt with the peasantry, either as agricultural tenants or as lawbreakers. In the former case in particular they are unselective, since the majority of peasants were tenants of one sort or another: the few who remained outside the organization of the large estate or manor are by definition undocumented and thus cannot be studied. Even in the latter case, court records, they are fairly wide in scope: in particular they are just as likely to document women as they are to document men.[56]

Peasant landholding,[57] like aristocratic landholding, was in principle dependent on past and future service, and was intended to support the tenant, though the payment of wages became increasingly common either to supplement this (because landholdings were small) or as a substitute for it (perhaps if there was no land at all available, or for occasional work by someone not attached to the manor). Landholding was hereditary, largely as a matter of convenience and because when a peasant joined a manor he normally bound not only himself but also his descendants to the land. Since women were regarded as equally capable of fulfilling most rural work they were free to inherit land in principle as well as in practice, either from their father or their husband, provided that they could fulfil the particular work obligations attached to it. But brothers or sons took precedence, though this is perhaps a misleadingly legalistic way of looking at a society where the land really belonged to the family, who shared out the responsibilities attached to it presumably on the basis of skills and physical suitability. Women would for instance be responsible for any obligation of textile work owed to the lord, as well as for poultry keeping.[58] One point that should be stressed is that for much of the period, in much of western Europe, simplicity (not necessarily squalor) was so much the norm in peasant households that 'housework' in the modern sense was no great burden. There was very little furniture, virtually no washing to be done, few spare clothes to be made, purchased or cared for. Cooking was rudimentary and often not done at home: bread was often baked in the lord's oven or that of a richer neighbour.

Evidence which is beginning to emerge suggests, however, that we need to be very wary about assuming that the life of a peasant, whether male or female, was so harsh as to be completely dehumanizing.[59] Obviously by modern western European standards it was austere in terms of material comfort: so, come to that, was the life of the elite. It could be extremely precarious, not so much because people regularly starved to death (for it was in their lord's interests not to let them) but because malnutrition made them vulnerable to disease, infant mortality and early death, and because they were at the mercy of forces, whether natural or economic, over which they had no control. But the picture of the medieval peasantry as passive accepters of their fate is beginning to look increasingly false. Within the structure of the manor community (the only one that usually influenced their lives) they took considerable responsibility for their own destiny, according to their place in the power structure of the community. Since the family was all important at this level too, one can assume that women had a roughly equal share of responsibility. The peasantry expressed very definite views on any outside forces (the church, the monarchy or the aristocracy) which occasionally intruded: one French village fought a legal battle over forty years and several generations, and involving appeals to Paris and Rome, over their legal status.[60] Peasant revolts[61] against local aristocracy, the national government and the monarchy became increasingly common in the crisis of the fourteenth and fifteenth centuries, and our evidence, fragmentary and biased as it is, suggests a significant awareness of the issues involved, though the information available to the rebels must have been very scanty. Persecution of peasants for heresy brings to light their lack of passivity in religious belief too,[62] though their theology was often idiosyncratic. There too women were deeply involved: indeed safety from persecution for heresy depended on family loyalty, especially loyalty of husband and wife.[63] Overall one could say that where the power structure significantly affected them the peasantry shared in responsibility: where it did not normally do so the peasantry attempted to intervene only occasionally, when necessary, though when they did so their level of awareness suggests that they habitually kept a careful eye on the wielders of power to check on whether they were fulfilling their responsibilities.

Whether we can extrapolate from the apparent equality of peasant women and men on the economic level to an equality on this political or quasi-political level is at present difficult to say. Women do not seem to have taken part in peasant revolts. Although it is likely that modern historians have not investigated the possibility of female involvement, contemporary records of the revolts, concerned as they often are with the bestiality of peasant actions in raping women and massacring children, would almost certainly have noted female involvement in order to express and inspire further horror. Yet it would be most unsafe to suppose that there is any likelihood at all that women were more conservative, especially since there is ample evidence of female involvement in late medieval heresy.[64]

In the last resort the medieval peasant whether male or female had an ultimate responsibility to face God. Unlike their social superiors, the peasantry do not seem to have considered themselves responsible for the spiritual health of the community (hardly surprising since they did not have the power to influence it), and the little evidence available to us suggests that they worried relatively little about the spiritual quality of their own lives: what they were concerned with was a good death, by which they made their peace with God.[65] Like the higher classes of the laity earlier in the Middle Ages they do not seem to have felt that they were in a position to avoid sin on a day-to-day basis. Nor were they much interested in what constituted sin: in southern French peasant society for instance it was assumed that in general, fornication was not a sin if one enjoyed it.[66] Nor were they in a position to buy salvation by monastic endowment, though their enthusiastic and unexpected response to the First Crusade or to the Cistercian policy of recruiting 'lay brothers' from the peasantry, men who lived a semi-monastic life but whose primary responsibility was manual labour, suggests that they were prepared to earn salvation if the conditions were attractive. In the last resort though they believed, in spite of their surprising interest in theological speculation, that God was a reasonable father who did not demand perfection[67] but merely contrition at the last. Such a religion was both comforting and comfortable in a lifestyle otherwise characterized by a lack of comfort in either sense. Possibly they were aided in this by the oft-repeated biblical praise of the poor and criticism of the rich.[68]

(v) Voices from the market place[69]

By 1500 western Europe was heavily urbanized in a few areas, notably Flanders, Italy and southern Germany, though cities were of course by modern standards extremely small. Cities had their own social hierarchy, with an elite of aristocracy sometimes living on estates outside the city, various levels of merchants and traders, and an urban proletariat. The urban proletariat had fairly obviously been recruited from the rural peasantry. About the origins of the merchant class there has been considerable dispute[70] but certainly many must originally have come from prosperous but frustrated peasant families or from the landless class. The importance of this from our point of view is that it throws some light on the reasons why it was within the urban classes that women enjoyed the greatest degree of freedom and equality.

At the highest level of urban society household management was probably of sufficient complexity to provide a full-time occupation for a wife just as it did for the aristocratic wife. The husband might be away on business, just as the noble was engaged in fighting or government, so that the wife would be required to look after the business at home.[71] No doubt this is essentially why one finds widows engaged in mercantile activity at the very highest level, such as in the English wool trade.

Smaller businesses might involve either a partnership between husband and wife or, frequently, a woman running a separate business independently. Her right to do so was recognised in law, largely because this meant that her husband could not be held responsible for her debts.

Finally among the urban proletariat women are found as wage earners, though their wage rates were usually lower and they were more susceptible to exploitation because they tended to work part-time. What needs to be emphasized however is that there is no evidence of a feeling that urban women should be confined to domestic duties within the home, unless they belonged to the urban aristocracy and modelled their lives on their rural counterparts.

(vi)   Conclusion: Establishing a dialogue

If we ask ourselves 'what does it mean to be a woman in 1983?' our answer is likely to involve a wish to reject an identity forced on us by society and to find one for ourselves. If we worry that we are only 'Brian's Wife, Jenny's Mum',[72] ought we not to be asking ourselves how, in an historical context, we ever came to be so? If we discover that such a label reflects the values of a society which would have labelled Brian as Jenny's father (and at least sometimes as Josephine's husband) or Jenny as Brian's and Josephine's daughter, whereas our own society seems to see Brian and Jenny as individuals, then that discovery is surely a weapon. For that society is long dead, and its anachronistic echoes may turn out to be as vulnerable, in the light of our proclaimed knowledge, as any ghosts.

If we further discover that even in that long dead society there were women who resisted such restriction of their identity, and that these women were in fact accepted as proclaiming the great truths relevant to that society, is not this discovery as potentially exhilarating and encouraging as discovering our contemporary sisters? If we understand the forces that defeated them, are we not better equipped to avoid a similar defeat?

In the past we have perhaps not listened because we too readily despaired of understanding the voices. They can be heard in unexpected places. For instance art history might well seem a particularly unpromising field of inquiry for feminists, reflecting as it does the values of the powerful at their most blatant. Yet out of one sort of evidence available on the art history of medieval Europe, 'books of hours' (in effect private prayer books for daily use) there comes a voice that provides an excellent example of the value of listening in unlikely places.

Books of hours were individually designed and thus tell us a great deal about their aristocratic owners, often women, who clearly used the books constantly. One,[73] completed in February 1415, belonged to a French noblewoman, Mary of Guelders, who died in 1425. She had been married to the Duke of Guelders as part of a political alliance, and to cement the alliance it was important that the marriage should produce children.

One page of her book of hours depicts Mary of Guelders reading the book, which has been presented to her by an angel. God dispatches another angel to her, bearing a banner inscribed 'O gracious Mary'. Only by reading this does one realize that the childless Mary of Guelders is identifying herself with the Virgin Mary at the Annunciation, and expressing her prayer that God will reward her piety by sending her a child too.

In this one picture we can thus hear the voice of a woman attempting to use the power structure of her society to enable her to fulfil her desired role in that society. Granted she had not in all probability chosen that role freely, granted too she failed, for she died childless. But if we can hear her voice, maybe it is more likely that we shall be able to make someone hear ours.

Notes

1. D. Hay, *Europe in the Fourteenth and Fifteenth Centuries*, Longmans, London, 1966, p.59.
2. Heloise's correspondence with Abelard on the value of celibacy indicates this by implication: see B. Radice (ed.), *The Letters of Abelard and Heloise,* Penguin Classics, Harmondsworth, 1974, especially Letter 1.
3. See, for example, J.B. Ross and M.M. McLaughlin (eds.), *The Portable Medieval Reader*, Penguin, Harmondsworth, 1978, pp.78-9.
4. See below p.31 for the case of Christina Markyate.
5. Abelard and Heloise appear still to have considered themselves married, in spite of Abelard's use of the "bride of Christ" image. See below p.33 and Radice, *op. cit.,* p.109.
6. R.W. Southern, *Western Society and the Church in the Middle Ages,* Penguin, Harmondsworth, 1970, pp.314-15.
7. See below p.31.
8. Radice, *op. cit.,* pp.45-55.
9. These form the basis of Eileen Power's still unrivalled *Medieval English Nunneries,* Cambridge University Press, Cambridge, 1922.
10. Regrettably this is not taken up in W. Braunfels' monumental *Monasteries of Western Europe: the Architecture of the Orders,* Thames and Hudson, London, 1972.
11. See above footnote 3.
12. The most famous/notorious medieval parish priest must now be Pierre Clergue, the 'star' of a brilliant recent book by E. Le Roy Ladurie, *Montaillou,* Penguin, Harmondsworth, 1980. The book is based on

the investigation of a French village for heresy in the early 14th century. The priest, a double agent, was popular with his parishioners until his treachery was discovered. Boccaccio's *Decameron* also suggests popular affection for the lecherous priest.

13. S. Painter, *William Marshal,* John Hopkins Press, Baltimore, 1933, pp.284-6.

14. R.H. Bainton, *The Medieval Church,* Van Nostrand, Princeton, N.J., 1962, p.115.

15. D. Baker (ed.), *Medieval Women,* Studies in Church History, Subsidia, I, Basil Blackwell, Oxford, 1978, pp.15-30.

16. Radice, *op. cit.,* pp.137-8.

17. *Ibid.,* p.117.

18. Baker, *op. cit.,* pp.15-30.

19. *Ibid.,* pp.31-78 and 79-100.

20. G. Zarnecki, *The Monastic Achievement,* Thames and Hudson, London, 1972, Ch.2.

21. *Ibid.,* Ch.3.

22. Baker, *op. cit.,* pp.227-52.

23. One is quoted in K. Clark, *Civilisation,* B.B.C. and John Murray, London, 1969, p.40.

24. A fascinating study of the psychological/emotional side of monasticism is provided by J. Leclercq, *Monks and Love in Twelfth Century France,* Clarendon, Oxford, 1979.

25. Southern, *Western Society,* pp.314-18.

26. On Gilbert, see Ross and McLaughlin, *op. cit.,* pp.73-5.

27. Baker, *op. cit.,* p.222.

28. *Ibid.,* pp.205-26.

29. H. Mayer, *The Crusades,* Oxford University Press, London, 1972, Ch.2.

30. There is insufficient space here to deal with medieval medical theory and practice as it related to women. On this topic see V. Bullough, *Sex, Society and History,* Science History Publications, New York, 1976, pp.43-59.

31. *New Catholic Encyclopaedia,* McGraw-Hill, New York, 1967, vol.4, p.38.

32. T. Tentler, *Sin and Confession on the Eve of the Reformation,* Princeton University Press, Princeton, 1977, pp.3-27.

33. Southern, *Western Society,* pp.272-99.

34. *Ibid.,* pp.318-31, and Baker, *op. cit.,* pp.253-74.

35. *Ibid.,* pp.185-204.

36. Radice, *op. cit.,* Letters 5-7.

37. *Ibid.,* p.160.

38. *Ibid.,* p.214.

39. *Ibid.,* p.138.

40. The question has recently been discussed at length by A. Macfarlane,

The Origins of English Individualism, Basil Blackwell, Oxford, 1978.

41. Ross and McLaughlin, *op. cit.,* pp.369-78.
42. Radice, *op. cit.,* p.58.
43. Baker, *op. cit.,* pp.31-77 and 79-100.
44. Ross and McLaughlin, *op. cit.,* pp.369-78.
45. An example is given in Mayer, *op. cit.,* p.56.
46. The classic work on this is M. Bloch, *Feudal Society,* trans. by L.A. Manyon, 2 vols, Routledge and Kegan Paul, paperback ed., 1965.
47. M. Keen, *The Pelican History of Medieval Europe,* Penguin, Harmondsworth, 1967, pp.103-16, *passim.*
48. Clark, *op. cit.,* Ch.3.
49. E. Mercer, *Furniture 700-1700,* Meredith Press, New York, 1969, Ch.3.
50. E. Power, *Medieval Women,* Cambridge University Press, Cambridge, 1975, p.36.
51. See Baker, *op. cit.,* pp.119-42 for the example of St Margaret of Scotland.
52. Tentler, *op. cit.,* pp.162-232.
53. A recent article, M. Todd, "Humanists, Puritans and the Spiritualized Household", *Church History,* 49 (1980), pp.18-34, does this (but then argues, in my opinion unconvincingly, that counter-Reformation Catholicism downgraded the role of the family).
54. Painter, *op. cit.,* Ch.1.
55. We have however recently learnt a great deal more from the detective work of Le Roy Ladurie.
56. A fascinating recent work using such records is E. Britton, *The Community of the Vill,* Macmillan, Toronto, 1977.
57. Bloch, *op. cit.,* Vol. I, Part V.
58. E. Power, *Medieval People,* Methuen (paperback edition), London, 1963. Ch.II contains an interesting if rather imaginative account of peasant family life in the early medieval period.
59. Life at Montaillou, whilst hard, was certainly not dehumanizing.
60. M. Bloch, "From the Royal Court to the Court of Rome. The Suit of the Serfs of Rosny-sous-Bois", S. Thrupp (ed.), *Change in Medieval Society,* Appleton-Century-Crofts, New York, 1964.
61. M. Mollat and P. Wolff, *The Popular Revolutions of the Late Middle Ages,* George Allen and Unwin, London, 1973.
62. Montaillou is of course only known to us because of this.
63. Le Roy Ladurie, *op. cit.,* p.184.
64. Baker, *op. cit.,* pp.289-303 and 359-80.
65. Le Roy Ladurie, *op. cit.,* pp.225-40. See also Ross and McLaughlin, *op. cit.,* pp.512-5 for a greater emphasis on a good life.
66. Le Roy Ladurie, *op. cit.,* p.159.
67. Cf. the view of William Marshal (see above, n.13.).
68. R.W. Southern, *The Making of the Middle Ages,* Hutchinson,

London, 1953, Ch.2 Section (ii).

69.   The topic of urban women is dealt with particularly well by Power, *Medieval Women,* pp.50-70.

70.   The seminal work was H. Pirenne, *Medieval Cities,* Princeton University Press, Princeton, 1925, Ch.IV.

71.   This is the context of the text translated by E. Power as *The Goodman of Paris,* Broadway Medieval Library, London, 1928. See her discussion of it in *Medieval People,* Ch.V, and an extract from it in Ross and McLaughlin, *op. cit.,* pp.154-60.

72.   G. Wesson (ed.), *Brian's Wife, Jenny's Mum,* Dove Publications, East Malvern, 1975. The title comes from a poem on p.26.

73.   J. Harthan, *Books of Hours,* Thames and Hudson, London, 1977, pp.78, 80-1.

2

Patricia Crawford

From the Woman's View: Pre-industrial England, 1500-1750

(i)

Woman, says Simone de Beauvoir, is made, not born. 'No biological, psychological, or economic fate determines the figure that the human female presents in society; it is civilization as a whole that produces this creature'.[1] Thus to understand women's positions in pre-industrial England, we need to consider the social and economic circumstances which controlled their lives and shaped their understanding of what it was to be a woman.

We do not know the precise size of the population in England in 1500.[2] It was probably around 2 million, and some historians believe that the population had still not reached its pre-Black Death size of around 3 million. During the sixteenth century the population expanded beyond the largest size an English population had ever been — and kept on growing. By 1750 the population was about 5.7 million. This population growth was a European-wide phenomenon, and needs to be explained in terms of changes in patterns of disease, especially plague, in food resources and in family size and structure. Around the mid-eighteenth century, England's industrial development made the country unique in Europe.

All these basic social factors influenced the lives of women, but the lives of the individual women within the society at any one time differed greatly. England during the pre-industrial period was a stratified society. The hierarchy based on birth and wealth ranged from the poorest to the monarch. Everyone, men and women, derived their social status from their fathers, but women on marriage took the social status of their husbands. Thus, for example, while both the sons and daughters of a gentleman were gentry, a daughter lost her gentry status if she married a yeoman.

The main social groups in pre-industrial England were as follows. At the top, monopolizing the wealth and power of the community, were the peers and gentry who together made up the nobility. They comprised about five per cent of the population and owned most of the land, and were distinguished by a lifestsyle which involved no manual work. Yeomen, who may have equalled some of the poorer gentry in wealth, worked their farms themselves. In the towns there was a growing group of small traders. Yeomen farmers and tradesmen comprised the 'middling sort of people'. They all had some capital and their families usually shared in the common economic unit on which their livelihoods depended. Below these groups were wage labourers. They were vulnerable to fluctuations of trade, and during the sixteenth and seventeeth centuries many wage labourers were unemployed because England's main export, woollen cloth, was dislocated by wars in Europe. Some wage earners moved between the towns in winter and the countryside in summer.

Many people in this society were poor. Some historians estimate that about one third of the population was in danger of starvation if there were a bad harvest.[3] Those who lived at subsistence level had no resources at their disposal, and many tramped the roads in search of work, which made them liable to be classed as vagrants, whipped, and returned to their parish of origin. In theory each parish was responsible for relieving its own poor. Children under seven would remain with their parents and receive relief, but the older children would be bound to employers as servants.

The social and economic status of the family into which a woman was born determined whether she had enough to eat and the age at which she could afford to marry. Thus the lives of individual women differed markedly: the daughter of a gentleman would have plenty to eat and would marry at around eighteen to twenty, but the daughter of a poorer labourer would be accustomed to going hungry at times and would not marry till she was around twenty-six to twenty-eight years of age. This 'late' age at marriage for the majority of women in English society was typical of the marriage pattern for the whole of Western Europe at this pre-industrial period, and is one significant difference from the post-industrial pattern. But then, as now, the economic circumstances of a woman's family of origin influenced her social pattern and life. While the daughters of the nobility would be educated at home, and in the houses of female relatives, the majority of girls from poorer families would leave home between the ages of seven and fourteen to work as servants in someone else's household until they married in their late twenties. The tasks they would perform there would vary according to their own skills and the type of household: in the house of a yeoman, for example, they would participate in the basic work of providing food and clothing and keeping the house clean. In a great house, the house of a gentleman or nobleman, where the number of servants might range between five and thirty, their tasks might be more specialised. Some women were laundresses, some would clean and cook while others would wait on the lady of the house and care for the children. Being a servant for ten years or more before marriage was a part of life for the majority of women in pre-industrial England. Many girls went to London to be servants and lost their connections with their place of origin after they married and settled elsewhere in England.

One factor which influenced the lives of everyone in pre-industrial England was the mortality rate. Again, position in the social hierarchy influenced the experience of mortality for the individual woman and her children. The basic life expectancy at birth for any person was around thirty-five to forty years, but this gives a misleading impression of the population.[4] While it is true that there were more people under twenty as a proportion of the population – about half the population at any one time was under twenty in the pre-industrial period – many of those over twenty lived to a good old age. The life risks for the individual female child would be something as follows. There was a great risk of death in the first thirty-six hours of life from post-natal trauma. Subsequently, as some women who could afford to do so put their babies out to wet nurse, these babies were at risk. One in five of the babies born did not live to a year. Around the age of one, when the babies may have been weaned, female children may have been slightly more at risk as they competed for the household's scanty food resources. Before the age of five, another one in five children would die. Girls ran similar risks of death from disease and accident as boys, although in adolescent years they may have escaped the dangers of some violent deaths. By adolescence, many children would have lost one or both of their parents, and seen one or two of their siblings die. After their marriages in their late twenties, women entered a time of risk when they began childbearing. As lactation has a contraceptive effect, women who breast fed their babies may have had a child every two years or so. Thus, between marriage in the late twenties and the menopause around forty, women may have borne six children, of whom maybe four would have survived infancy. This pattern contrasts with that of women in the post-industrial period, such as in nineteenth-century Australia, where women married earlier and bore consequently more children. Women who survived until the menopause had a good chance of living to sixty or seventy. Wealthier women may have had rather less chance of survival: as they married earlier and put out children to wet nurse, they experienced more pregnancies, perhaps one each year. Anne Hatton, a gentlewoman, bore twenty-two children after her marriage in 1685.

According to the surviving parish registers, the majority of people in pre-industrial England lived their lives in small-scale domestic groups. Peter Laslett believes that a household containing three generations was unusual, and most of the households consisted of parents and children. Few people lived long enough to see their grandchildren. Distances and lack of transport restricted the chance of help to the nuclear family being given by a wider group of relations. In the poorer households, children would be sent elsewhere as servants as soon as they were old enough to be useful because their families of origin could not afford to feed them. More recent research in other sources suggests that household types were more varied. Not all households contained nuclear families and their children.[5]

Family connections were different for the gentry. Because the gentry married younger than the majority of the population, many of them lived to be grandparents. The gentry also had the means of communicating across the country: they owned horses, coaches (increasingly as the seventeenth and eighteenth centuries progressed) and they could write letters. In their great houses the records of their family connections could be preserved. Among this group, there were many different kinds of households. Their households were larger than those of the bulk of the population – up to thirty people perhaps – and might be multi-generational. Many an eldest son, on marriage, would board (or 'table') with his parents: thus his wife spent the first years of her marriage in the house which would ultimately be hers, but initially she was under the tutelage and control of a mother-in-law. Sometimes the couple might live with her parents: Alice Thornton, a gentlewoman, had 'all our table gratis' with her mother for eight years for herself, her husband, one man servant and three maids and nurses for her children. Matthew Henry, a Nonconformist minister, tabled for over a year with his wife's parents, and on his wife's death he and their baby daughter continued to live with them until, with the active assistance of his mother-in-law, he remarried.[6] The variety of household arrangements at this period is thus a caution against any too rigid interpretation of the numbers of people living in a household: compositions of households varied greatly.

Lives of women also varied according to whether they lived in the town or the country. Life in the village may have been small-scale. Women probably had few relations to whom they could turn for aid. They depended on their neighbours for help in childbirth and in sickness. A wealthy gentlewoman who lived in the country may have suffered from boredom and loneliness as her husband would probably spend some months in London for business each year. Town life offered more entertainment. Of the towns, London far outstripped all others in size by 1600. Those who lived in town – young girls who were servants – were more at risk from sickness and poverty than those in the villages, especially while plague remained a danger up to 1665 (the Great Plague). Many girls who went to London to make their fortunes were too proud to admit failure and return to their families when they were sick or unemployed.

Economic and social circumstances thus had varied effects upon women's lives. The leisured lives of women at the top of the social hierarchy were very different from those who worked in the fields. While all the institutions of the society – the church, the law, the administration – deemed women inferior to men and therefore subordinate, a noblewoman commanded respect from men who were her social inferiors. Women then, as many do now, took their social position from their male relatives.

(ii)

Women have always worked, although not always for wages. Women were employed in a variety of ways at the beginning of the sixteenth century. The Marxist view is that their economic position and employment opportunities deteriorated during the seventeenth and eighteenth centuries as England began to industrialize. Unfortunately we still do not have much information about women's work during this whole period. A pioneering study by Alice Clark in 1919[7] of the working lives of women in the seventeenth century has not yet been followed up, nor do comparable studies exist for the sixteenth or eighteenth centuries. Nevertheless, Joan Thirsk has recently suggested that industrialization during the later seventeenth and eighteenth centuries may have created new economic opportunities for women.[8]

It is important to appreciate that much of the labour of women, while not contributing directly to the *income* of the family, ensured its survival by producing food and clothing. Women also worked for wages. As agricultural labourers, their wages were fixed by the justices of the peace at the quarter sessions, usually at about one third those paid to men. If the family owned a small plot of land, women might share the agricultural labour as well as take responsibility for providing food and keeping house. We know little about the interiors and possessions of these poorer households. Inventories have survived for the contents of the cottages of some of the better-off labourers. In 1613, for example, Edith Coke left goods including blankets, sheets, kettles and cups to the value of £14.14.2. Other poorer houses consisted of one or two rooms, dirt floors and few possessions. Keeping house in such circumstances would not have been time-consuming. Many women contributed to the family's income by weaving or spinning. It was assumed that a woman's wages would be sufficient to keep herself and one child.[9]

The majority of women worked as servants for wages and board before they married. This was unskilled labour, although it might be at differentiated tasks. Some women acquired skills in crafts, particularly in the production of textiles. Women were spinners and weavers, and like other employees, were subject to the fluctuations of the market. They shared in the retail trades as relatively unskilled labour, and also participated in provisioning trades – as bakers, butchers, fishwives, millers, brewers and vintners. Some of these trades women carried on independently, sometimes as wives or widows, but Clark suggests that as the trades became increasingly capitalised, women were excluded.

The main professions of the church and the law were closed to women. In areas such as medicine and teaching, the development of these professions during the early modern period had the effect of excluding the untrained practitioner (that is, those who had not attended a university) and establishing monopolies. Women were restricted increasingly in medicine, and were primarily nurses. The midwives who had traditionally controlled child-birth were being replaced by 'male accoucheurs'.[10] Teaching continued to be an area of employment for women: the wife of the prebend of York who resigned 'betakes herself to get a living by teaching young children to sew'.[11] Elizabeth Elstob, an Anglo-Saxon scholar, was forced to earn her own living after her brother died in the early eighteenth century. Before she found a post as governess, she was forced to set up a small school for young children.

Many women with children lived alone because their husbands were away, perhaps at sea or as soldiers, or because their husbands had deserted them, or died. Economic necessity forced these women to earn an income. The wife of Edward Coxere, who was a sailor in the late seventeenth century, bore a daughter and lost a son while he was at sea, then began to keep a shop, 'there being a necessity for something to be done for a livelihood'.[12] Widowhood might be a difficult and unhappy time for a woman, depending on her social class and economic circumstances. Among the gentry, the widow's rights were governed by marriage settlements, but a wealthy widow might find herself vexed with legal suits in order to preserve her children's inheritances from either the Court of Wards (which was abolished in 1641) or from rapacious male relatives. Poorer women might find their parish provided some relief for them, particularly if they were too old to work. Sons and daughters were expected to provide for their aged widowed mothers, but the records of the church courts which provide evidence of disputes over the widow's rights to sit by the fire and to have food and light indicate that not all children fulfilled their obligations.

Exploring Women's Past

Widows of tradesmen might take over their husbands' business in the sixteenth and seventeenth centuries. There were, for example, women printers who were licensed after their husbands' deaths. In other cases, as can be seen from accounts of a diarist in Lancaster, widows of tradesmen with young children had been so busied about their domestic concerns that they had no idea of how to manage their husbands' businesses. Since even apprentices took time to learn how to run shops and to trade, these women were often forced to get a living for themselves and their children by a less skilled – and less lucrative – occupation, such as candle-making, using the proceeds from the sale of their husbands' goods as capital.[13]

It is perhaps easier to see the contribution which women made to their family's economic survival in this pre-industrial period than it is later. The majority of women worked for their livelihoods and ran the households which fed and clothed the male workers and cared for their children. Although standards of housing and living generally were improving between 1500 and 1750, the gap between the rich and the poor was widening, and life for the majority of people was a difficult struggle for survival, although, for an increasing minority of prosperous women, leisure was available.

(iii)

Patriarchal ideology influenced the ways in which men perceived women in the pre-industrial period. The greatest single influence on the lives of women (and of men too) was the Christian religion which informed the laws of England and its administration.

England in 1500 was a Roman Catholic country, but in the 1530s Henry VIII broke with Rome and subsequently, in the reign of his son Edward VI, a Protestant Reformation began. This Reformation, which made the Church of England a Protestant one, suffered certain vicissitudes and was never what the more extreme Protestants, known as Puritans, considered satisfactory. Consequently in England in the early seventeenth century there was a minority group of Catholic families concentrated in the north of England and isolated from national life, and an Anglican church, within which rival groups competed for changes. During the English Civil Wars, 1642-1649, Parliament abolished bishops and attempted to make the Church a presbyterian one. During these years of disorder, and subsequently during the Commonwealth, 1649-1660, there was a wider range of religious practice and belief. Many religious sects flourished in which women took a prominent part. Although the Anglican church's monopoly was restored with Charles II in 1660, religious dissent continued until toleration was granted in 1689 with the accession of William and Mary. In the eighteenth century the religious scene was more peaceful. Toleration allowed the Dissenters to worship as they wished, but the social composition of this group changed. Whereas in the reign of Elizabeth I at the end of the sixteenth century there had been people in all social ranks supporting change in the Anglican church in a puritan direction, the heirs of these Puritans in the eighteenth century were generally restricted to tradesmen. Dissent was no religion for gentlemen.

These religious changes over three centuries affected women. In some places women took a prominent part in defending the old religious establishments against those who wished to change the services and dissolve the monasteries. In 1536, for example, when the dissolution of St. Nicholas's Priory, Exeter was attempted, 'certain women and wives in the city' came in haste with spikes, shovels and pikes to defend it.[14] The dissolution of nunneries in the 1530s deprived women of what Margaret Ker has shown was an attractive alternative to marriage and the family.[15] Although some Catholic families continued to send daughters to nunneries abroad, there were no nunneries in England after 1540. The newly Protestant Anglican Church stressed the Bible as its source of authority, so that biblical ideas about women were more important than ever. The Bible offered various images of women, from Eve the author of man's downfall, to Mary, mother of the Redeemer. The emphasis of the English church fell on the creation myth, the implications of which were endlessly discussed. In one version of Eve's creation in Genesis, she was shaped from dust, in another, from Adam's rib. While some argued that her creation from Adam made her superior to him – the product of flesh rather than dust as he was – most stressed that the creation out of his rib made her a companion. (Creation from his head would have made Eve Adam's superior and from his foot would have made her to be trodden upon.)[16] Perhaps because Mary's role in the Catholic church was a large one, the Protestant church reduced her importance. Texts from Timothy about women being saved by childbearing were stressed in sermons.

Although these texts about women's inferiority and sinfulness formed the subjects of many sermons and were the basis of the domestic advice books of the early modern period, there were other stories in the Bible which women might read and use as alternative role models. When women petitioned Parliament during the Civil Wars and the members told them not to meddle 'in state's matters', they quoted the example of Esther from the Bible who risked her life to save her people.[17] Furthermore, although the majority of women might accept the versions of the biblical stories given by the preachers, not all did, as the following incident illustrates. A woman in childbed was 'not to be ruled', so those about her sent for a Lady Pickering, who exhorted patience, saying that 'this misery was brought upon her sex by her grandmother Eve, by eating an apple. "Was it?" says she. "I wish the apple had choak'd her".'[18]

Just as women had played a prominent role in heretical sects during the medieval period, so during the English Civil Wars of the mid-seventeenth century, when there was *de facto* religious toleration, many women joined religious sects.[19] There, to the horror of the conservatives, they preached and taught. Most of these sects were suppressed at the Restoration in 1660, but some survived, of which one of the most interesting is the Society of Friends, or Quakers, as they were known. The Quakers held many ideas in common with other sects. They stressed the importance of the individual soul, and the idea that there was neither male nor female in the Lord and that all were fellow creatures. Their refusal to show respect to any social superiors by taking off their hats – on the grounds that such reverence was due only to the Lord – enraged most of their contemporaries. In practical terms, Quakerism offered women an opportunity to participate more fully in worship than did the established Anglican Church. But although the Quaker women had more freedom than many, and much of the literature published by women in the later seventeenth century is by Quakers, they were restricted within the Society as it became more organized. Women's meetings were established for the discussion of separate issues and for charitable purposes, and some women, who considered it would be immodest to 'speak' in the Quaker mixed meetings, preached in these women's meetings. During the 1670s the Quaker movement was divided on a number of issues, and this question of women speaking with messages from the Lord was one to which may Quakers objected.

There was one important change at the Reformation which affected the status of marriage in England: priests before the Reformation were expected to be unmarried and celibate, but after the Reformation they might marry. Celibacy was no longer an ideal, and the Anglican – and Puritan – theologians all discussed this new doctrine of matrimony as an ideal state, pointing out that as God had designed marriage for man in the Garden of Eden, it was an institution of divine ordination. Protestant preachers emphasised the importance of companionship in marriage, but wives were still expected to be subordinate to husbands. In the good order and good government of families, said the preachers, lay the safety of the commonwealth. If wives and children were obedient, political authority was secure.[20] Yet not all women were obedient, nor were all able to reconcile themselves to their duties. One puritan gentleman was discussing marriage with a woman who was unhappily married. 'God', said Sir Symonds D'Ewes, 'decreed marriages in heaven; and when they are once accomplished, every man and woman ought to compose and frame their hearts to a persuasion that the husband or wife they enjoy is best for them'. The woman's rejoinder was brief and dry: 'Ay, if one could do so'.[21]

In some ways the Protestant doctrines assisted the position of women. As the Protestant church emphasised the role of the individual in his or her salvation, women had to save their own souls. Those who could read sought out their faith in the Bible. Women as well as men began to keep spiritual diaries from the later sixteenth century onwards, in which they examined their souls, their prayers, their daily activities, and tried to account for their time. The Protestant Reformation in the sixteenth century gave a great fillip to women's education, but the social upheaval at the time of the mid-seventeenth century Civil Wars made the rulers of England suspicious of education for men as well as women. By the eighteenth century the curriculum for women seems to have changed. Whereas Thomas More – admittedly an exceptional individual – taught his daughters Greek in the sixteenth century, the gentry of the eighteenth century were sending their daughters for lessons in dancing and deportment. Even when educational ideals did flourish, the curriculum for the education of girls differed from that for boys in the upper social strata. Boys might enter the University and study at Inns of Court. There were some boarding schools for girls in the seventeenth century, but in general girls learnt at home.

Historians have been interested in the different attitudes of the Catholic and Protestant churches to the question of the relationship between women and men. Natalie Davis has applied some of Alice Rossi's ideas about three models for talking about equality. One model is pluralistic, with women allowed to keep their distinctive characteristics in a hierarchical society: this is the Catholic position. Another is the assimilationist model. The subordinate group is raised by making it like the superior group, but still subordinate: that was the Protestant solution. The third model involves a transformation of existing roles, but neither church in the pre-industrial period approached this. That is, although Protestantism may have offered some advantages to women in England, some losses were sustained, and women remained subject.[22] Their subordination was reflected in the laws of England.

Because the Reformation in England in the sixteenth century was never a complete one, the administration of the Anglican church remained much as it had been under the Catholic church. The Catholic church had controlled the morals of the community via a system of church courts and these continued after the Reformation. The rituals associated with birth, marriage, and death remained under church control. The church decided who might be allowed to marry, and what a valid marriage might be. Canon law laid down that a woman must be twelve years of age, a man fourteen. The two essential ingredients of a valid marriage were the consent of the two parties and the consummation of the marriage. Thus a marriage which was not consummated was deemed invalid, and annulled. There was no divorce either before or after the Reformation, though the church might allow legal separation (this did not permit remarriage). In practice many people who were unhappily married tried to have their marriages declared invalid, and this was often possible on technical grounds. The only exception to this was for those wealthy enough to have a private act of Parliament passed for a divorce after the first case in 1666. Sexual offences were punished by the church courts which viewed the offences of men and women differently. In 1650 an act was passed to bring the law of England into harmony with the law of God: the death penalty was prescribed for adultery. By the Act's definition, a married woman who copulated with a man was guilty of adultery; a married man who copulated with a woman was guilty of fornication, which carried a lesser penalty.[23]

Men with property wished to leave this to their legitimate heirs, hence they feared that if women's sexuality were uncontrolled, children not their own might inherit. They sought to control women's lives so that they would not stray. Modesty was deemed a crucial virtue for women. Wealthier women – more at risk because they had more leisure – were praised for their busyness because a woman who was always busy about her household had no time to transgress. Reading and embroidery took up much of the time of leisured women in the sixteenth and seventeeth centuries. Lady Anne Clifford recorded that she made a cushion to pass the time. Others made flowered bed-spreads.[24]

Below the level of the wealthy propertied groups, the marriage of a woman depended on the consent of her relations who would help to set up a household. Prior to this consent, many women pledged themselves to marry. If sexual intercourse took place, the woman might find herself pregnant. Even if the man married her she might still find herself indicted in the church courts for pre-marital fornication, but if he would not, her lot was a grim one. After the passing of the Poor Law in 1601, her parish was responsible for maintaining her and her bastard child. As this required increased poor rates, she would be socially unpopular. She might also be physically punished with a whipping for bearing a bastard. After 1623, if her baby died and could not be proved by a witness to be dead at birth, she was deemed to be guilty of murdering it, a reversal of the normal procedure of English law at this date by which a person was deemed innocent until proven guilty.

The laws of England at this period were made by the monarch, the peers and the commons. Although there were some female monarchs during this period, the laws were made by the men of property. These laws assumed that women were inferior and were the responsibility of their fathers or husbands. Married women were not legally free to dispose of their own property, although settlements at marriage guaranteed them property at their husbands' deaths. The state of maximum legal independence for a woman in this society was widowhood where she was subject to the control of no man, although her male relatives might try to influence her.

Common law gave a poorer woman rights to one third of the property of her husband on his decease. The remainder was inherited by children. Inheritance customs varied from county to county during the pre-industrial period: in some areas female children may have inherited equally with males. This is in marked contrast to the undeviating pattern of inheritance among the families of the peers and gentry: the eldest male inherited the bulk of the estate and the title. This estate came to him on such terms that he could not sell or dispose of it among his children even had he wished to do so. Only by his own personal exertions could he hope to provide dowries for his daughters and some form of livelihood for his younger sons.

Women do not exist in a vacuum. At some stages of their lives all are members of a family. Recent historical research has suggested that the family underwent major changes between 1500 and 1800. The most significant change, Lawrence Stone argues, was in ideology by the rise of what he terms 'affective individualism'. Before the end of the seventeenth century Stone believes that relationships between husbands and wives were formed on the basis of property interests and that parents did not love their children. Children, he says, were brutally treated and even killed, and he quotes the sixteenth-century French essayist, Montaigne, who claims to have lost two or three children in their infancy with some sorrow, but not a great deal of regret.[25] Stone's view of such loveless marriages and unloving parents has been criticized. Part of his mistake lies, I believe, in his using male sources. If he had begun to read the letters which women wrote to their parents, their husbands and their children, he would see mothers concerned about their babies, anxious over their feeding, their ailments and their teething, discussing their clothing, their progress in walking, talking and movement, and revealing desperate grief on the deaths of their children. Nor do these attitudes appear in women alone: men were concerned for their children. Although the evidence of letters relates only to the tiny literate portion of the population whose letters have survived, it is evidence which should not be ignored.

During all the changes between 1500 and 1750 one notion remained remarkably constant: women were weaker than men. Because of their inferiority, it was deemed that they should be subordinate. It is fascinating to observe that although the *reasons* for women's necessary subordination might change, the axiomatic inferiority of women remained.

(iv)

The main biological events in women's lives focus on reproduction – menstruation, conception, pregnancy, abortion, child-birth and lactation – but even these 'naturals' of women's lives are interpreted in a cultural mould which gives them social meaning. In particular, the implications of medical explanations of women's biology are important. In this section, I want to discuss both the biological determinants of women's lives and the cultural interpretations of the biological facts.

The basic premise of the medical models was the inferiority of women. In 1500 medicine was dominated by the ideas of the second-century Roman physician, Galen, who believed human beings were influenced by a balance of elements in their bodies. Women's bodies were cold and moist while those of men were dry and hot. Women's anatomy was described as a variant of men's: women's reproductive organs were those of men, internalized. The ovaries were called the female testicles. But women were less efficient machines. They concocted more blood than they needed from the food they took in, so this excess was discharged monthly. Menstruation in itself made women liable to all kinds of disorders as they accumulated putrefying blood in their wombs, the fumes from which rose to trouble their brains. Women who did not menstruate when they should have done were believed to be in a dangerous state. Physicians advised blood-letting, lest the woman fall into sickness. During the sixteenth century there was much discussion in the general literature about whether woman was a mistake or not. There was a belief that Nature, in creation, sought always for perfection: a male. If Nature erred a female was produced. Gradually this ceased to be debated as physicians recognised that woman had a purpose in the reproduction of the species. Woman was 'an house created for Gestation and Generation'.[26]

In the mid-seventeenth century there was a change in scientific and medical ideas which has been described as a revolution. Physicians began to question and to challenge the old Galenic assumptions and to base their clinical practices on observation and experiment. Concurrently with this, physicians gained in assurance and professional confidence, and distanced themselves from women who had taken a large part earlier in the healing of the sick. Men involved themselves in the delivery of babies and the position of midwives deteriorated. At a popular level it is doubtful if this made much impact on what women believed about their bodies and its functions, but among the upper sections of the society the physician began to assume importance as a family adviser.

The main biological events for women which physicians explained were related to reproduction. There were several medical theories about how conception occurred during the sixteenth century. The main idea was that both men and women released their seed during copulation and that from this mixture a child was formed. The menstrual blood which the woman accumulated was used to nourish the foetus. Another theory was that the male seed shaped a child from the mass of menstrual blood: the man provided the active principal, the woman the matter of the foetus. The implication of the first theory for women's sexuality was a positive one: women had to enjoy sex in order to conceive a child. Advice books from the sixteenth and seventeenth centuries tell couples how to achieve what amounts to a simultaneous orgasm. On the negative side, this theory of conception, when carried over into a legal context for the judgment of rape, meant that the woman who conceived after rape was deemed to have consented and enjoyed the sexual act.[27]

By the end of the seventeenth century the discovery of the microscope and the recognition of sperm stimulated a major controversy on the process of conception (or 'generation', as it was called). Scientists argued that the child was pre-formed in the spermatozoa, or that the 'egg' contained all future eggs (like a series of boxes inside boxes). Either the male or the female was the exclusive source of life. The implication of this for women's sexual pleasure was commented on early in the eighteenth century as being resented by women: no longer was their sexual pleasure necessary for the process of conception and they 'take it ill to be thought merely passive in those Wars wherein they make such vigorous Encounters'.[28]

Menstrual blood continued to be viewed as the source of foetal nutrition. Women opposed physicians letting their blood during pregnancy for 'they thinke all the nourishment is drawne from the childe'. Furthermore, since it was believed that breast milk was simply menstrual blood diverted to the breasts and there whitened by the nipples, any pregnant woman who was breast-feeding was advised to wean her baby immediately lest it be starved, for as Luther explained in the sixteenth century, the child in the womb would take all the cream leaving only skim milk for the one at the breast. Ideally, a breast-feeding woman should avoid sexual intercourse lest this provoke menstruation (and so deprive the child of nutrition) and a subsequent pregnancy. These attitudes are clearly revealed in the discussion of the selection of wet-nurses who should be separated from their husbands. In practice, it does not seem as if this taboo on sexual intercourse with a lactating woman was always observed, because we can see from family records that a number of women weaned their babies after they were pregnant or after they thought they were pregnant.[29]

Not only did the woman contribute the nourishment of the foetus: her imagination shaped the child's appearance. The likeness of a child to its father or other relations was believed to be the consequence of the mother's thoughts. If she thought of her husband, her child would resemble him. Maternal longings were taken seriously, as any frustration of the mother's wishes would affect the child. Any frights which a pregnant woman received would appear on the child in the form of birth-marks. These ideas continued into the eighteenth century, and at a popular level, probably longer.[30]

Menstruation was viewed by men with anxiety and there were biblical taboos and medical reasons why no man should copulate with a menstruating woman. The Bible had declared that the child of any such union would be weak, leprous and disordered, and although it was not clear from the Bible whether these Levitical taboos were based on a recognition of medical facts or were a punishment from God for those who disobeyed, the medical theories of this pre-industrial period justified the taboo. Since a child was formed by both men and women spending their seed, a child could be conceived during menstruation, but the child would be deformed because the seed would be choked with menstrual blood. Since the menstrual blood was believed to have great and dangerous power – it might blast crops, kill bees, blunt knives and such like – it seemed logical that it would harm a forming foetus. Any deformed child was therefore viewed as a punishment of its parents for the misdeed of copulation during menstruation.

So long as it was believed that women produced seed as well as men, women were recognized to have sexual needs. This seed might accumulate and cause illness, and one of the disorders to which young girls and widows were subject came from retention of seed. The main medical remedy was sexual activity, and thus marriage was advised as a cure. This disorder, which was sometimes called greensickness, was one which can be seen as a consequence of the medical theories. Sex was believed to be necessary, therefore those who were deprived were liable to fall ill. In the same way, menstruation was necessary and those who suffered from amenorrhoea were believed to have greensickness (this term was used for a variety of disorders in young girls), or mother fits (the womb was commonly referred to as 'the mother'). This diagnosis exposed women to a variety of remedies – drinks, powders, fumigations, pessaries and even blood-letting. While some remedies may have been harmless, blood-letting would have contributed to anaemia in women.

Because medical theory recognized the importance of sexual activity, it makes no sense to see the late sixteenth and seventeenth-century Puritans as hostile to sex. They, like the rest of their community, believed sex to be necessary for health as well as procreation. The questions they discussed were how much sex and when. Like everyone else who advised on the subject, Puritan preachers and writers assumed that sexual activity should occur only between a married couple. Since Solon, a pagan, had advised that three times a month was a desirable rate of sexual activity, Puritans thought that those with Christian liberty should not exceed what the pagans prescribed. Excessive sexual activity was discouraged and here again medical theory buttressed Christian teaching. Seed was a highly refined distillation from the food and blood which human beings produced: 'a distillation of the fifth essence' they sometimes called it. 'Spending' too much of this seed (the language is of interest) would weaken the body. Men were in more danger of this than women, for women were always wanting to conceive and bear children, hence they were always seeking man's seed. They 'snatch seed as hungry dogs do a bone' said the physician Lemnius. Too much sex made a woman's womb slippery and caused abortions. Furthermore, the Puritan belief that love was necessary in a marriage was buttressed by medical beliefs. A woman had to love her husband if her womb was to open to admit his seed. If husband and wife hated each other, when their seeds did meet they would reveal the same aversion and no child would be conceived.[31]

It should be stressed at this point that what we are looking at is medical theories, and what these reveal are the assumptions of the literate, male minority. In terms of understanding the ideology of a patriarchal society, these ideas are of great importance, for medical theories support ideas of female weakness and inferiority, although, as we have seen, the medical ideas take female inferiority as one of their axioms. The problem of popular belief, and in particular, of women's beliefs, is much harder to elucidate. The surviving sources are much fewer. There is one general advice book written by a woman, Jane Sharp, in the seventeenth century, and incidental comments on matters obstetric and gynaecological in the almanack books of Sarah Jinner, but the ideas and assumptions in these works are identical with those of men.

There are some sources available which take us closer to women's own ideas. These are their commonplace books which contain, amongst the recipes and household hints, medical remedies for a number of the recognized gynaecological disorders – greensickness, stoppage of the terms (amenorrhoea), overflowing of the courses (dysmenorrhoea) and barrenness. Many of these remedies are identical to those in printed sources, but others differ, having magical qualities. For example, a cure for excessive menstruation was that blood should flow into a hole with a three cornered stake; to provoke menstruation, a branch of mulberry should be tied to the arm. We can catch glimpses of a group of women advising each other across boundaries of social status: one woman copied down a remedy which she had from a poor woman begging alms at the door.[32]

Another less direct source for women's ideas is their depositions at the quarter sessions for illegitimate pregnancy. Women are very positive about which of several sexual encounters led to pregnancy. Susan Draper, for example, admitted to sexual intercourse with a blacksmith on a number of occasions but it was a month before Whitsun 'hee did then begett her with child'.[33] Is Susan Draper taking seriously the popular literature which says a woman may know she is pregnant by the shutting up of her womb, by the feeling of pleasure, and such like? In fact, one of the most difficult questions in medical practice during the seventeenth century was to determine pregnancy: there seemed no reliable guides.

What knowledge of birth control did women have? Women obviously knew that sexual intercourse was necessary for conception, and sometimes there are hints that abstinence was the main known contraceptive. Lactation was seen to delay pregnancy: there are printed observations on wealthy women who hired wet-nurses who had a baby every year while those who breast-fed their own babies often had two years between babies. But in terms of a reliable contraceptive for the individual woman, lactation is of limited use, for its effect depends on the amount of other food the child takes and the regularity of the stimulus. Ovulation may resume any time from three to eighteen months.[34] Withdrawal, or coitus interruptus, was known as a male method because the Bible condemned Onan who, to avoid impregnating his late brother's wife, spilled his seed upon the ground. (In the eighteenth century the term 'Onanism' had shifted in meaning and was used to describe the 'sin' of masturbation).

Abortion is not a contraceptive, but it is one way of controlling fertility. Women obviously believed that many of the remedies to precipitate menstruation would also cause abortion, and they went to doctors asking for the restoration of menstruation so that they would receive abortifacients. Presumably the female sub-culture exchanged prescriptions. There are interesting hints of knowledge of abortion from the comments of one woman, Deborah Brackley, who was questioned for illegitimate pregnancy. She had contracted to marry her fellow servant George Jewell in 1649. Over the next two years she had several times feared she was pregnant, to which he made a variety of responses:

> at one time hee said hee was now avenged of her, att another time
> hee told her that shee could not be with Childe & though the
> docters tould her soe yet they were fooles And if shee were with
> childe shee knew what things to take to bringe it goinge, & advised
> her to take Phisike.[35]

The comment 'shee knew what things to take' is suggestsive, and
maybe Deborah tried them; if so they were ineffective, for she was
in danger of serious punishment, which could have included a
whipping, and public shame from her pregnancy in 1651.

It is part of my argument here, that if reliable means of contraception or abortion had been known, more women at the time would
have used them, and there would also be something about these
remedies in the surviving evidence. The first mention of condoms
is in the eighteenth century, and again I would argue from absence
of evidence: if there had been condoms around in Restoration
London, a well-informed sexually active male such as Samuel Pepys
would have known about them.[36]

Accounts of women in the eighteenth century who were on trial
for the murder of their new-born babies reveal a picture of women
who were determined not to allow a pregnancy to destroy their social
lives. These girls had concealed their pregnancies in the households
in which they were servants – no easy task, given lack of privacy
in accommodation – and then had given birth without making a
sound which would arouse suspicion. They had then disposed of the
baby, sometimes in 'the house of office' or in the pond, and
attempted to carry on as usual. Again, these desperate actions point
to a picture of women who believed they had little choice about the
consequences of their sexuality.[37]

There are social factors which affected fertility as well as the
deliberate attempts by men and women to control fertility. In
addition to the late age at marriage, malnutrition led to amenorrhoea
in women and so infertility. A French historian, Ladurie, has shown
from a study of birth registers after famines in late seventeenth-century France that there were few births during the famine.
He deduced that this was caused by amenorrhoea by correlating the

pattern with that which occurred in the Netherlands in 1944-5 when there was near-starvation – and trauma – after the German invasion.[38]

Sexuality for women in the early modern period was unavoidably linked with child-bearing. Lacking a reliable means of contraception, women's lives revolved around pregnancy, lactation and the nurture of children. The cultural meaning given to these biological events was, however, a reinforcement of the notion that women were inferior, and the medical theories about female weakness underpinned many other parts of the patriarchal ideology.

(v)

In discussing the social and economic conditions of pre-industrial England, I have tried to make women visible in a way in which they were not always visible to their contemporaries, or to later historians. (One seventeenth-century physician, for example, wrote of 'a fellow' who lived in Kineton and had twenty-seven children of whom none lived above a month.)[39] In this section I want to turn more directly to the words of women themselves using evidence from the period of the seventeenth-century.

Women's words survive in a variety of sources; sometimes these sources are created by men, or by institutions controlled by men. When women visited physicians, they spoke of their anxieties about child-bearing and their grief for the deaths of their children. Menstrual disorders they might link with their child-bearing capacity: 'she hath feareth and grieveth she have no children more because she hath been troubled with the redds so much'. Pregnancy, if the women were unmarried, brought them into the quarter sessions for examination: there they spoke of consenting to sexual intercourse on promises of marriage from fellow servants, or from men they met on the roads. Elizabeth Pittey, for example, said that at first she refused sexual intercourse, 'but the said Westaway pressinge her unto it againe & againe att last she condescended'. Few of these women could sign their names. Some said they had been seduced by their masters or his son.[40]

Records of women's conflicts with their husbands provide some evidence of the issues which women disputed. In the Court of Star Chamber Viscount Fenton complained that his wife Marjorie had torn out of the Bible the chapters relating to wives' duties to their husbands. There were clashes over domestic management. In his will, Gilbert Earl of Clare complained of his wife allowing all the linen to be ruined because she sent it out to be washed, following 'that lazy trick of her mother's', instead of supervising its washing by servants at home. She was always gadding around the town and pleasing herself. In the life of his wife, Richard Baxter said that he objected to Margaret's insistence that the rooms be scrubbed as clean as the plates: he thought that the servants' time would be better employed in reading good books. In this, and the following case, the wives were of higher social origin and 'breeding' than their husbands, and obviously sought to maintain their families in the standard to which they were accustomed. Bishop Bedell's wife wanted to dress her children with 'elegance and neatness of habit' but her husband protested and insisted that they wear plain clothes.[41]

While physicians' case books and court records can be valuable to the historian for the lives of women, they must be used with extreme caution for the women themselves did not generate the records, and their words have been filtered through a medical or a legal model. Fortunately, women themselves created and left an enormous number of records. They wrote autobiographies and kept diaries, some of which have been subsequently printed. They wrote lives of their husbands, and some of these were published at the time, such as those by Margaret Cavendish, Duchess of Newcastle and Theodosia Alleine. Other biographies, such as that of Lucy Hutchinson, and autobiographies, such as those of Anne, Lady Halkett and Ann, Lady Fanshawe, were published later. Women also wrote many letters, and although subsequent cataloguers dismissed many as of little historical importance, they contain a mine of information about women and their lives. Some collections of women's letters have been printed and are well known, such as those of Brilliana Harley, Dorothy Osborne and Lady Russell. Women also left commonplace books in which they recorded recipes, household hints and various cures for sicknesses and disorders. They kept household accounts.[42] They wrote and published books.[43] These sources provide evidence about women's feelings on a range of subjects.

Marriage was, for women and men, an important step. Some women reveal anxiety about marriage or unwillingness. Ann Henry, in 1689, was unhappy at the thought of leaving home. In the 1630s, Mary Boyle was living 'so much at my ease that I was unwilling to change my condition'. Some wanted to marry for love. Dorothy Osborne wanted to marry William Temple, but as both sets of parents opposed the match, she had some years in which to reflect upon the question of marriage for love in her letters to Temple. She censured a gentlewoman of her acquaintance who persuaded herself that a man with an income of £2,300 per annum was better than an income of £1,200 and a man she loved, and she regretted the fate of a woman who was sacrificed by her family to an unpleasant husband. Dorothy's brother, who opposed her marriage with Temple, consistently argued that people who married on the strength of the kindness they had for each other were disappointed and later unhappy, whereas those who married for sensible reasons – like the sizes of their respective fortunes – would find that love developed after marriage. Dorothy thought this far too uncertain a basis for marriage. Her brother thought that passion for a husband was dangerous: Dorothy argued that 'reason and religion teach us to govern our passions'. She and Temple did finally marry. Their fortunes were not, in fact, widely disparate, so their discussion about the role of love in marriage was between a couple in the same social stratum. Dorothy was not alone or unique in her determination to marry one she loved. Other women commented on relations who, though married to 'a good estate', yet did not enjoy much comfort. Mary Boyle, daughter of the powerful and wealthy Earl of Cork, fell in love with a younger brother who was, though of good family, of small fortune. She defied her father to the extent of refusing to marry anyone else, and when her father gave his consent to her marriage to Charles Rich, she confessed in her autobiography that she 'thought of nothing but having a person for whom I had a great passion'. Earlier, when her father presented to her the man he desired she would think of as a husband, she confessed to an extraordinary aversion to the man 'though I could give my father no satisfactory account of why it was so'. Presumably the aversion was sexual, and her father may have accepted her statement because he knew, according to the current medical theories, that no child would be born to a woman who had an aversion to her husband.

The families of other women took less interest in their marriages. Perhaps the women were orphans, or they had lost touch with their parents. These women may have gained more freedom in their choice of a husband. From the diary of Samuel Pepys we can piece together the story of the courtship and marriage of their two servants, Jane Birch and Tom Edwards. In February 1668 Pepys's wife Elizabeth told him that the pair planned to marry. Pepys decided to give them £50 – a generous gift. But matters did not run smoothly between the couple. In August, when Tom said he didn't want to marry her, Jane was raving in 'a fit of jealousy about Tom, with whom she is in love', so that it took four or five people to hold her down. This 'fit' to which Jane succumbed would be diagnosed according to the contemporary medical literature as the consequence of thwarted passion: in girls, the Mother, or womb, must ever and anon be fuming up to their throats upon the least disturbance of their Amours'. Some fell into 'most terrible fits of the Mother, five or six in a day, upon a rupture of a Marriage'. By March of 1669 Pepys was putting some pressure on Tom to marry Jane, telling him he would not keep him as a servant after Jane had gone. Two days later Tom agreed and on 28 March 1669 the couple married with gifts of £80 from the Pepyses. Pepys thought Tom 'looks might smug upon his marriage'.[44]

Some women were very happily married, as their letters and comments reveal. They praise their husbands as an 'honest and kind husband', or a 'religious, prudent, and a loving husband'. Women mourned the deaths of their husbands in moving language. Lady Russell wrote of lacking 'the dear companion, the sharer of all my joys and sorrows', lamenting 'I want him to talk with, to walk with, to eat and sleep with'. A Quaker woman wrote more simply, 'my loss is very great in divers respects, I often think'. In a different context, a widow pleading for the wardship of her children disavowed any intention of remarriage: 'so many devils go in shapes of men'.[45]

Many married women wanted children. Anne Bradstreet, a gentle-woman living in New England who wrote poetry, noted in private that

It pleased God to keep me a long time without a child wch was a great grief to me, and cost many prayers and tears before I obtained one.

Sarah Henry kept a diary. A few weeks after her marriage to John Savage her diary became absorbed in the fluctuations of her hopes and fears of a child for over two years until she finally conceived.[46]

During pregnancy, many women were anxious. Anne, Lady Harcourt wrote of 'my exhorbitant fear of my travayn'. Alice Thornton prepared for her death before the birth of her eighth child. Elizabeth Joceline secretly bought a new winding sheet. Mrs Godolphin wrote instructions about what should be done for her child should she die giving birth (as in fact she did). Brilliana Harley asked her husband to pray for her while she waited for her delivery. Jane Turner feared that her baby would be deformed, yet 'notwithstanding all my fears it was free from blemish'.[47] The examples are numerous.

Many women came safely through child-birth and rejoiced, like Jane Turner, in 'a goodly lovely babe'. For women of gentry status the sex of the child was of vital importance: sons and heirs were wanted. Anne D'Ewes's announcement to her husband of the birth of a daughter in 1640 shows her attitude:

It hath pleased God now againe the nineth time to restore me from the peril of child-birth: and though we have failed in parte of our hope by the birth of a daughter yet wee are likewise freed from much care and feare a sonn would have brought.

She went on to say that God would send them a son if he saw good. Brilliana Harley had better news for her husband: 'I make haste to tell you under my owne hand that it hath pleased the Lord to Bles us with another sonn''. Some women died in childbirth. Anne Bramston, who fell into labour six weeks before her time, was warned by the physician that she would probably die when he tried to deliver her. 'She replied, she expected death, she hoped she had made her peace with God' and she died two days later. In her twelve years of marriage she had borne ten children although only two were alive at the time of her death.[48]

If women wished to nurse their own babies, they may have been overruled by their husbands' authority, as was Elizabeth, Countess of Lincoln, who believed that this was a cause of her babies' deaths. Ann D'Ewes, who wanted to breast feed her baby son, was advised 'by such as were about her' (presumably other women) 'that the child should not suck any other till her breasts were fully drawn and made fit for it'. The medical belief at the time, which the women shared, was that colostrum was bad for the baby, and that the milk of any other woman was less fit for a child than that made from the blood of the mother who had already nourished it in the womb.[49]

Women took pleasure in their babies and in their children. Katherine, Duchess of Buckingham, wrote charmingly of her daughter clapping her hands in time to music. 'I wood you were here but to see her now', she wrote to her husband who was in Spain, 'shee is so full of pretye playe and tricks'. Women watched their children develop and observed their temperaments. A dying woman begged her husband to be 'sure to be kind to all the children, but especially I pray you to Jacke, whose sad apprehensive nature requires most kindness'. Mothers worried over their children's illnesses, and grieved at their children's deaths. And women's bonds with their children were taken seriously by the society at large. If a mother were to kill her child, the courts deemed her mad by definition, since her action was so unnatural. In many women there was a struggle between love of God and love of their children. The dying Lady Coltness spoke of being 'this night' with her son Johnie who had died earlier:

> Fy upon me! fy upon me: what is this I am saying of my son Johnie? I will be this night with my God.

Another dying woman told those about her that 'the great account why she desired to live was to take care of the religious education of her children'.[50]

Women of gentry status shared and shaped many of the dominant values. They were concerned about 'the family' and wanted to see their children married into 'good families'. The son and heir is often highly valued. Ann Fanshawe had three children sick with small pox. She writes in her autobiography that although she neglected the two eldest daughters, 'and night and day attended my dear son, yet it pleased God they recovered and he died'. Some women were self-deprecatory: 'I know you have more wit than a woman' wrote Brilliana Harley to her husband in 1626.[51] (Brilliana was Sir Robert's third wife. He was considerably older than she, which no doubt assisted his maintenance of authority. She was to die of pneumonia in their house in Herefordshire in 1643 during the Civil Wars defending the place against the Royalists while her husband sat in Parliament in London.)

According to the dominant ideology, women's modesty should have prevented their expressing views in public, yet about three hundred women published books during the seventeenth century. Most of them knew that their action required some apology or excuse. Others published anonymously so that their ideas would be taken seriously. They wrote on a variety of subjects: cookery, household management, religious duties and advice to children. They published almanacks and treatises on education. They wrote plays, poems and essays. Sometimes they wrote in defiance of family opposition. Elizabeth Avery's brother abused her for publishing: it 'doth rankly smell'. He questioned her identity: 'What will you make yourself to be?' and warned her that as a weak woman, Satan would easily make her fall. In publishing he considered she had made 'an attempt above your gifts and sex'. His sister had already answered him in her preface:

> though I may be counted mad to the world . . . if I am mad, as the Apostle said, it is to God.

Women published in defiance of censure: 'I matter not how I appear to Man' asserted Susanna Bateman. Sometimes women argued that their duty to God overrode their concern for modesty; sometimes it was their duty as a mother which directed them to leave some advice for their children. The Countess of Lincoln's justification was that as a mother, she had a special contribution to make. As God had blessed her with children, so He 'caused me to observe many things falling out to mothers, and to their children'.[52]

One of the most interesting groups who published were those whom I would term feminists for their concern to change the position of women and also for their anger at the condition of their sex. They were social determinists up to a point: usually they acknowledged that God had made them in some ways weaker than men, and denied that they aspired to superiority or even equality, but they argued that women were the products of a pernicious system of education. Some subscribed to conspiracy theories: it had been the policy of men 'to breed us low'. 'It is the policy of men, to keep us from education and schooling' asserted Sarah Jinner, an almanack maker. 'If we be weak by Nature, they strive to make us more weak by our Nurture' said another writer. Many women supported educational schemes so that women could gain knowledge. Some resented the fact that much knowledge was locked away from them in the Latin language which, while understandable by men of any education, was not generally taught to women. Women who did read foreign languages translated works for those who could not.[53]

Earlier I have commented on ways in which women were muted in their societies by not speaking the language of the dominant group. Women's education excluded them, on the whole, from professional modes of discourse. One fascinating example of how this 'muting' occurred comes from the work of Thomas Edwards in which he sought to expose the errors of the religious sects in 1646. Not the least of their errors was that they allowed women to speak, and Edwards gives an account of how Katherine Chidley, a woman who preached and published, attempted to argue a theological issue with one Mr Greenhill. He

> laboured to reduce to a short head all she had spoke. She would not hold to the stating of the question . . . but in stead of being satisfied or giving answer, shee was so talkative and clamorous, wearying him with her words, that he was glad to goe away, and so left her.[54]

Katherine Chidley did not accept the terms in which the minister sought to direct the discussion, but her attempt to explain her position is seen as 'talkative and clamorous'. The man refused to talk further and left. The incident brings sharply into focus the point about muted women and the paradox that they are seen as loquacious in their societies. Because what they wish to say does not fit within the

framework of the dominant ideology, their words are neither understood nor heeded, and so they are said to be talkative.

(vi)

One issue which interests me is that of autonomy. Given the
patriarchal society and the control of the wealth, power and ideology
by a male group, how did females respond to this? Were they
oppressed victims, or did they have opportunities for independence
and autonomy? Put in such general terms, the question cannot be
answered, but I should like to discuss some ways in which women
did achieve independence and at what price. This part of the discussion is rather more speculative than that which has preceded.

Dramatists of the Jacobean period explored the question of
women's power. They saw women achieving it by defying the social
norms and conventions. A woman such as Beatrice-Joanna in
Middleton's tragedy, *The Changeling,* defies convention and breaks
off her contracted marriage to one man when she sees another she
prefers. In order to dispose of the first man she allows him to be
murdered: she is, of course, punished with death in the end, but she
acted on her own initiative. Vittoria, the central character of John
Webster's play, *The White Devil,* dies proudly for her sins. She insists
her servant be killed after her:

> I will be waited on in death; my servant
> Shall never go before me.

One of the men who will kill her asserts she seems to tremble and
should dissolve with fear. This she denies:

> O, thou art deceiv'd, I am too true a woman,
> Conceit can never kill me. I'll tell thee what,
> I will not in my death shed one base tear;
> Or if look pale, for want of blood, not fear.[55]

Real women were also defiant. Ulalia Page, who was condemned to death for murdering her husband in 1640 did not express repentance for her action. She said that she had been forced to wed by her parents 'though my heart was linkt another way' and she used her own desperate action as a warning to parents not to force children into marriages against their inclination.[56]

In these examples women are asserting sexual power. Denied access to the more regular lines giving power, they used their sexuality to advantage. The mistresses of King Charles II wielded great political power, which contemporaries recognized. At lower levels in the society, men recognized women's sexual power, warning each other of the wheedling and coaxing ways of women: 'in the night they will work a man like Wax, and draw him like as the Adamant doth the Iron'. One man, charged with fathering a bastard in 1579, gave the following account:

> A little after Easter, her husband being dead, and she lying alone, she persuaded him [Henry Packer] to lie in her house, and the night she lay in one bed, and he in another, and in the night she [sighed] and he asked her what ailed [her] and she said that her feet were cold, and she willed him to come to her bed.[57]

Christian ideology could strengthen women's independence, in encouraging them to take their salvation seriously. Religious belief could make women defy the norms of behaviour: Quaker women, for example, preached and published because they believed this their duty. Even young girls might defy their parents or guardians for religion's sake. Mary Proude (later the grandmother of William Penn) wanted to hear sermons when she was ten years old, though the family with whom she lived disapproved. She therefore set off alone on Sunday afternoons to hear the preacher, though the family forbade anyone to accompany her. 'Sometimes a servant out of compassion would run after me lest I should be frightened going alone'. Eleanor Channel, an uneducated poor woman with many young children, had a message from the Lord she wanted to deliver to Oliver Cromwell in London in 1653. Her husband hindered her from going to London three times, but finding she was unable to sleep and was rendered speechless with anxiety, he was forced at last to consent. Once in London, she lacked £5 to give to the guards at the Lord Protector's courts; standing dumb in Fleet Street, she was dragged to Bridewell and whipped. Arise Evans, finding her there, took her to his house, listened to her, and published the work in her name, saying

> it may be more of God than we are aware of, and that by this Dumb woman, God will put all vain talkers to silence.

Alice Hayes, who became a Quaker after she had been married two years to a man she 'loved as my own Life', nevertheless insisted upon attending meetings. He took away her clothes to stop her, and threatened to sell all he had and leave her. She persisted, and in the end her husband acquiesced. Another Quaker woman, Joan Whitrowe, who lived in London, received a message that the Lord needed her in Bristol. She set off, on foot, leaving her husband and her children, including a baby of one still at her breast. When she returned ten days later they were all well. She seemed conscious that her independent action had placed her outside her society: 'I walk alone as a woman foresaken'.[58]

The ability to 'walk alone', to stand outside the social norms, was a source of power for women. Keith Thomas has shown how women, excluded from office in the established Anglican church, were attracted to the religious sects and to the role of prophet. Women had dreams, visions, and revelations. Messages from the Lord brought some women before the nation's political leaders: Elizabeth Poole was examined by the Army Council in January 1649 because she believed that while the Lord would have King Charles brought to trial, the Lord instructed them to touch not his life. Eleanor James appeared at the court of King James II to warn him to repent of this Roman Catholicism, and she wrote to the Pope to convert him also. The women prophets risked being branded as mad or as frauds, but in the role of prophet they were listened to more seriously than at any other time.[59]

Many earlier historians, from the eighteenth century onwards, have set out with the purpose of answering the question 'why are women everywhere inferior and subordinate?' In this chapter I have tried to eschew such a value-laden question and rather to describe the positions of women in English society between 1500 and 1750. Obviously there are many gaps in our knowledge, but until we have more information about various subjects, particularly about women's work, and more detailed studies of particular groups of women, we will not be in a position to offer larger theories about how their position changed. Part of my research has been an attempt to put women into the story, to look at what they say and what they do, because I would argue that by looking seriously at women and their contributions to society, the whole history of the period will look different. A narrative of the main political events with, maybe, a chapter at the end about 'social history' which includes women, children's literature and culture – all the bits which would not fit in the main story – will no longer be satisfactory. It will be seen to be only half the story. I have also, in writing about women, tried to avoid a model of society which gives a monopoly of vice to the dominant group and makes women 'the oppressed'. This makes women more powerless than they in fact were, and does not help in understanding the interaction between men and women and the ways in which women developed their lives, ideas, and at a more basic level, worked for their survival and that of their families.

Notes

Many sources survive relating to the lives of women in early modern England. Many works written by women survive, there are many letters, diaries and autobiographies. There are lives of women written by their kin and funeral sermons preached about them. There are also rich institutional records of women's collisions with the courts of common and church law. Some of these, surprisingly, are not equalled for nineteenth-century Australia.

For suggestions of further reading, see the section at the end of the book.

1. Simone de Beauvoir, *The Second Sex,* trans. H.M. Parshley London, 1953, p.295.
2. The following account of the social and economic circumstances in England 1500-1750 is based on a wide variety of sources. For those interested to follow up these questions, see "Suggestions for Further Reading" at the end of this book.
3. Peter Laslett, *The World We have Lost,* 2nd edn., London, 1976, Ch.5.
4. R. Schofield & E.A. Wrigley, 'Infant and child mortality in England' in Charles Webster, ed., *Health, Medicine and Mortality in the Sixteenth Century,* Cambridge, 1979, p.95.
5. Laslett, *World We Have Lost.* The work of the Cambridge Group has been questioned by Miranda Chaytor, "Household and Kinship: Ryton in the late 16th and early 17th centuries", *History Workshop,* 10, 1980, pp.25-60.
6. Alice Thornton, *Autobiography* London, 1875, pp.120-1; J.B. Williams, *Memoirs of the Life, Character and Writings of the Rev. Matthew Henry* London, 1828, pp.56-7.
7. Alice Clark, *Working Life of Women in the Seventeenth Century* London, 1919.
8. John Thirsk, *Economic Policy and Projects,* Oxford, 1978.
9. J.S. More, *The Goods and Chattels of our Forefathers,* London, 1976, p.44.
10. Jean Donnison, *Midwives and medical men. A history of inter-professional rivalries and women's rights,* New York, 1977.
11. D. Parsons, ed., *The Diary of Sir Henry Slingsby,* London, 1836, p.8.
12. E.H.W. Meyerstein, ed., *Adventures by sea of Edward Coxere,* Oxford, 1946, p.80.
13. J.D. Marshall, ed., *The Autobiography of William Stout of Lancaster 1665-1752,* Manchester, 1967, pp.125,132.
14. J. Youings, *St. Nicholas Priory,* Exeter, 1960, p.15.
15. See Chapter 2, above.
16. William Austin, *Haec Homo,* London, 1638, p.43.
17. Lawrence Stone, *The Family, Sex and Marriage in England 1500-1800,* London, 1977, p.339.
18. C. Severn, ed., *Diary of the Rev. John Ward,* London, 1839, p.102.

19. K. Thomas, 'Women and the Civil War Sects', in T. Aston, ed., *Crisis in Europe 1560-1660,* London, 1965, pp.317-40.

20. For example, Robert Abbott, *A Christian Family,* London, 1653, dedication. There is a large literature on Puritan ideas about the family. The best accounts are: L.L. Schucking, *The Puritan Family,* London, 1969; E.S. Morgan, *The Puritan Family,* New York, 1966; C.L. Powell, *English domestic relations, 1487-1653,* New York, 1917.

21. J.O. Halliwell, ed., *The autobiography and correspondence of Sir Simonds D'Ewes,* London, 1845, i, p.362.

22. N.Z. Davis, 'City Women and Religious Change' in *Society and Culture in Early Modern France,* Stanford, 1975, pp.93-5.

23. K. Thomas, 'The Puritans and Adultery: The Act of 1650 Reconsidered', in D. Pennington and K. Thomas, ed., *Puritans and Revolutionaries,* Oxford, 1978, pp.257-82.

24. V. Sackville-West, ed., *The diary of the Lady Anne Clifford (1590-1676),* p.40. See also Patricia Crawford, ' "The only ornament is a woman": needlework in early modern England', Third Women & Labour Conference Papers, 1982.

25. Stone, *Family,* pp.99,105.

26. Much of the documentation on which this section is based is in Patricia Crawford, 'Attitudes to Menstruation in Seventeenth-Century England', *Past and Present,* 91 (1981), 37-73. For a useful discussion of medieval ideas at a slightly earlier period, see Ian Maclean, *Renaissance Notions of Women,* Cambridge, 1980.

27. Michael Dalton, *The Country Justice,* London, 1655, p.351.

28. *Culpeper's Complete and Experienc'd Midwife made English by W.S.* 3rd edn., London, 1718, pp.20-22.

29. Martin Luther, *Works,* Philadelphia, 1967, *Table Talk,* p.321. James Primrose, *Popular Errours,* London, 1651, p.305; Alan Macfarlane, *The Family Life of Ralph Josselin,* Cambridge, 1970, pp.202-3.

30. L. Lemnius, *The Secret Miracles of Nature,* London, 1658, p.11; Janet Blackman, 'Popular Theories of Generation: The Evolution of Aristotles' Works. The Study of an Anachronism', in J. Woodward & D. Richards, ed., *Health Care and Popular Medicine in Nineteenth Century England,* London, 1977.

31. Lemnius, *Secret Miracles,* p.23.

32. Royal College of Physicians, MS 654, f. 73, MS 513, f. 37.

33. Devon Record Office, Examination of Susan Draper, about 8 months pregnant who signs with a mark, [22] Dec. 1652, Q/SB. Box 59, 33.

34. Roger Short, 'The evolution of human reproduction', *Proceedings of the Royal Society,* series B, 195, (1976), pp.3-24.

35. Devon R.O., Q/SB 58, Examination of Deborah Brackley, 3 Sept. 1651. From the twelfth century, consent to marriage made a valid marriage. No public ceremony was required to make a marriage valid and indissoluable; R.M. Helmholz, *Marriage Litigation in Medieval*

England, Cambridge, 1974, pp.26-7.

36. It is interesting that Pepys never had sexual intercourse with a woman until she was safely married. Much of his sexual activity was therefore mutual masturbation. He was also desperately afraid of venereal disease, so although he looked at prostitutes, he avoided sexual intercourse with them. A.S. Smith, 'Samuel Pepys: Sex and London Society 1660-1669' , B.A. (Hons.) thesis, Western Australia 1979.

37. R.W. Malcolmson, "Infanticide in the Eighteenth Century" in J.S. Cockburn, ed., *Crime in England 1500-1800,* London, 1977, pp.187-209.

38. E. Le Roy Ladurie, 'Famine Amenorrhoea Seventeenth to Twentieth Centuries' in R. Forster & O. Ranum, ed., *Biology of Man in History,* Baltimore, 1975, pp.163-178.

39. *Diary of John Ward,* p.98.

40. Devon Record Office, Q/SB 58, 19 Dec. 1653.

41. Stone, *Family,* p.325; Will of Gilbert, Earl of Clare, PCC 42, Ent 1689; R. Baxter, *A Breviate of the Life of Margaret Baxter,* London, 1681, p.80; *Life of Bishop Bedell by his son,* ed. J.E.B. Mayor, Cambridge, 1871, p.30.

42. For details, see G. Davies, *Bibliography of British History, Stuart Period 1603-1714,* Oxford, 1970.

43. G.C. Moore Smith, *The Letters of Dorothy Osborne to William Temple,* Oxford, 1928, pp.9, 69, 96, 120, 128, 138, 150, 177; Thornton, *Autobiography,* p.52; T.C. Croker, ed., *Autobiography of Mary Countess of Warwick,* London, 1848, pp.2, 10.

44. R. Latham & W. Matthews, eds., *The Diary of Samuel Pepys,* London, 1970, vols 8 & 9; Gideon Harvey, *Morbus Anglicus,* London, 1672, p.23.

45. John Croker, *Journals of the Lives and Gospel Labour of William Caton and John Burnyeat,* 2nd edn., London, 1839, p.329; Lady Newdigate, *Gossip from a Muniment Room,* London, 1897, p.94.

46. Anne Bradstreet, *The Tenth Muse,* (1650), Gainsville, Florida, 1965, p.45; Patricia Crawford, 'Attitudes to Pregnancy from a Woman's Spiritual Diary, 1687-8'. *Local Population Studies,* 21, 1978, pp.43-5.

47. Thornton, *Autobiography,* pp.145-8; Elizabeth Joceline, *The Mothers Legacie to her unborne Childe,* London, 1624; John Evelyn, *The Life of Mrs Godolphin,* Oxford, 1939, pp.80-1; B.L., Portland loan 29/72, 24 Feb. 1626; Kent Record Office, F.27, Journal of Jane Turner, 1670. Journal of Jane Turner, 1670.

48. Journal of Jane Turner, Sept. 1676; B.L., Harl. MS 379, f. 112, v.; B.L. Portland loan 29/72, 15 Apr. 1626; T.W. Bramston, ed., *The Autobiography of Sir John Bramston,* London, 1845, p.111.

49. D'Ewes, *Autobiography,* ii. 45.

50. B.L., Harl. MS 6987, f. 119; A. Clifford, ed., *Tixall Letters, or, the Correspondence of the Aston family,* London, 1815, p.190; W.K.

Tweedie, ed., *Select Biographies,* Edinburgh, 1847, ii. 503, 520. Michael Macdonald, *Mystical Bedlam. Madness, Anxiety and Healing in Seventeenth-Century England,* Cambridge, 1981, pp.80-5.

51. *Memoirs of Lady Fanshaw,* London, 1829, pp.10, 134; B.L. Portland loan 29/72, 17 Feb. 1626.

52. *The Copy of a Letter Written by Mr Thomas Parker,* London, 1650; Elizabeth Avery, *Scripture-Prophecies opened,* London, 1647; Susanna Bateman, Poem, London, 1656; Elizabeth Clinton, *The Countesse of Lincolne's Nurserie,* Oxford, 1628. I am writing a chapter about these women who wrote for publication for a forthcoming book edited by Mary Prior *Women in Pre-Industrial England: Studies in Social History.*

53. [B. Makin], *An Essay to Revive the Antient Education of Gentle-women,* London, 1673, pp.22-4; Sarah Jinner [Almanack for 1658]; Mary Tattlewell, *The women's sharpe revenge,* London, 1640, pp.40-1.

54. Thomas Edwards, *Gangraena,* London, 1646, repr. Exeter, 1977, i, p.79.

55. For a discussion of the ideas about women in the drama of Thomas Middleton, see Margot Heinemann, *Puritanism and Theatre,* Cambridge, 1980, Ch.11.

56. Ulalia Page, *The lamentation of Master Pages wife of Plimmouth,* London, [1640?].

57. *Pray be not angry: or the womens New Law,* London, 1656; F.G. Emmison, *Elizabethan Life: Morals and the Church Courts,* Chelmsford, 1973, p.13.

58. *Some Account of the Circumstances in the Life of Mary Pennington,* London, 1821, p.9; Elinor Channel, *A Message from God,* London, 1653; Alice Hayes, *A Legacy or the Widow's Mite,* London, 1723, pp.39-46; Joan Whitrowe, *The Humble Address of Widow Whitrowe,* London, 1689, pp.9-13.

59. Keith Thomas, *Religion and the Decline of Magic,* London, 1971, p.138.

3

Margaret Anderson

'Helpmeet for Man': Women in Mid-nineteenth Century Western Australia

In the middle decades of the nineteenth century, Western Australia was a tiny rural outpost of the British Empire, struggling, not very successfully, to establish itself as a viable economic community. Although within eighteen months of white settlement in June 1829 almost 2,000 immigrants had arrived in the colony, initial conditions did not encourage other settlers to follow suit and by 1850 the population had reached only 5,254. By contrast, South Australia, which was settled seven years later in 1836, had a population of 52,904 by 1850.[1] After 1850 population growth at the Swan River accelerated, at first because a small number of wealthy pastoralists persuaded the British Government to make Western Australia a penal colony, a decision which saw the arrival of nearly 10,000 male convicts and about 7-8,000 free immigrants between 1850 and 1868; later with the discovery of gold in the Coolgardie/Kalgoorlie area in the early 1890s. By 1900 there were about 180,000 people living in Western Australia, although they were still dispersed over a very wide area.[2]

In common with other nineteenth century English communities, Swan River society was essentially hierarchical, with wealth and power concentrated in the hands of a relatively small ruling class – a group of landowners, officials, merchants and professionals, who controlled both the labour market and the law, and who manipulated both to suit themselves as far as they could. For most of the period political power was even more concentrated: until 1870 the Governor, appointed by the Imperial Government, ruled with the assistance of only a small Legislative Council, most of whom were officials, with a few wealthy male colonists appointed by the British Government on the Governor's nomination. Twenty years of representative government followed from 1870, with the Governor assisted by a council of eighteen members (later increased to twenty-four) twelve of whom were elected, but the franchise was set to exclude both men without property and all women. From 1871 males over twenty-one years, who owned property worth £100, paid rent of £10 per year, or held a depasturing licence could vote, but candidates had to own property with a capital value of £1,000 or returning an annual income of £50. Even so the legislative powers of this group were very limited – one historian has described it as 'little more than an exclusive debating society', while real power remained with the Governor and the officials of his Executive Council. Full self-government was not attained until 1890, but even then property qualifications for both voters and members were retained and plural voting was allowed. Members of parliament were still unpaid and, of course, all women were excluded from voting, until an amendment to the constitution was successfully introduced in 1899.[3] Throughout the second half of the nineteenth century therefore women in Western Australia were effectively excluded from exercising any real political or economic power.

In fact in a very real sense nineteenth-century Western Australian women were a 'minority group' – even numerically: colonial men outnumbered women from the very early days of settlement. In October 1848, when the last census before the arrival of the convicts was collected, women represented only 39 per cent of the total population and this proportion fell over the next six years to only 33 per cent in 1854. Growth continued to be slow over the next two decades and women still only accounted for just under 43 per cent of the total population in 1880. This disparity was even greater in the adult population where men vastly outnumbered women, in proportions ranging from 78 per cent in 1854 to 65 per cent in 1881. Census data does not allow a precise examination of the marriageable population before 1881, but some indication can be gleaned from figures published in 1854. Of the single population aged twelve years and over in that year, some 82 per cent was male. Or, to put it another way, for every 100 single men aged over twelve years in Western Australia in 1854, there were only 22 single women. Over half of these men (55 per cent) were convicts. By 1881 improvement had been slight: 70 per cent of the marriageable population (including widows and widowers) over fifteen years was still male and there were still only 43 marriageable women for every 100 marriageable men.[4]

Neither were the sexes evenly distributed geographically, so that although there were 44 single females for every 100 single males over twelve years in Perth and Fremantle in 1854, the ratio in country areas was only fourteen. In the adult population (twenty one years and over) the ratios were even more dramatic – twenty one and four respectively. By 1881 the situation in Perth and Fremantle had improved markedly, with 68 marriageable women to every 100 marriageable men, but in country areas the old inequalities remained, with a ratio of only 34 to 100. Throughout the three decades of the mid-nineteenth century therefore the Swan River Colony exhibited a huge preponderance of men, a disproportion which reached exaggerated heights in the population 'available' for marriage.

The implication for women of their extreme numerical inferiority is still a matter for debate. In summarizing differing interpretations of the 'numbers theory' in Australia, Dixson particularly emphasizes the conflict between American and Australian historiographical interpretations of the same phenomenon. While Australian historians have tended to argue that woman's minority status contributed to her exploitation and low social standing, American history traditionally argues the reverse, relating the relatively high status of American women on the frontiers to their comparative scarcity.[5] It is also unclear whether contemporary belief that the paucity of women improved their material chances in life by bolstering their bargaining power in the marriage market – about the only avenue of upward mobility available to women at this time – has any basis in fact. During the second half of the ninteenth century all Australian women certainly had far better prospects of marriage than women in Britain, and Western Australian women may have been slightly more successful at finding husbands than their sisters in the other colonies. In 1881 only 3 per cent of women aged between 45 and 49 years had never married, although a staggering 44 per cent of men were in this category. But whether these women had managed to advance themselves through marriage, as immigration scouts in Britain often promised, is quite another matter. Although a survey of the occupations of men married between 1850 and 1855 in Western Australia did suggest that women showed a decided preference for husbands with the security either of property or a trade, and to the detriment of the majority, the labouring class, a comparison with the occupations of the brides' fathers revealed this same concentration in the 'higher' status occupations. In other words, there were simply more women of 'higher' social status. In fact, far from colonial women exploiting their scarcity to move up the social ladder, it seems likely that a sizeable proportion may have moved downwards on marriage. It is always difficult to discuss the social status or class position of women in past societies, since this depended on so many factors, some of them extremely subtle. Broadly speaking, a woman's status in colonial Western Australia derived from the social position of the men she lived with – her father first and then her husband. Comparison of the occupations of husbands with those of brides' fathers is one, admittedly limited, way of pinpointing changes in status through marriage. A very rough attempt to assess the marital mobility of the women in this group – rough because it is impossible to classify a man described in the marriage register only as a 'farmer' at all adequately – suggests that only about 15 per cent of women married in Western Australia between 1850 and 1855 actually married 'up'; 56 per cent married men of similar occupation grouping and fully 29 per cent married 'down'. Rather surprisingly these results are very similar to those calculated by Fisher[6] in her far more extensive analysis of the mobility of women married in Sydney in 1870 and 1887, although there was an excess of women of marriageable age in Sydney at this time. That so many women in Western Australia seem to have chosen marriage, even to a social inferior, is probably a reflection of the comparatively low status of spinsters in colonial society coupled with an almost total absence of employment opportunities apart from domestic service.

But however successful or unsuccessful colonial women may have been in manipulating the marriage market, what is quite clear is that almost all of them did marry and presumably most went on to bear and raise families in the colony. Some of them – a very few of the literate and wealthy – kept diaries which have survived and which reveal something of their lives from then on – their households, their family links and their daily activities – but of the majority we know almost nothing. They left no record of the sorts of households they lived in, whether alone, or with parents, or brothers and sisters; nor of their subsequent family experiences – how many children they had, or how many of those they managed to raise. What of Charlotte Preston for example, a seventeen year old blacksmith's daughter, who married shoemaker Edmund Ashton in April 1850? They went to live in Guildford where they stayed until about 1860 or 1861, when the family, by this time grown to include four children (one had died) moved to York. Ordinarily the Ashtons would not figure in the history books. Although Edmund finally managed to buy some land and by 1867 could describe himself as a farmer, he was not important enough to attract the attention either of his peers, or of the conventional historian. Neither he nor Charlotte wrote letters or kept a diary, or, at least, none which has survived. But the bare bones at least of their domestic experience can be pieced together from available records – from census listings and the entries registering their marriage and the births and deaths of their children, and it is to these sources that historians are now beginning to turn, hoping that the statistical reconstruction of families and communities might unearth more about the domestic experience of ordinary people in the past than the more traditional analysis of literary sources has managed. This is not to discount literary sources; the qualitative aspect of family life must always be important, but it is to suggest that without some quantitative evidence of women's experience in the past, the literary sources are analysed in something of a vacuum.

What follows is a brief summary of the reproductive histories of about 100 couples put together from the records of births, marriages and deaths held by the Registrar General's Department in Perth. The women in the sample were all married between 1850 and 1853 in Western Australia and bore their children over the next three decades – if they lived. All marriages between 1850 and 1852 were recorded and every 10th for 1853. The sample was restricted in time to facilitate searching through the birth registers. The subsequent reproductive histories of these families were built up by tracing their children through the index to the birth registers. The age at which their first and last children were born, the number of children they had and the intervals between them are all important indicators of what amounted to a very important part of colonial women's experience in the mid-nineteenth century.

Although it is impossible to be very precise about it, it seems likely that women in Western Australia tended to marry fairly young, at between about 19 and 21 years, so that their period of potential fertility was probably in excess of 25 years. (It is normally assumed in a 'non-contraceptive' society, that women's childbearing years end at about 45 years.) For most of the women in the reconstituted sample, maternity followed closely on marriage: 57 per cent produced their first child within twelve months of marriage, 76 per cent within 18 months and 85 per cent within two years. The average length of the first birth interval was fifteen months, although the median length was twelve months. However some of the longer first birth intervals, especially those in excess of two years, almost certainly represent second or even third pregnancies, with earlier pregnancies ending in miscarriage; so that colonial women may in fact have started on the reproductive round even earlier than these figures suggest. Just for comparison by 1970 in Australia this pattern had changed, although not as markedly as might have been expected, with 36 per cent of all couples producing their first child within a year of marriage and 61 per cent within two years.

Of course a significant number of these women were already pregnant when they married: 26 women, 21 per cent of those for whom information was available, bore their first child either before (two) or within seven complete months of marriage. About half of these babies were born within three months of marriage, so that about 9 per cent of brides were probably visibly pregnant on their wedding day. Unfortunately there was insufficient information to draw any real conclusion about the social origins of the women concerned, although at least four were servants and another two were widows. Of those whose father's occupation was recorded three were daughters of small traders, two of artisans, three of unskilled labourers and one only was a farmer's daughter. Only one woman of relatively high social status, the daughter of an army captain, featured in this group: she bore the illegitimate son of a Perth attorney and married him three months later. The men concerned were mostly farmers and labourers, but these were the two largest occupation groups recorded in the 1859 census. There is no indication of the relative status of the farmers in the group, whether large landowners or smallholders.

Although it is theoretically possible for a woman to produce a child every twelve months or so, an assumption often made about child-bearing experience in the past, such a high rate of fertility is, in fact, very rare. In the Western Australian sample families the second child was generally born about two years after the first, with successive children arriving at roughly two to two and a half year intervals, a pattern which seems to have been remarkably consistent in Britain, Europe and America from at least the seventeenth century onwards. The gap between babies did appear to increase slightly as the mother grew older, but this was by no means a clear trend and in some large families of ten children or more, the interval between children was a consistent 24 to 26 months throughout the childbearing years. In fact the most powerful impression gained from summarizing the total reproductive histories of all of the women was of an incredible consistency in childbearing experience over the life cycle: even towards the end of their childbearing years, these women still averaged less than three years between births. There is certainly no evidence of successful family limitation being practised. Of course it is important to remember that these figures are averages and that individual experience varied. In particular, it was not uncommon in larger families for there to be a fairly concentrated spate of childbearing, often for the first three or four children, before the intervals settled down. For example seventeen year old Charlotte Pollen married Edmund Ashton in April 1850 and their first child, Ralph, arrived promptly nine months later, in January 1851. Ralph was not quite seventeen months old when a second child, Edmund, was born and another nineteen months saw the arrival of a daughter, Alice, in January 1854. Thereafter the family grew rather more sedately, with birth intervals averaging between two and two and a half years until the eleventh and last child, Nathan, was born in May 1874. Charlotte was then aged forty.

The most powerful natural control on women's fertility at this time was probably lactation. As early as the mid 1950s a group of re-searchers in India established that lactation significantly increased the period of post-partum amenorrhoea (the absence of menstruation and ovulation after childbirth) provided that the infant survived for at least one month after birth and there was certainly a tendency amongst the sample families for a stillbirth or the death of a child in early infancy to be followed by a shorter birth interval than usual.

The median length of twenty four such intervals was sixteen months. It is fairly clear, at least for the literate classes, that women in Western Australia in the mid-nineteenth century expected to suckle their babies themselves, (although evidence from a later period suggests that single mothers, or poor women, were sometimes forced to put their children out to nurse so that they could continue to earn a living), and it may well be that individual physiological responses to lactation among Western Australian women – and the effects of lactation do vary considerably between individuals – are one explanation for both the length of birth intervals and the apparent variation in birth intervals between women. It might explain why Caroline Clinton, who married at seventeen and went on to bear children over a twenty-five year period, ultimately had fifteen children while Charlotte Ashton, also married at seventeen and whose childbearing years spanned twenty-four years, only had eleven, as we saw. The average interval between Caroline's children was twenty months, between Charlotte's twenty-eight months. Mary Ann Bourke also bore children over a twenty-four year period, but she averaged three years between births and finally had a family of nine children.

It is impossible to tell from existing diary sources, whether women in the colony routinely extended lactation in the hope of delaying conception, but a few comments hint at some such attempt. One woman, writing to her sister in July 1849 for example, remarked 'Mrs E. tells me she is *not* likely to increase just yet, she seems to be in good health and spirits';[7] but of course, 'Mrs E.' might just as easily have been referring to something else – her husband's sleeping separately on the verandah for instance – which was apparently also a common recourse later in the century.[8] Some contraceptives certainly existed in this period – the condom first appeared in the eighteenth century and an early diaphragm soon after the invention of vulcanized rubber in the 1840s – but whether such devices ever found their way to the Swan River, let alone its remote country districts, is another matter. Contraception was certainly not considered respectable and was roundly denounced by theologians and the medical profession alike for interfering with God's will with nature and for causing a host of degenerative diseases, including cancer. Coitus interruptus or withdrawal is thought to have been the most common contraceptive in use, although medical men disapproved of this even more strongly; and there are also records from very early times of various recipes for pessaries, simple cakes of flour and water were apparently used, or other preparations including plain lemon juice, which could be inserted into the vagina, but if any of these were used by women in mid-nineteenth century Western Australia, they seem to have had little result. The chief problem was almost certainly the profound ignorance even amongst scientists and doctors, about the functioning of the female reproductive system. Although from 1845 the ova were known to be released spontaneously, rather than on intercourse as was previously assumed, (following the animal model) the link between the ovaries and menstruation was still a matter of controversy in the 1870s and medical opinion tended to recognize the menstrual period as the most likely time of conception. So even the few women with access to a doctor's advice were not likely to be better off.

Not surprisingly there is much more evidence for the use of abortifacients than contraceptives in the colony and at least one universal cure-all, Holloway's Pills, advertised that particular property of its wonderful ingredients quite openly. In the *Perth Gazette* of August 1856 an advertisement claimed that a dose of Dr Holloway's Pills would 'correct and regulate the monthly courses, acting in many cases like a charm'.[8] While in 1862 they were claimed to cure 'all disorders peculiar to women', including 'any irregularity of the system', a recognized euphemism for pregnancy.[9] Most of these sorts of preparations were purges of varying ferocity, which probably did little actual harm, although they were unlikely to achieve the desired result either: others contained more dangerous compounds of mercury and lead in sufficient concentrations to cause poisoning. Instrument-induced abortions were also available in Western Australia in the later nineteenth century (and almost certainly earlier) although it seems unlikely that married women adopted this course very often: the risk was simply too great. They may, however, have welcomed a miscarriage on occasion. Mary Taylor, the wife of a gentleman farmer in the Albany region in the south-west of the Colony, recorded in her diary in 1873, 'a letter from Josephine [her niece] . . . I am so thankful the dear girl has lost her baby.'[10] There is also not much doubt that such repeated childbearing was seen by colonial women as a burden from which they would have preferred some escape. In letters they tried to reassure (and reconcile) each other. One Sydney woman, writing to her Western Australian sister, who was approaching yet another confinement, said in 1859:

> Do not regret the dear little strangers – God grant it may be a comfort to you. I hope before this reaches you the trial will be over.[11]

And a trial it undoubtedly was. Throughout the 1800s in Western Australia childbirth was both a painful and a relatively violent and dangerous experience, even with the gradual improvement in medical knowledge during the second half of the century. Between 1872 and 1881 in Western Australia an average of just over six women died for every 1,000 babies born, a mortality rate which was higher than that in Britain at the same time and even this may not take account of deaths from peuperal (or childbed) fever. Very many other women suffered all their lives from the after-effects of poor midwifery. The trauma of repeated childbearing at this time must have been increased by the certain knowledge that assistance in the event of complications was likely to be of only limited value and probably too late. The medical profession, which until the middle years of the nineteenth century had taken scant interest in midwifery, only began to introduce such training for its prospective practitioners in Britain in the 1850s and it was 1886 before proficiency in this area was a required qualification. Even trained doctors were severely hampered by imperfect knowledge and inadequate techniques until well into the twentieth century however and prolonged labour, especially with a child grown too large to be born, resulted in very high death rates. One doctor whose general textbook on midwifery was published in 1871, estimated the rate of death from Caesarian section, described as 'the most serious of all obstetric operations', at slightly less than half of all cases, and advised students to perform craniotomies instead. Craniotomies, which entailed inserting a hook to perforate the brain of the child, before removing the skull in pieces, was said to be used in one in every 350 deliveries in Britain, resulting in a maternal death rate of one in six. However Dr Milne suggested using a new crushing instrument, described as a vast improvement over older methods. He wrote:

> The advantage here is, that you may require only one introduction
> and one withdrawal, and thus happily and mercifully escape the
> weary and painful seizing and losing hold, pulling and picking,
> and ceaseless twisting and tearing, until the exhaustion of the
> operator is nearly equal to that of the hapless and suffering
> patient.

The operation could then be reduced from three or four hours to
fifteen or twenty minutes.[12] Horrifying as they sound, such methods
might at least have saved the life of one Mrs Warren, whose death
notice in the *Perth Gazette* in September 1856 described her as 'a
great sufferer for ten days in childbed'.[13] Colonial women certainly
took careful note of the maternal fortunes of their acquaintances,
discussing successive births and deaths in letters and no doubt,
amongst themselves. We can only guess at the anxiety which each
new pregnancy ushered in.

There is no direct evidence that married colonial women resorted
to infanticide, although there was a steady trickle of charges against
single women throughout the nineteenth century. Many of these
women must have endured intense pain, fear and loneliness, for of
course a successful infanticide mostly presupposed that a pregnancy
and birth remained undetected. Most of the women charged seem
to have been servants and of course their fate was horrific if their
pregnancy was discovered. They would probably have faced dismissal
'without a character' despite the shortage of servants and of course
the physical presence of a child would have made future employment more doubtful. Added to that was their immediate desperate
plight on dismissal, as they awaited the birth. It now seems incredible that advanced pregnancy could be undetected and that these
women could continue their extremely arduous duties right up to
and immediately after the birth but very many of them did so. One
example was published in the *Perth Gazette* in October 1867, when
one Louisa Lund was charged with concealment of birth.

The story ran:

From the evidence it appeared the prisoner was in the service of

J.B. Locke at Wannerup, Vasse; she was challenged by her master with being in the family way, but she denied being so, as she also did to other persons, or that anything more was the matter than a severe cold; she persisted in her denial until Tuesday the 11 of June, when her mistress on account of her suspicion being aroused sent for Dr Rossillotty, whom she would not allow to examine her until told the police would be sent for, when she admitted their suspicions were right, that she had been confined on the previous Friday, and on being further questioned as to what she had done with it, said she had wrapped it up in a bundle with a stone and thrown it into the river. On the 27 July, a man excavating sand in Mr Locke's garden found a bundle which contained the body of a full grown child, wrapped in two jackets, one of which was identified as having been given by Mrs Locke to the accused by whom it had often been worn.

The Jury found the prisoner guilty, and His Honor passed a sentence of four months imprisonment, to date from the day of the birth, thus giving the girl twenty-two days imprisonment from this day.

The relative leniency of this sentence is interesting as is the charge itself. In almost all cases women were not charged with infanticide – with murder – but rather with concealing a birth. In the seventeenth and eighteenth centuries the law was incredibly harsh. If a child was illegitimate, concealment of its birth was proof of murder, and the guilty mother was hanged. This act was repealed in 1803, but the charge of murder still warranted hanging. Undoubtedly because of this very few women were ever charged with infanticide. There was one in Western Australia during the 1830s, but she was acquitted. It is obvious that the courts looked with sympathy on these mothers and allowed the lesser charge, often even acquitting women of this, unless, like Louisa, they confessed. Stillbirths and deaths immediately after birth, were common enough, for sufficient doubt to surround such cases. This is clearly one instance in which the law did not reflect public morality. All in all however, contraception, abortion and infanticide notwithstanding, it is quite clear that marriage meant something very different to people in the nineteenth century. In particular it meant the rapid assumption of family responsibilities after marriage and a steadily increasing burden of responsibility throughout the wife's fertile years.

In fact most of the women in the sample of reconstituted families went on to bear large families, although not perhaps as large as is sometimes supposed. One woman had sixteen children altogether, two had fifteen, one had fourteen and three thirteen, but most families were smaller than this. Nevertheless only 5 per cent of the women who lived into their earlier forties ultimately bore three children or less, while about another quarter had between four and six children. In other words, nearly 70 per cent of the women in the group eventually had families of seven or more children, while 40 per cent bore ten or more during their fertile lives. The average number of children born to these women was about nine – a significantly larger number than women in Britain were bearing at the same time and probably more than most women in America as well. In fact so far, the completed fertility of women in the Western Australian sample is among the highest recorded in an English-speaking community.

This means of course that childbearing and rearing must have dominated the greater part of colonial women's adult lives. And in fact we find that only just over 20 per cent of the women who survived into their middle forties completed their childbearing in fifteen years or less. Fifty-five per cent of the women bore their children over twenty or more years, while for 16 per cent babies continued to arrive for 25 years or more. Only 6 per cent were aged under 35 years when their last child was born: 64 per cent were aged 40 or more, including two aged 45 years and four aged 46. By the time these younger children were approaching adulthood their parents would have been well into their middle to late fifties or early sixties. The majority of marriages did not survive such an extensive childrearing period, over 60 per cent of families experiencing the loss of one parent before the youngest children reached their late teens, although the children in only seven of 90 families were actually orphaned. Nevertheless some experience of death within the family circle was a much greater possibility than it is now. Although not high by contemporary standards, infant mortality in particular was a very significant factor and colonial women must have faced the possibility that each of their hardly-won children would not survive its first year of life. During the 1860s in Western Australia between 120 and 126 of every 1,000 babies born alive died within the first twelve months and although infant mortality in the sample families was actually lower than that in the total population, almost 60 per cent of these women still lost at least one child over their childbearing lives.

However overall, despite a mortality rate among both parents and children which seems high by modern standards, the reproductive histories of the women in the reconstituted sample suggests that most were ultimately responsible for large families: groups of eight, ten or more in a house were probably about average. With a new baby arriving every 24 to 28 months, these married women's fertile lives must have been dominated by recurrent childbearing and lactation with at least twenty of their adult years taken up with infant care.

The demographic pressures which kept women pretty well confined to the home were supported by an ideology, mainly articulated by the wealthy in society, which essentially served two purposes. In the first place, it attached great significance to home and family life and to woman's central role within the family, giving women's domestic activities a measure of status (although whether this was real or not is considered later in the chapter). Secondly it argued that woman was intended, by God and 'Nature', to fulfil a domestic role and hence, by implication, that she was unfitted for anything else. It was an ideology in other words, which seemed to place woman and her domestic role upon a pedestal, but which in reality functioned to ensure that she never attempted to climb down.

Articles on family life and on woman's function within the family, guarding the home, preserving stability, were popular throughout the middle decades of the nineteenth century in Western Australia's two weekly journals – the *Inquirer* and the *Perth Gazette*. Both reflected a view very common in the English-speaking world at the time, that society would not function in an orderly fashion unless the population was organized in stable family groups, where a proper regard for religion and a thorough respect for authority and the law could be instilled and reinforced. In the relatively new and untried society at Swan River the role of the family assumed even more importance than usual, so the argument ran, since it had to compensate for the weakness, or often the absence, of the restraining influence normally exercised by an established (and observant) community; by the Church and even by the law, since many very isolated areas were effectively outside the reach of the law for quite lengthy periods. In a rather rambling editorial, which began by discussing the servant problem but ended in a tirade against the vanity of women, who were accused of marrying only for 'position', the editor of the *Perth Gazette* stressed this point particularly.

In February 1874 he wrote:

> Our readers may say that we are trespassing on the province of the preacher. We wish the preachers of the present day would enforce the common duties of life upon us more than they do. It is of more importance that our wives should make our houses 'homes' than that a cross should or should not be put up in a Church.
>
> As a subject of general importance this may demand and we trust it will receive, consideration, but if it be of importance generally, of how great importance must it be to those who, living as so many of our fellow-colonists are obliged to do, as we might say, 'in the bush' are without society to compensate in some measure (can it in any measure?) for the blank, we shall not say worse, they find at home?[14]

Colonial woman's responsibilities were clear: she was to concentrate all her energies on preserving family life, the task allotted to her by God himself, thus preserving an orderly society and securing the happiness of all.

The implications of this set of ideas for women in the colony were profoundly important, since the whole credibility of the belief system which promoted the family as the principal controlling institution in society was almost entirely dependent upon a series of related ideas about the nature of womanhood and the role of women in society. By the mid-nineteenth century concepts of 'home' and of 'woman' were so completely intertwined, that each was effectively defined in terms of the other. To change woman was to threaten the family. As late as 1900 Dr Emma Drake, whose medical manuals were widely read in America and certainly available in Australia, argued defensively, in the face of what she saw as the growing threat of the feminists, 'as long as the world stands, woman must have her definite and specific work in it. So long as the home exists, woman will be its recognized centre'.[15] Throughout the middle decades of the nineteenth century in Western Australia this wife/mother image often referred to as the 'true woman', was the only role model presented to women, or at least the only model accorded any status.

A formidable list of qualities was demanded of the 'true woman'. She was to be graceful, gentle, patient, pure, pious, submissive and self-sacrificing, but above all, she was to be domestic, all attributes admirably suited to her role as 'helpmeet for man'. But it went even further than that, for it was also believed that such qualities were intrinsic to the very character of the true woman – a natural extension and expression of her physiology. Of course that meant that the woman who did not possess these qualities or, even worse, who seemed to reject them, was not only unattractive, but even unnatural. As the editor of the *Perth Gazette* blustered in 1874 in the course of a discussion on the 'women's rights question', 'we have been taught to believe that woman was created as an "helpmeet for man", if she is more she is without the pale – if she is less, she falls short of the true standard'.[16] The belief that woman was naturally more moral (in a sexual sense) and pious than man also lay behind her categorization as a civilizing force in society, quietly diffusing her controlling influence from her vantage point in the home. Anne Summers has described these ideas as the 'God's Police' stereotype.[17] This was certainly the image of woman most stressed in the Western Australian press. Under the heading 'Miscellaneous' in the *Perth Gazette* in September 1850 for example, was printed the following:

> We read in a Sheffield paper that 'the last polish to a piece of cutlery is given by the hand of woman'. The same may be said of human cutlery – that 'the last polish' to a young blade is given by his mixing with female society.[18]

On a less serious note, but still suggesting the popularity of the concept, Miss Eleanor Hunt, a wealthy Englishwoman who was related to the ruling class Harper family whom she visited in 1877, wrote in spirited fashion to Charles Harper in October of that year:

What howling swells you are now, with your wagonettes and pair of horses. Your wind and water mill, your garden and your most 'researché' dinners. You seem to have jumped from barbarism to civilisation since Mrs Grant's advent. Now own Sir, what marvellous influence we 'charming women' have. What would become of you poor miserable men without us? You would soon be sunk in a slough of barbarism and become absolutely unbearably horrible without us.[19]

Now from her letters Nellie Hunt was obviously a very intelligent woman: one of her cousins described her as 'very clever', but 'too self-reliant' to be a good marriage prospect. Quite clearly she could laugh at the stereotype, even while, probably, still accepting it. Others took it entirely seriously. 'Une Femme', who wrote to the editor of the *Perth Gazette* in March 1874, argued:

Where will you go in town or country and not observe that a man's true happiness is all centred in the little compass of his own domestic fireside hours. Whether he be citizen or settler, mechanic or gentleman, it is the same; and the influence of my own sex over such portions of a man's life I need hardly say is paramount. . . . the gay and worldly life [a reference to a current debate about the vanity of young women] bring in no happiness to the domestic hearth, but act as a destroying agent against the exercise of those virtuous and higher principles without which life is wretched, lonely and miserable.[20]

The ruling class men who administered the colony agreed with her: they also believed in the refining influence of female company and the steadying effect of family life and they worried incessantly about the number of unmarried men, especially unmarried convict men, in the population. Their answer was a vigorous campaign in favour of sponsored female immigration, which they kept up throughout the middle decades of the nineteenth century. The publication of each successive census from 1848 saw the Registrar General make some such appeal. In 1848 for example G.F. Stone argued

The relative proportion of the sexes in the total population, as exhibited in the General Abstract is unsatisfactory, and disadvantageous in the highest degree to the domestic, social and moral welfare of our community. In some districts there is a startling disparity, which a judicious introduction of female immigrants might remove.[21]

The steadily mounting proportion of convicts in the population heightened this anxiety considerably. In 1854, after drawing his readers' attention to the large number of unmarried men in the colony, Charles Sholl warned:

It is unnecessary for me to point out the moral evils likely to ensue from this inequality: or to do more than to allude to the crimes which such disparity is likely to give rise; but, as a means of averting the probability of such occurrences in this Colony, I would respectfully suggest that Free Female Immigration should be encouraged to a greater extent than hitherto, in order to adjust the balance between the two sexes.[22]

Various schemes for redressing the balance of the population were suggested, but one which was carried out saw the importation of a number of shiploads of women, many of them Irish needlewomen, fleeing the recent terrible potato famine. Some 464 sponsored single women arrived in the Colony between 1850 and the end of 1853, although 2,555 convicts arrived in the same period. Emigration agents in England also worked hard at inducing single women, especially 'respectable' domestic servants to emigrate, often stressing the material advantages to be gained from emigration, and there is more than a hint in some sources that many women were actually seriously misled about conditions in the colony. One contemporary, Janet Millett, who arrived in the colony with her clergyman husband in December 1863, later published her reminiscences of life in the colony and observed:

The strong demand for single women has induced those individuals to whom the task has been entrusted of meeting it to regard the case too much from one point of view only, and decent girls being found unwilling to emigrate to a penal colony, the fact that it is one has sometimes been concealed from them until after they have sailed, whilst in the meantime they have generally received a description of its merits altogether fabulous.[23]

But even so the emigration officials were not very successful at finding the numbers of single women Swan River's rulers wanted and some colonials began seriously to consider a suggestion from the British Government that the colony accept female convicts as well as male to balance the sexes. Other prominent settlers opposed the suggestion with great bitterness and debate raged throughout 1854. They did not disagree over the need for more women – in fact both sides justified their positions by stressing their belief in the ultimate responsibility of women and the family for the moral welfare of the community – but they differed violently in their willingness to accept convict women in this role. The ideological dilemma was this: if piety, purity and modesty were intrinsic to the female character, it followed that immorality, or irreligion were more difficult to countenance in women than in men. As the Reverend J. Brown put it at a public meeting on the 'female convict question' in June 1864, it was probably more difficult to reform female than male convicts, since,

Those means that under the divine blessing arrest *men,* are not so successful in recovering *women.* It has pleased the Almighty to give to woman as her safeguard an honest shame and modesty; and it is hard indeed to recall her to a virtuous path when these have been sacrificed to crime.[24]

The editor of the *Perth Gazette* agreed.

We do not wish to judge erring human nature too harshly, but it is universally admitted that crime in women is less easily eradicated than in men, for a woman who has once lost self-respect has lost everything.[25]

This tendency to see women as either ministering angels or shameless hussies has been discussed in detail by Anne Summers in *Damned Whores & God's Police* – catchy concepts which are very apt. Unfortunately, in attempting to explain these concepts in terms of the development of society in the convict colony of New South Wales, Summers has missed the essential complexity of the ideology involved. The categories were opposite but contemporary components of one view of women.

Acrimonious debate consumed the ruling class for most of 1854, but in the end no female convicts were sent. Perhaps the known opposition of Governor Fitzgerald finally tipped the balance in favour of the opposition. In any event, the task of reforming the large number of male convicts was left to the free female immigrants.

On the surface then, ruling class ideology ascribed very high – even exalted – status to colonial womanhood. As chief guardian of the family woman was responsible for preserving the social morality and ultimately the very structure of an ordered society: she alone, so the argument ran, could hold back the floodgates of moral chaos. Such responsibility may well have proved very satisfying to those colonial women who identified with the 'true woman' concept – even Nellie Hunt seems to have derived some gratification from such ideas – and it could well be that ruling class ideology gave meaning to even routine and laborious domestic labour, reconciling women to the housekeeping and maternal tasks which were more or less inescapable until later in the century. But how real was this status? It is supremely ironic that despite the lip service paid to women, they were not considered to equal men, even in the home. As in earlier centuries, within the family as without, women's subordination was both expected and enforced. In fact submission to male authority and deference to male opinion were said to be the basis of true feminity.

The rationalization for this apparent inconsistency was simple: outside the very limited realms of morality and mothering women were simply inferior to men – both intellectually and physically. The very qualities of gentleness, patience, purity and sympathy, which were supposed to equip woman so well for motherhood, and to make her such an excellent moral censor, were also said to justify her submission. This inequality was enshrined in the Christian marriage service, which required women to promise to obey their husbands (it also formed the basis of family law in the colony as we shall see later) and there is a good deal of evidence that at least some ruling class women in Western Australia took their vows seriously and genuinely tried to put their principles into practice in their own marriages. Of course this did not prevent women from exercising some authority, influencing their husbands 'behind the scenes' as it was often put, but they were not expected to show this power openly. As the editor of the *Perth Gazette* put it in 1874, again when condemning the women's rights movement, 'We had rather the influence, though felt, was unseen. This may be merely a manly, or unmanly prejudice, but it is a common one'.[26] The public face of woman was always to be deferential: many comments in the newspapers and in private letters and diaries written by men and women stressed that women should respect their husbands, look up to them and depend on their superior judgement. Of course if the woman herself was capable and intelligent, the man she married should be more so. A letter from a relative to Frances Bussell, one of an old ruling class family, on her marriage (finally) in 1873, made this point quite clearly.

> I was indeed very pleased to hear of your marriage to so good a man and one who is called superior. You know I always told you not to accept anyone any way yr. inferior, you are a, well I will not flatter you – but every woman should marry a man she can respect and reverence to, to ensure true happiness – you required someone whose management altogether surpassed yours dear friend because you have had to manage alone.[27]

As in the seventeenth century those who sought to 'explain' women's inferiority drew on a wide variety of sources, from the teachings of established religion to the theories of scientific and medical men. All assumed that men and women differed in their essential characters and that woman's character was dictated by her physiology. The scientific theories grew more sophisticated, but contempt for woman's intellect and distrust of her physiology lingered. Hysteria continued to be described by the Victorian anatomists as a 'woman's disease', an inevitable reflection of a nervous system which was simpler than man's with individual nerves which were smaller and more delicate and hence more prone to overloading or nervous collapse. This condition was often called neurasthenia. Educated women were thought to be especially vulnerable to neurasthenia because they were demanding more of their systems than nature had intended. Some scientists also argued that as women had consistently smaller skulls than men, their intellectual capacity must be proportionately less, allowing many conservatives to dismiss as absurd the first real attempts of women to gain access to higher education. However of even greater significance to nineteenth century women were those theories linking women's intellectual inferiority directly to her reproductive capacity. It was thought by many doctors and scientists at this time that the body was a closed energy system, so that energy consumed in developing one area could not be available for another. Development of both the brain and the female reproductive organs was thought to consume vast amounts of energy (although for some reason the male reproductive system was not so voracious), allowing scientists to argue that the brain and the uterus could not properly develop simultaneously. Women's intellectual growth was said to be interrupted by puberty and continually hampered thereafter; while women who ignored the warnings of Nature and forced themselves to study in competition with men, were charged with literally destroying their wombs. An article entitled 'Modern Mothers', which was printed in the *Perth Gazette* in 1868, warned that educated women were proving increasingly incapable of nursing their children.

> Again, as for the increasing inability of educated women to nurse their children even if desirous of doing so, that also is a bodily condition brought about by an unwholesome state of life. Late hours, high living, heated blood and vitiated atmosphere are the causes of this alarming physical defect.[28]

In other words, the very source of woman's 'femaleness', her reproductive capacity, was identified as the basis of her intellectual inferiority. Darwin's publication of the *Origin of Species* also sparked off a series of theories 'explaining' female inferiority in terms of evolution. It was said that men had 'adapted' to command and that their brains had developed for that purpose, while women had adapted to caring for children and pleasing men.

Now obviously not all of these ideas were understood in detail by the ordinary men and women of the Swan River Colony. Apart from anything else, Western Australia was hardly at the forefront of the scientific and literary community at this time. But there is striking evidence, in the form of a rather remarkable debate conducted by the Swan River Mechanics Institute in October 1853, that the worthy artisans who were members of that society had at least come in contact with similar theories if only in a very popular form. In a long discussion lasting over more than five sessions, they solemnly debated the question 'whether woman do or would possess the same amount of Intellect as man if they had the same advantages', finally deciding 'that they would not'. Some extracts from this debate, the minutes of which were kept in summary form, are reproduced here. The grammar and spelling have been left intact but the emphases are mine. It should be remembered by the way that there were also several men who argued in the affirmative.

Mr Gray: The time which has elapsed since men have borne rule sufficiently proves their adaptation for that purpose. For any individual to support a doctrine for woman's superior Rule or Government over man is contrary to Scripture to reason to common sense and appears great folly . . .

Mr Johnston: Man's mind is one Indivisible as hope fear etc. but all his Genius is derived from a particular part of mind . . . *a Girl is generally most forward in learning but only to a certain extent. After they arrive at a certain point they stop* but the boys succeed in carrying on their education and in pushing it to any extent. A woman does not have and should not have a Masculine mind.

Mr Fox: Men have a superior power of Intellect to Woman. Woman have a refined Intellect Man has a Masculine mind – each use it according to their sphere . . . Women are so constituted that they never have and if they had double the advantages either in education or in any other sense whatever their advantages might be they never will excell over the man . . .

A. Gray: Is of opinion that Women is not intended to Rule over man but that from Creation to the end of time the Almighty determined that man should rule not only every living creature but over Woman also – consequently woman have not an equal power of Intellect as men and altho' Education would much improve their reasoning faculties yet they never have and never can equal the men in sense of power of reasoning or in any particular wherein it is required . . .

The chairman then summarized the debate.

Has not heard a single argument against his proposition worthy of an answer altho' much twaddle has passed; has noted and brought before the Meeting all the Women he could who have distinguished themselves. Scriptures do not prove that women were ever intended to Govern. Kingly power is known to be hereditary. Intellectual power is not so. Has instanced several men with a power of Intellect who in their sphere have without Education in their various branches shown a power of Intellect and Genius which Women have not. Scriptures do not prove that Women should be public creatures altho' they do labour in the Gospel and be helpers therein with their husbands advice. Women never have had and never can have the same amount of Intellect and no one among us considers his wife his superior in Intellect to himself or superior in Governing powers, the Almighty gave Adam or man wisdom to give names to Brute creation he did not give it to Woman. Woman never will till the end of time give the same evidence of their superiority of Intellect or commonsense.[29]

Contempt could hardly be stated more directly. It is interesting that there was another shorter debate on a similar question in 1874. Proportionately more members were prepared to argue in favour of women's intellectual equality on this occasion, but once again the meeting finally decided in the negative.

Unfortunately for colonial women, the men in the Mechanics Institute were not in any way unusual. The Western Australian press shared their contempt and published a steady stream of articles ridiculing women, their capabilities and activities, throughout the second half of the nineteenth century. It is interesting that the climax of interest and comment seems to have been the decade from the late 1860s to the 1870s, coinciding with the first successes of the movement for access to higher education by women in Britain, America and Australia and more importantly, with the organizational beginnings of the women's suffrage movement in Britain and America. It is hard to avoid the conclusion that men of the Swan River, as elsewhere, felt profoundly threatened by such radical changes and reacted by releasing a barrage of ridicule and scorn designed to keep colonial womanhood at least, firmly in her place. One or two examples are sufficient to establish the tone of much of this comment. One article entitled 'Feminine Tact' was reprinted from the London *Saturday Review,* a famous opponent of the women's rights movement, in 1867 and set out to argue, partly by judicious use of language, that whereas male tact stemmed from mental acuity, female tact was instinctive, based in sympathetic feelings, and inferior. Once again the emphases are mine.

> One can see by experience how entirely a *clever* man's tact differs from the tact of a *refined* woman. A woman's is made up chiefly of keen and sensitive *feeling,* with which shrewdness and mental grasp have nothing to do. Some kind of natural instinct enables her to sympathise with the passing sensations of those around her . . . this capacity of woman acquires partly from the ordinary training of women, which quickens their sensibility, and partly from the habit of observing and studying small matters, which is a necessity of social and domestic life . . . [male tact] springs not from the heart so much as from the *head* . . . male tact depends on the power of reading character. Though the observation of women is both accurate and infaute, it aids them rather to understand the *feelings* of those into contact with whom they are brought, than to form a just and complete estimate of their propensities or their ruling passions. This latter and more *thorough* insight into character requires a real knowledge of the world, and an acquaintance with the ordinary habits and actions of *men,* which women cannot and ought not to desire to possess. It would not be much use to them if it were theirs. The act of management is distinct from the art of pleasing, and a managing woman is not as much an ornament to her sex, as a woman who by her sensitiveness knows how to charm and to sympathise.[30]

Other articles put forward an argument which was probably more powerful – the notion that intelligence and femininity were incompatible; that intellectual women were 'unwomanly' and unattractive. It is an idea which has proved remarkably resistant to social change. A piece entitled 'Beauty and Brains', published in December 1868, put this point quite clearly and incorporated what was to become a familiar threat – that men would not marry clever women, or at least clever women who were foolish enough to show their intelligence. The author began by arguing that beauty, while admirable in itself, was a poor basis for marriage: brains were desirable, but with reservations.

> Men do not care for brains in excess in women. They like a sympathetic intellect, which can follow them, and seize their thoughts as quickly as they are uttered, but they do not care for any clear or special knowledge of facts. Neither do they want anything very strong minded. For most men indeed, the feminine strong mindedness . . . is a quality as unwomanly as a well-developed biceps or a huge fist would be. It is sympathy, not antagonism, it is companionship, not rivalry, still less supremacy that they like in women; and some women with brains as well as learning – for the two are not the same thing – understand this and keep their blue stockings well covered by their petticoats. Others enthusiasts for the freedom of thought and intellectual rights, show theirs defiantly, and meet with their reward. Men shrink from them.[31]

It is interesting that concern seems to be for the preservation of the form, rather than the fact, of masculine superiority.

We can only speculate about the effect of these and other even more contemptuous articles on women in colonial Western Australia. We cannot know how many women even read them: after all, colonial newspapers were expensive and cannot have had extensive subscription lists.[32] On the other hand neither newspaper was likely to antagonize its readers by publishing material they would find repugnant: at the very least the editors must have assumed a readership tolerant of such views. Thanks to modern sociology we also know that such continual and universal condemnation, coupled with rigid socialization from birth and the absence of alternative role models, cannot have left colonial womanhood, or at least ruling class colonial womanhood, unscathed. Certainly if there were any 'strong-minded' women in Western Australia at this time they did not leap to defend themselves or their sex in the press, as modern women would do. Literally only two or three women had letters published in the press throughout the period from 1850 to 1880 and two of these commented specifically on domestic matters.

In the meantime there is evidence to suggest that some ruling class women accepted the ideal of femininity as set out in the press. In a letter to her mother from England, where she was holidaying in 1875, Mary Harper had this to say about her hostess, Nellie Hunt, whose comments on the civilizing power of women were quoted earlier in the chapter.

> She is a very generous and liberal girl but is not a happy one. She is always craving for someone on whom to bestow her affections – but unfortunately though she is very clever and very generous she is not a lovable disposition she talks loud and argues with men and is too self reliant. I often feel very sorry for her . . . Mrs Collins and I were talking of her yesterday and saying that she would not be happily married for she has never been used to give up her wishes or inclinations to anyone.[33]

The phenomenon of spinsterhood is discussed in more detail in Pat Jalland's chapter below. There were very few women in Western Australia at this time with the economic independence of a Nellie Hunt, let alone the contentious intelligence which might have allowed them to stand outside their society. Indeed it is unreasonable to expect them to have done so. The women's suffrage movement probably represented the most 'radical' opinion in this period and even this movement did not question prevailing concepts of femininity to any great extent. In fact its adherents justified woman's increased participation in society by arguing that the world would benefit from her moral influence and gentleness.

The very common description of women as the 'weaker sex' partly reflected this concept of femininity, with its accompanying contempt for women's intellectual ability; but also drew extensively on beliefs about women's physiology. Nineteenth century doctors' ignorance about the functioning of the female reproductive system has already been mentioned and it is not surprising to find that many of them were very uneasy about the functioning of the uterus in particular. Historians in Britain and America have pointed out that it tended to be seen as a dangerous organ, perpetually in danger of malfunction and because they also believed it to be vitally connected with other major organs in the body, in particular with the nervous system, it was said to dominate women, both mentally and physically, in a continually disruptive cycle from puberty to menopause. No doubt this sort of argument also lay behind current attitudes to menstruation, although Crawford's chapter shows that this prejudice has a very long history. In the nineteenth century some doctors argued that during menstruation blood and other vital energy was diverted from the brain and other organs leaving women mentally unbalanced and particularly prone to hysteria throughout the menstrual period. Such arguments were particularly useful to those opposing the entry of women to higher education and the professions. However there is no sign that women in Western Australia at this time actually found menstruation debilitating: certainly their diaries reveal no regular patterns of 'illness' or interruption of their frequently arduous round of duties.

Nevertheless the concept of the 'weaker sex', in the physical sense, was clearly well established in mid-nineteenth century Western Australia. The term was used over and over again in the press and in advertisements for patent medicines. One which purported to be an article about the universal cure-all and abortifacient Holloway's Pills, was printed in 1857 and ran –

In another sense than the unkind one of Hamlet, we may truly say 'Frailty, thy name is woman', liable that all the safeguards that medical skill can throw around her should always be within her reach . . . man's province is action, and action is the handmaid of help, but woman, at every stage of her existence, is more or less fettered by household cares, and is in a measure debarred from that free exercise in the air, which contributes so greatly to physical vigour. Her sedentary habits, the tyranny of fashion, and more than all the *perils inseparable from the position she fills in the economy of nature,* subject her to much pain and suffering. Hysteria, fainting fits, nervous headache, coldness of the extremities and *many local complaints, especial to her organisation,* are among her physical afflictions, and maternity, the fountain of her purest happiness, too often brings sickness and sorrow in its train.[34]

Once again the emphases are mine. Another advertisement for the same product, popular two years later, referred to 'the local debility and irregularities which are the special annoyance of the weaker sex, and which, when neglected, always shorten life.[35]

These beliefs about the delicacy and unpredictability of female physiology, coupled with the great social need to keep women in the role of civilizing homemaker and mother, underlay much of the opposition to the idea of women's emancipation, opposition which dominated comment in the colonial press of the late 1860s and 1870s. These ideas represent the 'other side' of the true woman ideal – the contempt for woman's actual intellect and physiology which accompanied popular veneration of an abstract femininity. At first the response to the British and American women's demands for change was characterized by an amused condescension which did not take the movement seriously. In January 1861 for example, under the general heading 'Varieties', the *Perth Gazette* published the following quip: 'at the Women's Rights National Convention, Mrs J.E. Jones presented a declaration declaring "that woman's sphere cannot be bounded", – a self-evident proposition to all who live in this age of crinoline[36] but by the late 1860s the real threat of the movement was apparent to the colonial press and its response became increasingly virulent. 'God' and 'Nature' were lined up on the side of the status quo as women were accused of stupidity, of selfishness and finally of race suicide if they tried to move outside the home. As the editor of the *Inquirer* earnestly argued in a lengthy editorial on the subject of women's suffrage in March 1874.

There is no more important question under discussion than woman's position, and none more delicate and, at times, perplexing. Objections to female suffrage may be entertained by men who have the strongest desire for the emancipation of the sex from social fetters, and whose aspiration is to make her, intellectually as well as morally, the companion of man. Perhaps woman's worst enemies are not so much those who would unduly repress her, as those who would unduly push her forward; and make the movement to redress women's wrongs offentimes ridiculous, by claiming ultra woman's rights. In their calm moments the most silly of talkers and writers will admit that there is a difference between the two sexes . . . the line must be drawn somewhere . . . there are savage nations that have not manifested the same solicitudes, and where women do discharge the tasks which hitherto in civilised life have been confined to man, but with the inevitable result that the race decays and dies. It is pleasant enough for the Maori and our own aborigines to throw manual labour on the sex, but the curse falls upon the unborn children. The advocates of the extension of the franchise to the fair sex can here gather the lesson that Nature's laws are not to be violated with impunity.[37]

Yet paradoxically, despite the theoretical status of the 'true woman' and despite the fact that woman's domestic role was supposed to be the link holding families and hence society together, woman's actual work was almost universally described as inferior to man's income-earning activities. Often such comparisons were made in passing, the implication being that the difference in importance was too obvious to be spelled out, but every once in a while this contempt surfaced more directly. It was expressed most forcefully in a long letter signed by one 'Silvanus' and published in the *Perth Gazette* in May 1874. Silvanus seems to have been a gentleman (at least his letter shows evidence of a classical education), with a social conscience and his prime concern was to expose what he saw as the widespread exploitation of (male) servants in the colony. In his argument he instanced both long hours of physically exhausting work and little time off as special grievances, but he reserved his greatest contempt for employers' common insistence that general servants perform even the 'degrading' tasks normally allotted to female servants. Whether Silvanus' views represented merely personal disgust, or whether they did, in fact, reflect the resentment of many colonial general servants, it is impossible to judge – I have found no record of the opinion of any male servant on the matter – but the tone of the letter is so immoderate, the language used so forceful that it must reflect a deeply felt contempt for the tasks almost all colonial women were expected to perform, and perform gladly.

> Not only is he [the general servant] underpaid for the actual number of units of work done, but the nature of it at times is of the most objectionable character. The poor general servant must be now a man, and anon a woman; now dig the garden, and now scrub a floor . . . to a man, especially a Briton . . . who may be considered the man of men, it is most repulsive to be called upon to handle the dish cloth as a rule, and the scrubbing brush, on the knees, when occasion requires; to say nothing of washing kitchen towels; and if it be not so who will make me a liar and my speech nothing worth? . . . it makes a fellow blush to write it, much more to do it. Were the pay at all commensurate to the amount of work performed, ignoring for a moment the degrading description of some of it, there would be less cause for complaint.[38]

Where women's work could be so widely disparaged, either subtly, in the course of commenting on other matters, or openly, as in this last example, there seems little chance that women themselves could inspire real respect. Veneration of an idealized, feminine moral guardian was offered instead. In other words although women through the family were supposed to control men, men structured both their ideology and their institutions to control women.

This was no less true for poor women, although the 'true woman' concept, if they had even heard of it, must have seemed completely alien to the lives many of them led. Nevertheless the ruling class in the colony judged the poor by their own (theoretical) standards and in fact, as we saw earlier with their efforts to import immigrant women to marry convict men, concentrated a good deal of effort on extending their hegemonic control to the domestic lives of the labouring class. If they were ultimately unsuccessful, as does seem to have been the case, it was not for want of trying and throughout the second half of the nineteenth century they used the major institutions of colonial society – the Church and the law – in a continuing attempt to reproduce the 'ideal' family at all social levels. This of course included keeping women properly submissive to their husbands.

117

Throughout this period the teachings of the Church on marriage formed the basis of family law and despite a number of reforms in the second half of the century, the twin christian concepts of the permanence of the marriage tie and the subordinate role of the wife within marriage remained largely untouched. Until 1863 in Western Australia as in England until 1857, divorce was possible only through an act of the British parliament. Within marriage a woman owned no property in her own right, unless elaborate settlements were drawn up, nor was she legally entitled to leave her husband's protection. A husband was also bound to maintain his wife. The 1863 Matrimonial Causes Act provided for the first time for judicial separation, to be obtained by the wife or husband on the grounds of adultery, cruelty, or desertion 'without just cause' for two years or more. The Act also provided for the protection of any property the wife might acquire through inheritance, or by 'her own lawful industry' to be effective on the granting of the decree; and the payment of alimony for her maintenance by the husband.

It also allowed for divorce, but the double moral standard enacted ensured that this was extremely difficult for the wife to gain. A husband could obtain a divorce simply on the grounds of his wife's adultery. A wife had to prove either incestuous adultery, bigamy, rape, sodomy, bestiality, or adultery accompanied by cruelty or uninterrupted desertion 'without reasonable excuse' for two years or more. Moreover although whenever a petition for dissolution of a marriage was presented by the wife, both she and her husband were required to give evidence, a wife was not necessarily called to answer a husband's petition. Since much of the evidence produced at this time was necessarily circumstantial (as, for example, being found in a room with one another alone, or even writing and receiving compromising letters), the possibility clearly existed for collusion between a husband and a 'lover'. This possibility was discussed in an article in the *Perth Gazette* written in 1857 in response to the English act, although it was never raised in any of the trials. A husband could still claim damages from his wife's lover.

In 1879, following a similar act in Britain and after some prompting from the local press, the Divorce Act was amended to clarify the position of a wife suing for judicial separation on the grounds of cruelty. It allowed for a judicial separation with maintenance to be granted if a husband was convicted of an aggravated assault on his wife and provided that the court was satisfied 'that the future safety of the wife [was] in peril'. At the discretion of the magistrate, custody of any children under ten years could be granted to the wife. In principle this amendment represented an important step forward for women in the colony, but in practice the courts interpreted it so narrowly that it was of little help to most women. For despite these apparent reforms, the law in Western Australia continued to reflect ruling class family rhetoric and functioned above all to keep husbands and wives together. There were also sound economic motives for this, as deserted wives or widows with children faced a very precarious future in the colony and were often forced to apply to the government for assistance.

But the administrator's motives were not all economic. The summaries of cases heard in the Court of Divorce and Matrimonial Causes suggest that magistrates in Western Australia believed in the immense importance of the marriage tie in society as a whole and were loath to sever it in individual cases, even where the circumstances seemed to satisfy the letter of the law. In one full judgement which remains – and unfortunately most do not – the principle of wifely submission was also upheld as a necessary ingredient in marriage. In fact the judgement hinged on it. This meant that it was extremely difficult for Western Australian women to use the marriage laws at all, but in particular, it was almost impossible for them to escape domestic violence, which was extremely common, through the intervention of the state. Firstly the requirement that to gain a judicial separation a woman had to prove to the court's satisfaction that her life, limb or health was endangered, must have limited success to those who had been victims of extreme brutality. But more importantly the 1879 Act referred in its definition of assault to established law governing assault in general, which, in the relevant paragraphs dealing with women, or boys under fourteen years, allowed a case to be dismissed if the court found the 'assault and battery to have been justified, or so trifling as not to merit any punishment'. In practice this section allowed the presiding magistrate to move beyond a consideration of the facts of the acts of violence themselves, to an examination of the wife's behaviour in the period preceding the assault and an assessment of the extent to which she conformed to prevailing concepts of woman's role. In effect it enabled a magistrate to place the woman herself on trial, as the case detailed below amply demonstrates. Parts of this judgement have already been reproduced elsewhere, but the process of argument is important enough to justify its inclusion again.

In 1886 Bridget Tant petitioned the court for a judicial separation from Francis her husband of twenty-eight years. In her evidence she claimed that Francis was 'given to habitual intoxication', that he frequently ill-treated her, on one occasion beating her and chasing her out of the house with a hatchet, on another chasing her with a seven pound weight in his hand. After the hatchet incident Bridget had a deed of separation drawn up and supported herself and her children with a greengrocery shop, under constant harassment from her husband. In dismissing her petition Judge Stone argued on the basis of established precedent, that wives were only entitled to judicial separation on the grounds of cruelty if they could prove that their behaviour to their husbands had been properly submissive and dutiful. The implication is clear: that the preservation of family life was of first importance and this was essentially woman's responsibility, in the face of which her own comfort or happiness mattered little. The judgement is lengthy, but it is important to follow the process of argument. Stone said:

Although the Courts do not require many acts of cruelty to be proved to entitle a person to a judicial separation they do require something more than a single act to be proved, if that single act has been committed during a long course of cohabitation between the parties. If a person could apply to the Court for a judicial separation simply on the grounds alleged in the 5th paragraph [which detailed the incidents] without giving evidence in support to show that the conduct was likely to be repeated, the Court would be flooded with hundreds of petitions by parties treated in this way. I am glad to say although in other countries the sacredness of the marriage tie is little thought of, in our country judges are loth to interfere with the position the parties have agreed to take upon themselves as man and wife, unless for some very grave cause. I do not say that in this case I am at all satisfied with the evidence that has been given by the petitioner and the corroboration sought to be adduced in favour of the allegations in the petition. *At the same time I think she would have proved sufficient to entitle her to the protection of the Court but for her own conduct in the matter* [my emphasis]. With reference to these applications I will read from 'Browning on Marriage and Divorce p.105'.

'It is necessary that the acts of the husband by which the wife's health or safety is said to have been threatened should not only be proved and the alleged consequences plainly deduced from them, but their motives examined and their causes considered and the conduct of the wife herself by way of provocation must not only be taken into account but her demeanor even under unmerited oppression or provoked cruelty must be studied by the Court . . .

If a wife can insure her own safety by lawful obedience and a proper self command she has no right to come to this Court. [My emphasis] . . . So in Best vs Best the Court said "No wife can solicit the interference of the Court to protect her even from illtreatment which she has drawn upon her by her misconduct; she must first at least seek a remedy in the reform of her own manners". In Taylor vs Taylor the wife was held not entitled to a divorce by reason of cruelty as it appeared she was a person of bad temper and had not behaved well and dutifully to her husband . . .'

[Stone admits the substance of Bridget's claims of illtreatment.]

But as I said before that alone is not sufficient to my mind to justify me in granting a judicial separation, taking into consideration the circumstances which surround the married life of the parties . . .

At first I thought the respondent was a man given to very intemperate habits – a man who wasted his living and substance in profligacy and used the hard earnings of his wife and family for that purpose, but I am inclined to think after having heard the evidence on both sides that the position of the parties is this: The wife is a thorough business woman but a determined self-willed woman. She has several intelligent daughters and she has carried on a business to assist in the keeping of the household but I do not think that there is evidence to show that the husband has altogether neglected his duties as a husband and a father. I think he has also contributed by his labour to the success of the household, but I think that the wife is a person of that character that she would resent any interference on the part of the husband in any matters of business; and that whenever he has been irritated that irritation has arisen solely from the want of tact and the length of tongue of the petitioner herself . . . *If the wife who is supposed to be in subjection to her husband does not keep herself in that position but tries to keep him under and make him come and cringe to her for anything he may want and if he chooses and attempts to assert his rights as her lawful husband and she then commences to irritate him with her tongue she cannot expect this Court to assist her.* [My emphasis.] Her duty is to try and live peaceably with her husband and to put up to a great extent with his failings and shortcomings. If she has done that and then proves to the Court that notwithstanding all her efforts to make his life peaceable and happy her life or limb is in danger she is entitled to come here and on proof of the facts to get a judicial separation, but until she has established that the Court cannot assist her.[39]

The subjection of wives to their husbands was in this way directly enforced in mid-nineteenth century Western Australia: in fact Stone's judgement was tantamount to official recognition of a husband's right to enforce the marriage vows of obedience with violence if necessary. It was only in cases of spectacular and continuous brutality that the law acted for women at all. Even this much protection was only available to comfortably-off women: poor women could only hope for temporary relief by charging their husbands with assault in the ordinary police courts and there is no evidence that police magistrates were very sympathetic to their plight. Although some repeated wife beaters were given short prison sentences, most were merely fined, or even cautioned and dismissed. Even the fines were nominal. The usual fine for men convicted of assaulting their wives in York in the 1860s was 5 shillings with 5 shillings costs – precisely the same as that for ordinary drunkenness.

Of course not all women accepted their subordinate role; Bridget Tant, for example, presumably did not. Other women expressed their dissatisfaction with their husbands more directly and small numbers of women appeared from time to time in the police books charged with assaulting their husbands. The York occurrence books chart some of the history of Mary Ann and Job Church.

9 October 1858. A Warrant has been granted by W. Cowan Esq. J.P. York for the Apprehension of Mary Ann Church charged on the information of Job Church with constant Drunkenness and Abusive Language to her Husband and her Husband is Still in Bodely fear the said Mary Ann Church having Broke his leg.

Mary Ann was arrested, but was in trouble again in December.

23 December 1858. A Warrant has been granted by L.J. Bayly Esq. J.P. York for the apprehension of Mary Ann Church charged on the information of Job Church her Husband with Assaulting him and Neglecting him when Sick.

She was arrested again: the marriage vows could not be so disregarded. The next year Job apparently decided to even the score.

3 August 1859. Warrant has been granted by L.J. Bayly esq. J.P. York for the Apprehension of Job Church charged on the information of M. Church is Wife [sic.] with threatening to cut her throat and Beating her.[40]

A tiny proportion of women attempted more permanent damage. The Guildford police station recorded the following incident in September 1859. 'Arrested Margrett Allen for having firearms in her possession this evening, for the purpose of shooting her husband James Allen found a Pistol and caps in her possession'. Not surprisingly the courts took a dim view of such cases of wifely aggression and seem to have fined the women more heavily than they did men convicted of the same offence. In December 1866 in York, for example, Levi Holme was fined 20 shillings, in default 14 days in Fremantle prison for assaulting his wife (a second offence) and an equivalent amount for assaulting the arresting police constable. His wife, who was charged with 'fighting with her husband', was fined £2, in default 1 month's imprisonment in Perth Gaol. A similar variation can be seen in fines imposed on men and women for drunkenness and obscene language. In March 1862 for example, Mary Murphy was charged in the Fremantle Court with using obscene language. She was fined £1 or ordered to serve 21 days in prison. Thomas Baker, who had appeared on the same charge the day before, was fined five shillings with five shillings costs. Police officers found drunk were also fined more heavily than ordinary wrong-doers. In June 1861 P.C. Bird was confined in York for being drunk and using obscene language. He was fined £1 which was at least double the usual penalty. No doubt presiding magistrates reasoned that both women and police officers were supposed to set the community a moral example. Not surprisingly, women who were seen to have rejected ruling class ideals of sexual morality, 'fallen women', were often judged harshly in other matters. Poor women applying for government assistance had to show that they 'deserved' relief, by living an exemplary life.

But these women were unusual. More commonly women appeared in the police records as victims – of domestic violence and of what seem to have been a surprising number of violent attacks on women (and children of both sexes) in society at large. Between 1860 and 1880 in Western Australia there were fifteen charges of rape and about fourteen for a carnal assault on a child under twelve years – an average of one or two each year, in what was still a very small community. But the York police reports also reveal a constant stream of other 'minor' incidents, which must have represented a permanent reminder to women of their special vulnerability. In York in 1860, for example, the following incidents were recorded in the station's occurrence book:

7 February. Received information that a man named Henry Whitfield, ticket of leave had attempting to break into a room at Mr S.G. Meares where a Woman named Mrs Humphreys where sleeping with an attemt it is supposed to commit rap on her . . .

12 March. A warrant has been granted . . . for the arrest of Richard Holton charged on the information of John Cosgrove with Grossly Insulting him at is own house and forcing his Daughter away aged 15 years and 8 months . . .

13 June. A warrant is granted for the arrest of George Sun charged on the information of William Pims with assaulting his Wife with a Criminall intent . . .

25 August. P.C. Wickly and P.C. McMullin locked up James Tavern being given in charge by Mrs McGin [?] . . . for being drunk and Breaking into her House . . .

29 August. A Warrant has been granted . . . for the arrest of John Spinner charged on the information of Mr W. Edwards for being at his Dwelling House occupied by is Sister at about 2 am on the . . . [?] Instant.

Although the details of rape cases were always 'unfit for publication', the colonial newspapers managed, nevertheless, to convey sufficient of the circumstances leading up to the attacks, to convince women of their vulnerability.

The conclusion generally drawn in the press was that woman's special vulnerability in Western Australia reflected the extreme imbalance in the sexes and especially the proportion of convict men in the total population. But recent discussion of sexual assault on women in contemporary society by Susan Brownmillar and others emphasizes that rape is far more an assertion of power, than an expression of sexuality and it seems more likely, given the incidence of violence against women (and, incidentally, women at all social levels) both within the family and without, that such assaults reflected above all woman's inferior status in the nineteenth century and the popularity of an ideal of femininity which was heavily dependent on female submission. In other words, that the ideology which amongst ruling class colonists placed an idealized, submissive femininity on a pedestal, also contributed to woman's widespread brutalization. The realities of nineteenth century colonial women's lives were a far cry from the lofty ideals.

Notes

1.   P. Statham, 'Swan River Colony 1829-1850', in C.T. Stannage (ed.)

A New History of Western Australia, University of Western Australia Press, 1981, p.181.

2. See R.T. Appleyard, 'Western Australia: Economic and demographic growth 1850-1914' in Stannage, *New History,* p.219.

3. B. de Garis, 'Self-government and the emergence of the political party system 1891-1911' in Stannage, *New History,* p.346.

4. Western Australian Census, 1881, Part III, table 2 (based on corrected figures in these tables).

5. M. Dixson, *The Real Matilda,* Harmondsworth, Penguin, 1976, pp.193-7.

6. S. Fisher, 'Sydney women and the workforce 1870-90' in M. Kelly (ed.) *Nineteenth Century Sydney,* Sydney University Press, 1978, pp.100-102.

7. A letter dated 11 July 1849 held by Mrs M. Wilson, Cottesloe, W.A.

8. *Perth Gazette,* 1 August 1856, p.6.

9. *Perth Gazette,* 30 May 1862, p.4.

10. M. Taylor, MSS. Diary, 1 January 1873-31 December 1875, Battye Library Accession No. (from here shown as B.L.) 1191A, 27 April 1873.

11. Letter dated 20 February 1859 held by Mrs M. Wilson, Cottesloe, W.A.

12. A. Milne, *The Principles and Practice of Midwifery with some of the Diseases of Women,* Edinburgh, E. and S. Livingstone, 1871, pp.260-97.

13. *Perth Gazette,* 26 September 1856, p.2.

14. *Perth Gazette,* 13 February 1874, p.2.

15. E.A. Drake, *Purity and Truth: What a Young Wife Ought to Know,* Philadelphia, Vir Publishing Co., 1902, p.66.

16. *Perth Gazette,* 17 April 1874, p.2.

17. A. Summers, *Damned Whores and God's Police,* Harmondsworth, Penguin, 1975, Ch.9.

18. *Perth Gazette,* 29 September 1850, p.4.

19. E. Hunt to Charles Harper, 31 October 1877, Harper Family, MSS. Letters, B.L. 2244A/16-43.

20. *Perth Gazette,* 13 March 1874, p.3.

21. 1848 Census in *Western Australian Government Gazette,* 19 December 1848, p.3.

22. Western Australian Census, 1854, p.3.

23. E. Millett, *An Australian Parsonage,* London, E. Stanford, 1872, p.333.

24. *Inquirer,* 7 June 1854, p.3.

25. *Perth Gazette,* 5 May 1854, p.2.

26. *Perth Gazette,* 30 January 1874, p.2.

27. M. to F. Bussell, 28 November 1873, MSS. Bussell Papers, B.L. 337A, Box 4, packet 5.

28. *Perth Gazette,* 29 May 1868, p.3.
29. Perth Library Institute, MSS. Records, Vol. I, B.L. 1830A, 3-31 October 1853.
30. *Perth Gazette,* 22 February 1867, p.4.
31. *Perth Gazette,* 11 December 1868, p.4.
32. In March 1859 the cost of the *Perth Gazette* was sixpence per issue or 5 shillings per quarter. Neither journal seems to have published its circulation figures.
33. M. Harper to Mrs. Harper, 27 December 1875, B.L. 2244A/1-15.
34. *Perth Gazette,* 29 May 1857, p.4.
35. *Perth Gazette,* 18 March 1859, p.6.
36. *Perth Gazette,* 4 January 1861, p.3.
37. *Inquirer,* 18 March 1874, p.2.
38. *Perth Gazette,* 8 May 1874, p.3.
39. W.A. Supreme Court, MSS. Record Books, Divorce and Matrimonial Causes, 1863-1900. Held at the Supreme Court. Entry for 1886.
40. From the Occurrence Books kept by the York Police Station. B.L. 1141 (restricted access only).

4

Patricia Jalland

Victorian Spinsters: Dutiful Daughters, Desperate Rebels and the Transition to the New Women

The Victorian spinster was judged by her contemporaries as a human failure, condemned by stereotype to a lonely life of futility, ridicule or humiliation. Recent studies of the middle-class spinster in Victorian society have concentrated on the minority who became governesses, writers or emigrant gentlewomen. Historians have neglected the majority of middle and upper-class spinsters who performed a vital social role within the family. These spinsters were not brave or desperate enough to emigrate, and their families had sufficient means for outside work to be socially unacceptable. Such women were generally dependent on family charity, but it was not a one-way process. They frequently repaid any financial debt in kind, and the extent of the family's obligation to these women merits further analysis. Thousands of spinsters cared for ageing parents until their deaths; they acted as surrogate wives to bachelor brothers, without the personal rewards reserved for wives; they became resident maiden aunts, permanent childminders and nurses, and unpaid housekeepers.

This essay will examine the roles of the middle and upper-class Victorian spinster and the varying reactions to those roles, through a series of case studies. This analysis forms one part of a larger project examining the life cycles of Victorian middle and upper-class women, from 1870 to 1914. The major sources are the private papers of more than sixty families connected with British politics, where a father, son, brother or close relative was a member of parliament (obscure or otherwise) and where an extensive collection of letters and papers has survived for the women in the family.[1] The spinsters were the women most rapidly relegated to family and historical obscurity. This was the result of their status rather than their numbers, determined by a predominantly male social value system. One spinster usually remained in each generation of the larger Victorian families, suggesting this was sometimes the consequence of a policy of parental pressure. Yet very few of these spinsters left any historical record of their lives. Family papers were generally kept by the husband or sons of the married women, and most spinsters emerge only as occasional shadows in the background of their more fortunate married sisters' correspondence. In the vast majority of these family papers, the spinsters are represented only by passing references or rare letters of gratitude and condolence. But in a dozen families, the lives of spinsters can be reconstructed to varying degrees, making possible an analysis of the special functions and problems of unmarried women in domestic life. Each spinster must be seen in the context of her own family, as part of a series of individual case studies, illuminating different aspects of spinsterhood.

Spinsters were not a new problem in the nineteenth century, though the Victorians wrote as if they had invented 'redundant women'. From 1600, between ten and twenty per cent of European women remained permanently single. At any one time, about one-third of all women under thirty were likely to be unmarried.[2] A correlation has even been suggested between the increase in witchhunts in the sixteenth century and the rising numbers of spinsters. Unusual women who lived alone, without the protection of husbands or fathers, posed a threat to conventional society.[3] Lawrence Stone has argued that the rising numbers of unmarried women were 'a new and troublesome social phenomenon' in the eighteenth century; their numbers increased from about five per cent of all upper-class girls in the sixteenth century to more than twenty per cent two hundred years later.[4] The industrial revolution benefitted working-class spinsters more than those from the higher classes. Industrialization opened up greater employment opportunities outside the home for working-class spinsters, especially in factories and domestic service where single women predominated. By contrast, the impoverished spinster of the middle-class had little option but to teach. Any other occupation was considered socially unacceptable, and a limited education in the 'accomplishments' provided no vocational training. It was commonly assumed in the nineteenth century that the redundant women were chiefly concentrated in the upper classes, and that few working class women remained permanently single.[5] It is more logical to conclude that the middle and upper-class spinster was more conspicuous rather than more numerous.

The Victorians rediscovered the problem of the surplus female with the assistance of the statistical evidence provided by census material. The 1851 census caused considerable concern, revealing 1,407,225 spinsters aged between twenty and forty, and 359,969 confirmed 'old maids' over forty. In the years 1851 to 1911, between twenty-nine and thirty-five per cent of all women aged twenty-five to thirty-five were unmarried; and between fifteen and nineteen per cent of women aged thirty-five to forty-five were unmarried. In 1871, 'for every three women over 20 who were wives, there were two who were widows or spinsters.' The problem of 'redundant women' was largely created by a natural demographic imbalance between the sexes. The 1851 census first highlighted the excess of females over males in the population, showing that for every one hundred males in England and Wales there were 104.2 females. This imbalance slowly but steadily increased after 1851, reaching 105.5 females to every hundred males by 1881, and 106.8 by 1911.[6]

The chief cause of this demographic imbalance was the higher death rate of males from birth onwards. Although more male babies were actually born between 1851 and 1871, this numerical advantage vanished by the end of the first year of life, and females outnumbered males in increasing proportions with each decade of life.[7] This preponderance of females existed in most European countries in the nineteenth century, and for the same reason. It is tempting to speculate that higher male mortality rates caused the excess of females reported in Europe since the sixteenth century; and that the imbalance was only corrected by advances in medical science after 1900 which increased the survival rate of male babies in the first year of life.

Other factors contributed to the Victorian imbalance, though to a lesser degree than the high male death rates. Male emigration played a part, since three males emigrated for every one female, the figures in 1881 being 123,467 males to 40,840 females.[8] Of course, male emigration from Britain played a far more important role in creating the surplus male population in colonial Australia, which was the reverse of the British problem. Males also served abroad in the armed forces and the colonial service. Among the upper classes there was also an increasing tendency to postpone marriage until the man's income allowed him to support a family at the appropriate social level. In his private actuarial survey of 1874, R.C. Ansell found that the average age at marriage for middle and upper-class males who married between 1840 and 1870 was about thirty. This compared with the census figure of 27.9 years for the 1870s for the male population as a whole. Ansell found that over 20 per cent of the surveyed males married after the age of thirty-three, and his tables demonstrated the marked tendency to postpone marriage among the upper classes from 1840 onwards.[9]

Contemporary Victorian attitudes to spinsterhood established the cultural framework of rejection. Victorian social theorists, novelists and doctors reinforced ignorant social assumptions about the sexual, mental and physiological abnormality of spinsters. The radical publisher, Richard Carlile, was a progressive advocate of contraception, but even Carlile agreed in 1838 that old maids belonged to 'a sort of sub-animal class', because deprivation of the passion of love produced 'a sad mental defect':

> It is a fact that can hardly have escaped the notice of anyone, that women who have never had sexual commerce begin to droop when about twenty-five years of age, that they become pale and languid, that general weakness and irritability, a sort of restless, nervous fidgettyness takes possession of them, and an absorbing process goes on, their forms degenerate, their features sink, and the peculiar character of the old maid becomes apparent.[10]

It was commonly believed that the sexually-frustrated spinster was especially liable to hysteria, despite the obvious contradiction with the conventional medical opinion that, 'in general, women do *not* feel any great sexual tendencies'.[11] In the second half of the nineteenth century, the prolific writings of Herbert Spencer influenced social theorists and reflected contemporary prejudices. The contradictions in Spencer's arguments about unmarried women illustrated the inconsistencies in Victorian attitudes:

The not infrequent occurrence of hysteria and chlorosis shows that women, in whom the reproductive function bears a larger ratio to the totality of the functions than it does in men, are apt to suffer grave constitutional evils from that incompleteness of life which celibacy implies.[12]

The arguments of writers like Spencer and Carlile reinforced the resistance to spinsterhood of even the most intelligent females. In 1889, Marion Ashton exulted that her unexpected marriage to James Bryce, at the age of thirty-six, would release her from the empty, repressed life of the single woman:

I feel now (and have felt for a long time) as if my nature had been stunted and as if something that might have grown and expanded under other conditions was simply existing, would gradually wear out like my body, shrivel and grow old and decay.

The deepest pain in her 'struggle for duty' as a spinster 'was this load of self-repression' combined with the knowledge that half of her nature was being rejected. Had she remained unmarried, she felt she would have become cynical, hard and self-contained.[13] Beatrice Potter, before her marriage to Sidney Webb, was afraid of the harmful effects of continued celibacy. She found qualities that were masculine, 'somewhat abnormal', and 'exceedingly pathetic' in the increasing number of women 'to whom the matrimonial career is shut'.[14]

It was also assumed that respectable middle-class Victorian spinsters would direct their energies and frustrations into religion and philanthropy. Beatrice Potter recognized in 1886 that if she remained a spinster, her sexual and emotional feelings 'must remain controlled and unsatisfied, finding their only vent in one quality of the phantom companion of the nethermost personality, religious exaltation'.[15] This was remarkably perceptive, anticipating Peter Cominos' modern explanation in terms of sexual sublimation through religion:

While gentlemen were urged to conquer their sexual instincts by complete sublimation through work, genteel women, barred from work and confined to the family circle, sublimated through religion, 'the only channel' through which the sexual emotions could be expressed 'freely without impropriety'. Women realized ideal-love in the religious sense.[16]

One other aspect of Victorian social thought which explains the restricted role of the spinster was the belief in the natural separation of the spheres between the sexes. It was widely accepted, even by many suffragists, that physiological and intellectual differences between the sexes fitted males to the public sphere and females to their domestic world. Margaret Anderson's chapter has shown how the 'true woman', who married and produced children, was also idealized in Western Australia. The rationale for 'separate spheres' was obviously based to a considerable degree on the female child-bearing role, which inevitably devalued the childless spinster. Yet the unmarried middle and upper-class woman was restricted to the domestic sphere just as rigidly as her married sister. In many cases this meant subordination of the unmarried daughter to the will of the authoritarian father, especially if the mother had died: 'At least one [daughter] usually remained unmarried, the special servant for the father in his old age'.[17]

This concept of the spinster's primary duty was accepted un-questioningly by the most intelligent and able women. Frances Power Cobbe wrote in *The Duties of Women* in 1881 of the absolute obliga-tion for daughters to care for their parents. In her own case, nursing her father for many years involved considerable personal sacrifice.[18] Beatrice Potter in 1883 rationalized her position as the eldest unmarried daughter, acting as mistress of her father's household after her mother's death:

It is almost necessary to the health of a woman, physical and mental, to have definite home duties to fulfil: details of practical management, and above all things, someone dependent on her love and tender care. So long as Father lives and his home is the centre for young lives, I have mission enough as a *woman*.[19]

Charlotte Bronte in the 1840s followed the same line of duty as Frances Cobbe and Beatrice Potter, trying to convince herself that 'the right path is that which necessitates the greatest sacrifice of self-interest'.[20] But Charlotte Bronte resented the frustration, loneliness and waste of her life in a remote village, doomed to care for a cantankerous and selfish father. Where Charlotte Bronte channelled her frustration into her novels, Lady Constance Lytton half a century later turned to the women's movement. Her earlier musical and artistic ambitions had been thwarted by the domestic demands of her parents on their spinster daughter. As late as the First World War, Vera Brittain still resented the expectation of subservient dependence at home 'which has always harassed the women now in their thirties and forties'.[21]

Victorian literary fiction is a rich source for stereotypes and assumptions about unmarried women. The dominant literary image was of the spinster as a victim and social failure. Victorian novels emphasized the sad fate of the ageing old maid, trapped in the parental home and treated like a dependent child until sour middle-age. The plight of Thackeray's Julia in *The Newcomes* was typical: 'Being always at home, and under her mother's eyes, she was the old lady's victim, her pin-cushion'. Mr Osborne in *Vanity Fair* tyrannised his middle-aged daughter, who became resigned to her fate as a 'lonely, miserable, persecuted, old maid'. Charlotte Bronte's personal anguish was revealed in *Shirley,* where she condemned the sheer waste of single women's lives, 'degenerating to sour old maids, envious, backbiting, wretched, because life is a desert to them'. Mrs Gaskell provided a rare portrait of a whole society of widows and spinsters in *Cranford.* Miss Matty's one chance of married happiness was sacrificed early on the altar of Cranford's concept of social respectability, leaving her with 'a mysterious dread of men and matrimony' as she joined other sad ladies suffering from repressed sexuality in a society without men. Even George Gissing's *The Odd Women,* with its emphasis on the independent new woman, provides ample evidence of the conventional stereotype of the spinster. The feminist, Rhoda Nunn, was well aware of the problems of the average spinster: 'A feeble, purposeless, hopeless woman . . . living only to deteriorate . . . due to the conviction that in missing love and marriage . . . she had missed everything'.

Victorian social conventions and laws were based on the mistaken assumption that all women would marry. But, as Julia Wedgwood complained in 1869, 'women spend the best part of their lives in preparing for an event which may never happen'.[22] Charlotte Bronte's Caroline Helston protested in *Shirley:* 'what does it signify whether unmarried and never-to-be-married women are unattractive and inelegant, or not?'. George Eliot, Dickens and Thackeray also ridiculed an education supposed to train spinsters for a life they were unable to lead. John Stuart Mill argued that the fundamental cause of the spinster problem lay in the defects of women's education; a single woman 'is felt both by herself and others to be a kind of excrescence on the surface of society, having no use or function or office there'.[23] Women without husbands were anomalies in a social system where marriage and motherhood were conceived as the sole female vocations for middle and upper-class women.

The following case studies suggest that the real problems of the spinster were rather different from those of the imaginary old maid portrayed by contemporary novelists and theorists. As we have seen elsewhere in this volume, there was a considerable gap between the dominant ideology about women, images of them in literature, and the reality of their lives. Harsh material considerations caused flesh and blood spinsters more suffering than sexual deprivation or 'premature physical decay'. They were usually financially dependent on male members of the family – often a sufficient justification for their exploitation. Their social and economic position was exceptionally vulnerable, for they faced the possible loss of home, status and function in life with the death of a father or the marriage of a brother. Spinsters often had an ill-defined role in the family, with little recognition that they were individuals with interests, needs and identities of their own. The quality of the spinster's life varied with the stages in her life-cycle and also according to the nature of her familial relations. Angie Acland, for example, was contented in her earlier years, because of her affectionate relationship with her mother, but miserable during her subsequent years of service for an unappreciative father. The real hardship often came with the bereavement of the closest relative and during the ageing process.

Three types of spinster emerge from this study. The majority accepted Victorian assumptions about single women and played the traditional role expected of them. These dutiful daughters were socially constrained and they tended to see themselves in terms of the stereotype, as passive, acquiescent and unhappy. The lives of the majority probably justified this poor self-image, though some, like the King sisters, did achieve a measure of contentment. There were two extremes on either side of this stereotypical spinster. A tiny minority, on the one hand, rebelled against the role which society and the family attempted to impose on them, and sought escape through invalidism, drugs or other desperate means which were often both self-destructive and disruptive of normal family life. At the other extreme, a rather larger minority had the capacity to transcend the stereotype of the unfortunate spinster. They carried out their domestic obligations efficiently, but they also found fulfilment as independent 'new women'.

(i) Dutiful daughters: the stereotypical spinster

The stereotypical spinsters who acquiesced in their role will be examined first, using as case studies Sarah Acland, Elizabeth and Agnes King, Mary and Katharine Bryce, and Alice Balfour. The lives of Sarah Acland and the King sisters illustrate the most common experience of such spinsters, caring for elderly parents over many years and losing their sole role in life when those parents died. Sarah Angelina Acland, known as 'Angie' by her family, was the only daughter of Sir Henry Wentworth Acland, first baronet and Regius Professor of Medicine at Oxford. Sarah was born about 1840 into a large academic Oxford family, with a devoted mother and seven brothers. Angie had poor health from childhood, and also suffered from a fairly serious disability which left her lame, only walking with sticks. She was often sent away from Oxford as a child to climates more favourable for her health. It was not surprising that she remained single, since her poor health made her marital prospects bleak, and she was the only daughter.

After 1875 the happy family circle gradually collapsed, because of Mrs Acland's death and the sons' marriages. Angie's life grew emptier as her brothers left home and married. The great blow fell for Angie in 1878 with the death of her beloved mother. A year later she had morbid thoughts of following her: 'I miss her more and more, and shall be thankful if I may so do my work here that I may soon go to her'.[24] Her mother's death sealed Angie's fate. As the only daughter, she was now required to look after her father for the next twenty-two years until his death in old age. His health and comfort became the major considerations of her life, especially as she had promised her dying mother to 'do all in my power' for him.

Angie Acland's role was clearly defined from 1878 as her father's dutiful daughter, housekeeper and social secretary. She idolized her father, having immense admiration for his medical work and his academic reputation. But their relationship was formal, as if she were a business secretary rather than a daughter. He appeared to keep her at a distance as he went about his own busy life. Years later she recalled: 'As time went on I not only wrote out the cheques for [Father] to sign, but signed them all for him. My hands were full with the large and busy household and managing the stables'.[25] Her letters to Dr Acland always dealt first with his correspondence and appointments before she could 'trouble you with my affairs'. She consulted him on all decisions about her own movements, usually concluding, 'I hope you will think that all was done as you would have wished'.[26] She carefully compiled all the household accounts, sending them to her father for his correction and approval. Her tone was always subservient and submissive. Angie's life was not happy, as her new sister-in-law, Caroline, recognized, when she offered to 'give you help and comfort and if it may be to brighten a little your life, which I well know is sad and difficult'.[27]

The full recognition of the nature of spinsterhood came to Angie on the death of her father in 1900. He may not have made her particularly contented, but he had given her life its purpose for twenty-two years. After the funeral Angie wrote to her brother William:

> I shall never be the same again. I feel an old woman now that my only object in life is gone – and cannot imagine what I shall do – if I still have to live on. All my interest in life has so entirely gone during the long nursing of Father. My great comfort has been that he clung to me more and more to the end.[28]

William unwisely attempted to lift Angie out of her self-pity with a gentle reproach, provoking a sharp response from his sister: 'I do not think that I deserve your scolding or "think that things always go wrong". Of course you who have a comfortable home and a wife cannot the least realise what it is to lose Father and home and position in a moment'.[29] Angie felt uprooted at having to leave the old family home at her age and move to a more economical house. Her physical ailments increased and she felt desperately lonely: 'I sometimes feel as if I could not be meant to live, circumstances all seem so against me'. She understood her main problem: 'No place can be happy which centres round self and I have nothing else round which to centre and no object in life'.[30] Fortunately her brothers helped her through the worst of the crisis, finding her a nurse-companion and giving her a £25 quarterly allowance. She also acquired some new sense of purpose through increasing involvement with the Acland Nursing Homes, though philanthropy could not entirely fill the void in her life.

Elizabeth and Agnes King shared Angie Acland's fate in that they devoted much of their lives to caring for elderly parents. But they escaped Angie's loneliness and frustration because they were clearly contented in each other's company. The King sisters were probably fairly typical spinsters, who only escaped the usual obscurity of such women because their niece, Margaret Gladstone, happened to marry the Labour leader Ramsay MacDonald. Their father, Rev. David King, LL.D., was a Scottish Presbyterian minister, while their mother came from a gifted academic Scottish family. The two boys and three girls were brought up in a strict regime of earnest piety and endless church services. The parents were authoritarian, insensitive and possessive, so that their eldest daughter, Margaret King, had a hard struggle to leave the parental home for marriage to Dr Gladstone in 1869. Mrs King complained bitterly that Margaret's husband was like 'a robber who has carried off a treasure without making any compensation – and I feel bereaved and cold and hard and unkind and miserable'. Margaret finally replied to her mother's painful protestations of passionate love and grief with the argument: 'you know if I had stayed at home I should not have been a nice little baby any more but an old maid, and you don't approve of old maids'.[31]

Unfortunately, Elizabeth and Agnes had little choice but to stay at home with their parents, as old maids. Agnes was fourteen and

Elizabeth a few years older when their sister, Margaret Gladstone, died after the birth of her first child, another Margaret Gladstone, in 1870. The family had moved from London to Edinburgh in 1869, separating the two girls from their childhood friends and cousins. From an early age they had to cope with their father's mental breakdown which started on his retirement in 1869. Rev. King's condition deteriorated rapidly, with the tragedy of his daughter's death in 1870, followed four years later by that of their son David at sea. Elizabeth King lamented that it was 'dreadful to witness his suffering' and despair. During these miserable years, Agnes and Elizabeth became more protective of their parents and 'so much use and comfort to them all at home'.[32] Even at the age of sixteen, Agnes was anxious about a very brief absence: 'I do not like the idea of you and Papa, neither of you very strong, without one of your children'.[33] Filial love and duty were powerful elements in the two daughters, supported by a deep religious faith. They had less spirit of independence than their sister Margaret, and the tragic circumstances tied them to the family home for life.

For twenty-six years after Margaret's death, they cared for both sick and elderly parents until Mrs King died in 1896. The surviving correspondence suggests that they accepted their spinster role with religious acquiescence, made easier by their affection for each other. They moved back to London in the 1870s to be near their childhood friends and their motherless niece, Margaret Gladstone. The devoted aunts found much pleasure in the time they spent with Margaret as she grew up, and later with her children. They lived on a small private income, Agnes passing the time painting pictures and gardening, Elizabeth attending classes in cabinet making, and both engaged in charitable work.

The love between the sisters made spinsterhood a tolerable state. Agnes was unable to cope with Elizabeth's prolonged final illness from 1911-14, coinciding as it did with her niece's death in childbirth in 1911. The strain of nursing her beloved sister through an agonizing illness was too much. Inevitably she compared her own mental breakdown with that of her father forty years earlier, and like him she suffered a religious crisis. A series of 'prayers during the long struggle' revealed the intensity of her despair and grief at the impending separation from her sister: 'The trial I am going through is too great for me, my mind feels shaken from its foundation, and love, which has always been the mainspring of my life, love of God and love of my dear sister – seems drifting away'. She felt guilty about her suicidal thoughts, terrified her mind was going, and exhausted by insomnia and grief. She was unable to come to terms with her sister's 'great suffering', or the prospect of living without her: 'For more than fifty years my sister has filled [my thoughts]. Every joy has been a joy because it was a joy to her, every interest was an interest for and with her – I have no support and cannot stand alone'.[34] Elizabeth and Agnes King were more fortunate than most other spinsters who sacrificed themselves for their parents. After their parents' deaths they were content in each others' company and had sufficient means to live an independent life. Agnes' grief at Elizabeth's death was closer to that of a widow who had lost a husband, though the widow's social status would have been higher and she would probably have been able to transfer her affections to her children and a wider circle of friends.

The Bryce sisters and Alice Balfour also fit the stereotype of the Victorian spinster, but in one significant respect they were more unusual than the women examined so far. Their lives of service were dedicated to their brothers, rather than their parents, and their brothers were the focus of their existence. James Bryce's two sisters, Mary and Katharine, doted on their brilliant brother. After their father's death in 1877, the sisters transferred their affections to James, their younger brother. He became Regius Professor of Civil Law at Oxford in 1870, and ten years later began a long career in parliament, winning a ministerial position in 1886. Katharine and Mary focused their entire lives on James, who was a surrogate husband to them both. They never married, despite social opportunities in their earlier years, and they clearly assumed that their brothers, James and Annan, would stay single also. Mary Bryce, as the elder sister, kept house at 35 Bryanston Square in London, and acted as hostess for her brothers. Their letters to James might be mistaken for those of a wife, with many expressions of affection, as in 1887: 'Have we not much to be thankful for in our love for each other increasing as the years go on. My loving wishes dear one'. The sisters constantly fussed over his welfare: 'take great care of yourself – of cold and getting out of railway carriage [sic] – do be particular about tidiness dearest'.[35]

The sisters also acted as social and business secretaries to James, managing his affairs and providing encouragement for his political and literary aspirations. They were delighted when in 1880 the news came that 'the dear *Member*' had won his first seat, and were highly ambitious about his political future. They were concerned that his lecture tours abroad might endanger his political career. In December 1883, Katharine urged him to return from America as soon as possible, 'to make a noise for a week or two . . . on these burning questions of housing of poor etc. . . . You must keep in with the people down there'.[36] Mary meanwhile encouraged him to ingratiate himself with Gladstone by writing a book about America, which Gladstone said was needed just then: 'I mean to manage that you shall write it – '. She was true to her word. Five years later she was busy organizing the publication of *The American Commonwealth* with Macmillan, and arranging to submit the book for a competition, and for A.V. Dicey to review it in *The Times*.[37]

The lives of the two sisters disintegrated with the unexpected late marriages of both brothers in 1889. By this time their beloved James was fifty-one and they were shattered by his marriage, even more than by Annan's. In January 1889 the sisters were displaced by Annan's wife, Violet, as the new mistress of 35 Bryanston Square. Violet was at first deceptively submissive to her formidable sisters-in-law, and Mary reported to James that 'Violet seems inclined to put confidence in me and consults me about everything'. But signs of tension existed already: 'Kath and I are in the studio all day and back drawing-room in evening as we only meal with them'.[38] Three months later, the problems created by three mistresses in one household intensified. Katharine complained to James: 'I don't think Violet is very satisfactory, but I never had very much confidence in her. She is moody, and wants to get us all out of the way I think'.[39]

Unfortunately for the spinster sisters, James also deserted them for marriage only six months after Annan. Though they found Marion more acceptable than Violet, the sisters clearly could not cope with the collapse of their settled lives and went into a depression. By the end of 1889, family unity was completely disrupted and the spinster sisters left the family home. Only hints of the terrible rifts were recorded in their correspondence. Mary mentioned 'an unpleasant time' at Bryanston Square before they left, and feared that 'Annan will say all sorts of things about us which it would only vex us to hear'. Mary claimed that she restrained herself and said 'nothing against Violet except that I could not arrange the home matters with her for I found her manner tried me'. When James reproached the sisters in December for their behaviour, even threatening to cease communications, Mary replied:

> While naturally shrinking from additional pain I have yet no wish to put myself out of your life. It is only that I realize more fully than you could do the new order of things and the necessity in the nature of things for the difference between the past and the present.[40]

The two sisters never recovered from this double shock. The transformation in their lives was immense and, already in their forties, they were unable to adjust. Their interest and sense of value in life had previously come vicariously through their brothers. But now Violet had displaced them as mistress of the household, and Marion took over their role as manager of James' academic and political affairs. Mary wrote sadly to James in December 1889, reminding him of their lifetime 'of perfect love and trust' together, accepting that the expression of his affection must be altered by his marriage, and confessing to 'torturing thoughts – that I have lived too long'. Six months later Mary sought solace from despair in religion:

> Certainly life has lost for me much that made it not only sweeter but better for ones moral nature. And it is worse now than if it had come earlier when one had years to look forward to – a future in which the past could in some measure have been forgotten. But happily one has some work which can yet perhaps be done and if only one could more vividly and constantly realize God's presence and his purpose being worked out tho it is in much tribulation, the pain and sense of loss and of failure wd. not be so great as it often is.[41]

After 1889 their lives were like those of many other lonely, ageing spinsters with no great interests or occupation. The change was reflected in their letters, which became far shorter and duller, with little to record and small reason for History to remember them. Mary became a companion nurse to her invalid mother until her mother's death in 1903, filling her letters with the smallest details of her mother's ailments. Mary was a lonely woman, badly in need of a challenge and some stimulation. She took herself off alone for an annual holiday in Suffolk each year, which she devoted mainly to golf and cycling. She busied herself in committee work, joining the Executive Committee of the Women's Liberal Federation, and she followed every step of James' career with letters of encouragement. Katharine's response to the crisis was quite different. She adopted the role of the invalid, though the precise medical problem was unclear. She frequently went off to take 'bath cures' abroad or to recuperate at the seaside. The invalidism and the search for cures gave some meaning to an otherwise empty life. Mary's response to the crisis was the more positive, aided by better health and fortified by her religious convictions, and perhaps also by having been accustomed to take some initiatives in life as the elder sister.

Alice Balfour's case is sadder than the Bryce sisters. Her devotion to her brother was more obsessive, and her own talents were greater. Arthur Balfour never married, to release his sister from her chosen bondage, so she only ever attained prominence as the sister and housekeeper of A.J. Balfour, philosopher, scholar and Conservative prime minister. After their father's death in 1856, the three daughters and five sons were brought up at Whittingehame, the family estate in Scotland, by their domineering mother. Alice was a casualty of her mother's strict evangelical Christianity and her concentration on her male offspring. The three sisters disliked each other and were 'unanimous in affection only to Arthur, Frank and Gerald – the three sons who did well in the world'.[42] Alice became mistress of Whittingehame in 1876, after the death of her mother and the brilliant marriages of her two sisters. Alice worshipped her eldest brother, Arthur, from childhood. He came of age as heir to Whittingehame in 1869, with a £4 million fortune and abundant charm – the centre of a dazzling intellectual, social and political world. Arthur never married, though he was surrounded by beautiful and talented women who easily came under his spell.

Alice Balfour acted as surrogate wife and general factotum for her famous brother. She had to manage the huge house at Whittingehame, with the two large families of Eustace and Gerald often in residence, and the numerous servants. A typical entry in her 1898 diary read: 'Busy all day with preparations. Betty, Frances, 7 children and 5 domestics arrived. Tomorrow I expect 7 more'.[43] She also had to organize the whole household for the annual moves to London for parliamentary sessions. In London, she constantly entertained politicians to dinner and frequently attended the House of Commons' debates afterwards. All this was a great burden because Alice disliked household management and had to work very hard at it. Her frustration at spending so much of her life at uncongenial tasks erupted in 1885, when she decided to send away most of their Whittingehame servants and live only 'in a corner of the house – because I don't like housekeeping'.[44] Alice simply could not cope with housekeeping if anything shattered her routine, such as servants giving notice. Her excessively strict regime and her tendency to bossiness were probably over-compensation for lack of natural gifts as a housekeeper, combined with a sense of resentment and insecurity.

Alice's life was made unbearable by an open feud with her suffragist sister-in-law, Lady Frances Balfour, who was unhappily married to Alice's alcoholic brother Eustace. A direct clash of personalities was intensified by the rivalry between the two women for Arthur's affections. The spinster sister, as his housekeeper, saw him more frequently, but was in a vulnerable and somewhat humiliating position. The sister-in-law saw him less often, but received more real affection from him, which helped compensate for the inadequacies of her marriage to his brother. Quarrels frequently erupted because Alice loved children and was accused of meddling with the upbringing of Frances' five children. Arthur Balfour attempted to ignore the continual undercurrents of hostility and jealousy within the family circle, unless they erupted into full-scale hostilities. The climax came in 1897, when Frances accused Alice of interfering in the affairs of her alcoholic husband, Eustace. Alice was charged with 'disgusting conduct' and 'lack of breeding' because she 'cross-examined' the doctor about her brother's drinking habits. By Frances' account, Alice had been 'hunting Eustace with missives about his debts and the quantities of spirits drunk at Whittingehame'.[45] There followed a family crisis, described by A.J. Balfour as 'an outbreak which would do credit to a fishwife'. The effect of Frances on Alice was 'like a hot iron approaching a raw place', and Arthur finally issued his sister-in-law with an ultimatum. If Frances could not live in peace with Alice, then her family must visit Whittingehame only as occasional guests rather than habitual residents: 'By "peace" it must be distinctly understood that I do not mean "armed neutrality". Alice is your hostess: it is partly by her money that the Whittingehame life is rendered possible. For both reasons she has a right to cordial civility'. Arthur pointed out that Alice was the chief victim of Frances' attacks and she was not capable of fighting her own battles.[46]

The situation did not improve beyond 'armed neutrality' in the years that followed. In 1905, Betty Balfour reported from Whittingehame to her husband Gerald that Frances' 'presence with Alice destroys all sense of ease and comfort, and I feel as if the Whittingehame burden had been again hitched to our backs'. A few days later, Betty reported 'Frances in a very bad mind – generally abusive . . . in her fiercest mood about Alice . . .' Naturally the atmosphere in the house was 'odious'.[47] The feud between the two women continued after Eustace's death, with Frances expecting special treatment as a widow, though she had shown none to Alice as a spinster.

Not surprisingly, Alice was often miserably unhappy in a role which did not suit her, made worse by the violent family quarrels. She clearly envied other women their married state, as the letter she sent on Mary Gladstone's engagement in 1885 suggested: 'It is such a comfort to have one's duty in life put so plainly before one as yours probably will be in the future. It is one of the drawbacks of remaining unmarried that one has not those plain duties put before one'.[48] Alice would not have been human, given her love of children, had she not envied Betty and Frances their children. She also resented being taken for granted as housekeeper and hostess. The continual friction with Frances depressed Alice badly, and at times she gave in to 'great fits of gloom, especially at meal times'. Alice in despair in 1887 unwisely confided her sense of failure to Lady Haddington, saying that she 'knew she bored everybody, and [that] life was not worth having for her'. But the crux of Alice's despair was her complaint that she 'never got eno' love from those she cared for'. This came at a time when Alice was evidently getting on Arthur's nerves, and he was showing his irritation. Lady Haddington was too close to the truth for comfort when she told Alice that she had 'wasted her affection in a kind of idolatry'.[49] Mary Gladstone Drew understood all of this when she wrote to Arthur Balfour, after a Whittingehame visit in 1899, asking him to show Alice more affection:

> Alice's life is a grind and her adoring love for you is not enough in itself to give her the amount of happiness to which her goodness and unselfishness entitle her, – it *wd.* be *bliss,* if you could manage to sometimes give her a word of loving kindness and apprecia-tion e.g. a little extra kiss, or touch, or word, or gift, showing that you think of her – she is far too loyal ever to complain, but her life is dust and ashes for 2 reasons, Frances' brutality and your coldness. You never write or utter to her except on business, and yr. time is too full to think much of her and she wears yr. mother's glorious jewels, and has plenty of money and luxuries and comforts and these things rather shut our eyes to the barrenness of her heart.[50]

Alice was a talented woman with pursuits of her own, but she was incapable of making a bold move towards an independent and happier life. She was a gifted artist who exhibited her paintings at the Royal Academy. She also took a keen and knowledgeable interest in music, and in natural history. Philanthropy provided an outlet for her maternal instincts and her evangelical faith. She showed much concern for the welfare of the Whittingehame tenants, and shared Octavia Hill's belief in the beneficial effects of 'proper supervision' of the respectable poor in well organized workhouses. Her consider-able administrative skills and numerous contacts were put to good use in her foundation of a Nursing Association in East London in 1898 for the training of nurses. But her own talents and interests were usually subordinated to those of others. Maggie Cowell-Stepney, another sympathetic friend who understood the trials of women without husbands, sent Mary Gladstone a sensitive analysis of Alice's plight in 1904:

> Oh yes we guessed it all, long before we went to Whittingehame

– though *then,* the desperate tragedy of it, made all one's blood boil. I often long for her to throw it all up, and him, for herself and her own soul, (as Ibsen advises). She has an enchanting life all ready for her – a real Artist's life – her painting is *professionally* good, and in her own line she would be in the first rank. But would she be happy away from him, and could she give him up, except to a wife? – If only he married happily perhaps she might.[51]

Alice never made this bid for personal fulfilment, and was listed in *Who's Who, 1916* only as the 'sister of Rt Hon. A.J. Balfour, M.P.'

The majority of middle and upper-class Victorian and Edwardian spinsters accepted their lot. After all, their real choices were very limited. The degree of unhappiness they experienced depended on their individual circumstances and personality, but few of them appear to have been really contented and fulfilled.

(ii) Desperate rebels: the escapist spinsters

Two minority groups, however – the independent 'new women' and the 'desperate rebels' – were not willing or able to accept the traditional role and status of the spinster in the appropriate submissive manner. The rebels could not tolerate spinsterhood and sought escape, demonstrated in the most positive and courageous form by emigrant gentlewomen like Mary Taylor.[52] But the forms of escape open to spinsters who accepted the authority of the paterfamilias, and who were trapped by family expectations and obligations, were necessarily limited. They could only protest through invalidism, hysteria, religious fanaticism and other types of self-destruction. For a number of these women, it was a short step from obsessive hypochondria to excessive dependence on drugs and alcohol.

The spinsters who sought escape experienced profound role conflict and used desperate measures to resolve a situation they could not tolerate. Helen Gladstone, Evelyn Murray and Marianne Malcolm all retreated into invalidism. This was not uncommon for gifted Victorian spinsters, trapped in a social situation which prohibited the use of their talents. Alice James, for example, sister of the famous brothers Henry and William, spent her forty-three years in psychosomatic invalidism. It can be argued that hysteria, chlorosis, and other classic Victorian female diseases often arose out of role conflict, creating an alternative existence for women who found the conventional role impossible.[53] Helen Gladstone and Evelyn Murray both experienced harsh treatment because they refused to conform to their families' notions of respectable spinster behaviour. They were highly intelligent young women, badly in need of a challenging role and occupation in life. But with no legitimate outlet for their intellect and emotions, they found ultimate refuge in invalidism, drugs and exile. Marianne Malcolm's sad story is a reminder that, even without unacceptable family responsibilities and expectations, the loneliness, social isolation and lack of status of the Victorian spinster could seem intolerable. She tried to find meaning in her life through religion, invalidism and drink, complicated by a hopeless infatuation for Alfred Milner.

W.E. Gladstone's sister, Helen, was the daughter of a wealthy Liverpool merchant, and grew up in a family which regarded the frail invalid as its model of the ideal woman. Although Helen was born in 1814, several decades earlier than the other women in this essay, she merits inclusion because of the intrinsic interest of her story, as well as for the parallels with Evelyn Murray half a century later. Helen was the last of six children, born when John and Anne Gladstone were middle-aged and had lost interest in young offspring, except for the precocious William, Helen's senior by four years. Mrs Gladstone was an intensely pious evangelical woman with a morbid obsession with death and suffering, and a narrow philosophy of man's natural depravity and the need for self-discipline. She was also a neurotic hypochondriac who gradually became a full-time invalid, served by a devoted husband and family. Helen was increasingly isolated and neglected in a home dominated by illness. She spent the years from 1823 to 1829 watching her beloved elder sister, Anne, die slowly of tuberculosis. When the two eldest sons also showed symptoms of the disease, Mrs Gladstone had a genuine outlet for her obsession with disease and death. Meanwhile, Helen received only sporadic education from inadequate governesses, while her three brothers were away at school and university. Helen had grown close to William while Anne was dying, but afterwards Helen was demoralized by William's unfavourable comparisons between herself and the idealized dead sister.[54]

In these circumstances, it was scarcely surprising that Helen gradually joined the family invalids, in search of attention. Though apparently a healthy child, she had been treated as delicate from birth. By the age of sixteen she was suffering from an unspecified illness, involving spasms and bowel problems and frequent consultations with doctors. She was dosed with medicine of all descriptions, but only laudanum provided relief. Laudanum, or tincture of opium, was widely used, habit-forming and dangerous. But the illness gave Helen a role in her family, and at last she became the focus of her mother's attention. She recovered briefly in 1835 to perform the first positive role of her life in caring for her dying mother, but rapidly reverted to invalidism afterwards. At the age of twenty-one she was the only child still living with the elderly father in his rambling new home at Fasque in Scotland. She was isolated in a splendid prison with no friends, little prospect of marriage and no hope of a career. The consumption of laudanum increased and she spent many hours of her futile days in bed. William criticized his sister's behaviour as self-indulgent and wilful, prescribing a rigid regime of self-discipline and prayer. He failed utterly to realize that a highly intelligent woman without a family or a function might share his own need for a worthwhile occupation.

From the age of twenty-four Helen rebelled more openly against her family, which was insensitive to her frustration, and made no effort to help her find any kind of positive role in life. In 1838, her family had the sense to send her abroad in an attempt to remove her from a destructive situation. However, she used her first freedom from family supervision to fall in love with a man who would have been considered most unsuitable by her family. But the parents of the Russo-Polish aristocrat of Greek orthodox faith themselves considered the marriage unsuitable and the brief love affair was vetoed. Helen again became a recluse at Fasque, with no interest in life. She was an advanced opium addict by her mid-twenties, eating little and sleeping most of each day, regarded by William and her father as almost depraved. Her moody silence was broken only by quarrels over her extravagance on clothing. Helen was desperate: 'I am as a dead branch . . . offering no-one fruit or flower, for I am more beaten down than in any former illness'.

In 1842, she chose the most extreme form of defiance, by adopting the Roman Catholic faith, which William detested. William was self-righteous and shocked, not least by the press reports of 'the record of our shame', and had no appreciation of the support and consolation which the Catholic ritual provided for Helen. To his credit, John Gladstone refused to follow William's advice to expel Helen from the family home, but her expenditure and way of life at Fasque were more rigidly circumscribed. An attempt to establish a life for herself in Germany in 1844 ended in hysterical emotional scenes followed by a coma induced by a laudanum overdose. Presumably she could not cope alone, given her addiction, and the consequence was another emotional crisis designed to regain attention. Despite the strictest confinement on her return home, the family failed to keep opium and alcohol away from Helen, and her condition deteriorated, with symptoms of 'clenched hands, locked jaw, and inability to speak except in hysterical bursts'. Severe emotional scenes accompanied visits for medical treatment, reaching a climax in Edinburgh in 1848, when Cardinal Wiseman appeared to perform a miraculous cure with a sacred relic. William was inevitably profoundly disturbed by the public notoriety which Helen's cure achieved. The sustained improvement over the next three years resulted from continual attendance during her father's final illness, which for the second time in her life gave her a positive role as a nurse.

Helen was thirty-seven on her father's death in 1851, and she went almost immediately to Rome. She frequently accused her brothers of not caring for her, while at the same time expecting them to pay her heavy debts. She even had an audience with the Pope and requested him to pray for William. By 1855 she was in the care of a religious community in Rome, having relapsed once more into heavy dependence on opium. She finally became a professed nun – the ultimate challenge to her High Church brother William. Helen became more stable during the last twenty years of her life. For some time in the 1860s she returned to London, reduced her drug intake, became cautiously reconciled to her brothers and rejoiced when William became prime minister. She died in 1880 in Cologne, aged sixty-five. Even at her death-bed, William tried to shake her conversion, convinced that it had been opium-induced self-delusion. She saw herself as a victim of her male-dominated family, unable to perform the role expected of her as a female, but incapable of finding an alternative role which could provide fulfilment. Her rebellion against her fate took the form of opium addiction, while she sublimated her intellectual and emotional drives through religious exaltation. The insecurity of her life was probably determined as an adolescent. It was too late for her to learn to become independent afterwards, especially given the problems of her drug addiction and the self-righteous intolerance of William.

Fifty years later, the situation was no better for Evelyn Murray, one of seven children born to the seventh Duke of Atholl, and the last of three girls. The family papers reveal nothing about Evelyn till 1890, when she was twenty-two, and experiencing major problems with her health and her parents. She was reported as being very 'pulled down' because she had refused to take medicine, and then starved herself for a week. This suggests a possible case of anorexia nervosa, in rebellion against her parents. Two years later, she was evidently suffering from 'persecution mania' after a nervous breakdown, following a dangerous case of diphtheria.[55] She was treated for a grave nervous disorder, which the doctors seem to have diagnosed as neurasthenia, an illness increasingly common in young, single upper-class women. As Lorna Duffin recently noted of neurasthenia: 'the diagnosis closely matched the dilemma which was faced by these women in their struggle to reconcile their desire for independence with the demands of family and society that they fulfil the conventional expectations of the female role'.[56]

Evelyn's parents were well aware that her hostility to them contributed to her illness. The Duchess admitted that 'if it had not been for me she could nearly have got over it'. Evelyn was an intelligent, strong-minded girl who had struggled for years against her parents to attain some sense of her own value and identity as a person. Her rebellion took the form of 'a sullen frame of mind' towards her mother, disregarding her parents' wishes, sitting up almost all night and 'remaining out after dark hours'. In 1892, the Duchess was again exasperated that her daughter failed to take advantage of the London Season: 'She is restless. She avoids Balls and goes to Battersea museum almost every day. She does not like riding out in a carriage. When will it end?'[57] The conflict between mother and daughter, and the regime imposed on the twenty-four year old Evelyn at Blair Castle, was illuminated further by an ultimatum from the Duchess to Evelyn in June 1892, establishing the conditions for Evelyn's continued residence at home: 'I *must* have *respect* and *obedience*. I do not want to stop your Gaelic or any of your amusements if you will do them in moderation and not neglect other duties . . . if you come home you will quite make up your mind to do *all* I wish in everything including your dress'.[58] Lady Evelyn failed to conform to her parents' stereotype of appropriate female behaviour. She was not passive, docile and obedient. She preferred reading late at night, visiting museums and learning Gaelic, to the social round that would win her a suitable husband. Evelyn's case was not helped at this point by the failure of her two elder sisters to marry. All three daughters were becoming something of a liability in a family where the future of the three more precious sons took priority.

The Duke and Duchess responded to Evelyn's prolonged ill-health with anger and resentment, treating it as part of her general insubordination. Their reaction was to send her abroad, to relieve them of the problem. Evelyn resentfully opposed the first banishment in 1891: 'As you are so anxious to be rid of me almost the whole year round, you need never see me except at meals unless you wish and I will keep out of Mama's way as much as possible'. Her father's authoritarian reply to this hurt appeal for attention revealed a total lack of sensitivity: 'When your father decides to provide for you elsewhere for a time, you cannot insist on remaining at home'. Her mother complained that 'all this has caused me to take bad diarrhoea'.[59] Her grandmother wrote a harsh letter to Evelyn in exile:

If a daughter is a source of discomfort at home (instead of happiness and delight as *you might be*) a Father can send her away and she must live wherever he provides a home for her. It cannot be expected that you can be placed in a home as comfortable or congenial as the one from which you have by your own conduct exiled yourself – It is not for your own pleasure that you are living abroad – Your eventual return home will I believe depend on your own frame of mind. Should you come to see how undutiful, and unkind and cruel you have been to your mother – you should then write straight to her.[60]

This was hardly a wise letter to a lonely girl they thought to be suffering from a nervous breakdown, and only recently recovered from diphtheria.

An attempt at reconciliation failed in the following year, indicating once more that Evelyn was not prepared to live at Blair Castle on her parents' terms. By December 1892, the Duchess accepted the doctor's 'sensible' view that Evelyn should 'go on a long voyage in a sailing ship to Australia/New Zealand in charge of a competent person – he says an entire change would benefit her health'. If Evelyn objected, the doctor felt this voyage should be enforced for medical reasons.[61] Emigration to Australia might have been good for Evelyn, if only to give her a chance to establish a life of her own. Instead, she was sent into exile in Belgium, knowing this time that she would never return to Blair Castle.

Lady Evelyn remained in lonely exile in Belgium for the rest of her life. Her identity was kept a close secret, and the few people she ever met believed she was an orphan with no near relatives. Constant reports were sent back to her parents by a 'lady companion', and by a doctor who was treating her for insanity, until he finally declared her cured. Evelyn refused to communicate with either parent, writing only to her cousin, Emily Murray Macgregor, and, from 1900, to her younger brother Hamish. She even had a protracted dispute with her father over the extent of her financial support: 'I wonder my father sent me away if he did not wish to pay for it – perhaps it is too long ago for him to remember that I was forced'. It was finally settled in 1896 that Evelyn was to receive no more than £25 per month under any circumstances, with an extra £5 to pay for her companion.[62] Even as late as 1904 she protested against the Duke's continued demand for receipts for payment of her companion: 'It seems a very childish and unnecessary proceeding and was I suppose instituted as an annoyance – as I am hardly a child by this time and on the road to 40, I can surely be supposed to arrange my affairs at my own discretion'. Evelyn arranged in 1907 that she should never be required to communicate with him again and that he should be contacted only on her death.[63]

The futility and emptiness of Evelyn's existence were part of her martyrdom. In 1899 she told her cousin Emily: 'As I always think of the past everything here almost seems like a dream. It is almost as if I wasn't living. Everything is so completely indifferent to me that I hardly notice how the time passes'. She thought continually about her estranged family at Blair and brooded on the injustice of her father's treatment:

> I have spent [my life] entirely wrapped up in my own thoughts and quite oblivious to my surroundings, perhaps the fact of being completely unable to take an interest in anything or anybody has saved me from falling into temptations into which many others would have fallen who have been left entirely alone and friendless at the age I was then . . . 23 . . . my life might have been completely ruined in a very different way and I have only myself to thank that it has not been so. Papa knows enough of the world to know this and that is *one* of the reasons I could *never* write to him again not even now. A girl can have her life ruined when it would be nothing for a man and just these years between 20 and 30 should be the best of one's life.[64]

Evelyn's existence was far removed from such moral degradation. Her interests and human contacts were minimal. In 1911 she commented that 'my occupations are music and embroidery on a large frame', and she gave part of her allowance to the destitute. The only object of her affection was a pet parrot, her constant companion for sixteen years. She feared it was dying in 1910: 'My parrot is to me what an only child could be to someone else'. From 1899 her correspondence revealed the wish to die: 'I do so often feel as if I should just like to lie down and shut my eyes and die like that'.[65]

A final reflection on the tragedy and wasted potential of Evelyn Murray's life is provided by a letter to her brother in 1900:

> If one stakes everything on one ideal as I did, if one has to give it up suddenly one's life is a blank. But for a boy it is very different, you will see more of the world than I had the opportunity of doing and will not have your mind warped by having to live in one groove.[66]

Evelyn initially had literary or possibly academic aspirations, which were wrecked by her parents' opposition. Her rebellion against her parents was negative and finally self-destructive. Even though she was exiled, she made no effort to create a new life of her own, but lived within the confines of genteel martyrdom and neurasthenia.

The papers of Alfred Milner reveal glimpses of the pathetic life of a spinster who found escape through alcohol and religion. Alfred Milner's mother died in 1869, when he was fifteen, while the family was living in Germany. His father, a doctor and morphia addict, sent the boy to attend classes at King's College, London, staying with distant cousins, an elderly Mr Malcolm and his twenty-seven year old daughter. Milner's wife subsequently recorded with disapproval: 'Miss Malcolm lived mainly at Church, spending all Sunday there and many weekday hours. She was very intemperate, and the frequent references to "illness" mean that . . .' According to Lady Milner, for two years Alfred 'had to look after the cousin whose house he lived in and whose intemperate habits made the home miserable'.[67]

Marianne Malcolm welcomed the fifteen-year-old cousin to her home 'as a young brother'. Given the sudden, tragic collapse of Alfred's family, it is scarcely surprising that she became a mother substitute and the focus of his affection and gratitude. A month after his mother's death, Alfred wrote to Marianne: 'If anything can make up to me a loss, which you know can never quite be retrieved, it is surely *your* kindness and your love, which is as strong, or stronger than any sister's love could be'.[68] In 1872, she congratulated him on becoming a Balliol Scholar: 'here on earth the one heart that loves you best my darling is almost too full of joy and thankfulness – I would just put my arms round you and say one little word before you sleep tonight if I could – it is hard to be away from my Boy, at the moment of his triumph'. Three years later, Alfred declared that time had strengthened their ties, which could only be broken by death.[69]

Mrs Arnold Toynbee commented later that Alfred's friends urged him to devote less time to Marianne, as the relationship was jeopardizing his future. She was already drinking while he was at Oxford, and her health continued to deteriorate as she became increasingly dependent on his affection. She wrote frequently of being 'done up' and 'quite broken down' in health. But for thirteen years Alfred remained loyal and shared a home with Marianne when he worked in London, arguing that 'she looked after me when I had no one else'.[70] Milner finally broke away from his cousin in 1883, when he was twenty-eight and Marianne forty. He wrote at great length to justify his painful decision that they must live separately, to give him the 'absolute disposal of my own time' vital to his career as a journalist. He could no longer cope with her possessive nature and absolute devotion. Their joint life had been one of 'constant friction', involving many bitter disputes. He argued that living separately would enable them to sustain their old relationship: 'You are the person in all the world to whom I am most bound by duty, by common memories, by old affection'. But duty was by this time predominant. Milner promised to see Marianne frequently, to walk by her bath chair while she remained crippled, and to take her out for drives after her recovery. He would supplement her income to make her life as comfortable as possible, and provide her with a personal maid.[71]

Marianne died two years later, apparently from pleural tuberculosis and alcohol poisoning. Her diaries for 1884-5 give an entirely one-sided view of their relationship after Milner left her house. She lived in a fantasy world of love for her 'darling Boy', who visited her nearly every day. The diary is a pathetic record of obsessive love, delighted when he was 'hardly out of my sight – he pets and nurses me as tenderly as ever'.[72] She resented Milner's life outside her sick room, particularly his increasingly successful involvement in politics. Apart from Milner's company, her only pleasures, when she was well enough, were five or six church services a week. But the diary chiefly records the collapse of her health, mentioning rheumatic pains, neuralgia, depression, pleurisy, and congestion of the liver and right lung. By the end of 1884, Marianne welcomed death: 'to linger on always feeble if not actually *ill* is hard'.[73] Milner remained devoted, attentive and affectionate to the end, while she had the final satisfaction of a fatal illness to command his attendance at her sickbed.

(iii) *The transition to the new women*

The final category of spinsters was a rather larger minority with the capacity to transcend the stereotypical role. They carried out their familial obligations efficiently, but also found fulfilment as independent 'new women' or 'bachelor women'. Most women in this category were exceptional in their circumstances, intellectual gifts and inner resources. Some were well-endowed mentally, others had the advantage of a good school education and a degree of financial independence, and most were fortunate in that domestic demands did not consume the greater part of their mature lives. The leaders of the women's movement who remained single naturally fall into this category. Constance Lytton, for example, turned to the suffrage movement as an outlet for her frustrations against society, and Emily Davies found fulfilment through the women's education movement. Others found a role in the more traditional female sphere of philanthropy. From the 1880s the women's movement at last made it easier for a minority of able and independent single women to find satisfaction in a career outside domesticity. The women's movement challenged the ideal of womanhood which implied marriage and motherhood, particularly when that ideal was statistically unattainable for many spinsters.

A growing body of literature from the 1860s onwards argued that single women had the capacity and the need to lead worthwhile lives. Frances Cobbe in 1862 contended that celibacy was a viable way of life for women, and that single women must learn to support themselves in independent lives of dignity.[74] Josephine Butler in 1869 refused to admit that it was every woman's duty to marry: 'There is abundance of work to be done which needs men and women detached from domestic ties; our unmarried women will be the greatest blessing to the community when they cease to be soured by disappointment'. Harriet Martineau argued that women must become independent for practical, economic and demographic reasons. Barbara Leigh Smith believed that women must be trained for work and not expect to be supported by men 'if they are to stand as dignified, rational beings before God'.[75] By the 1890s numerous tributes were made to the achievements of single women, even by writers not entirely sympathetic to the goals of the women's movement. Lady Jeune noted in 1898 that modern thought and education had raised women intellectually, enabling thousands to choose their own careers and successfully pursue independent personal goals. Stephen Gwynn commented in the same year that ambitious women could now choose between marriage and a career, promoting the growth of a new class of 'ladies who live entirely by themselves and work for their living'.[76] George Gissing in *The Odd Women* in 1893 depicted Rhoda Nunn as the champion of the surplus women, aiming to train them 'for the world's work'.

Such writing provided support for a growing minority of courageous and independent 'new women'. Women in this category have already received attention because of the growing interest in the early leaders of the women's movement, such as Emily Davies and Frances Power Cobbe. The intention here is to consider briefly three women in these political families who fall within this category – Lady Gwendolen Cecil, Gladstone's daughter Helen, and Elizabeth Haldane. Lady Gwendolen is perhaps a borderline case in that her life essentially revolved around her famous father, but in some respects she was far more emancipated than most spinsters in political families. Born in 1860, she came from an aristocratic family which respected individualism and eccentricity, even in its female members. Like most girls of her class, she was denied a formal education, despite her considerable intellectual and literary gifts. After her elder sister's marriage, when Gwendolen was twenty-three, she shared with her mother the responsibility of household and estate management at Hatfield, and there was no question of her leaving home. She was considered no great match, with her plain angular features and lack of interest in the doings of society, and she made little effort to improve her chances of marriage. She was also assertive and self-opinionated – characteristics more readily appreciated by the Cecil family than most Edwardian husbands. Like all the Cecils, she preferred the company of her remarkable family to that of other people, so it was no great sacrifice to devote twenty years of adult life to her parents. If she suffered any emotional deprivation from single life at Hatfield, which seems unlikely, then it could be argued that her religious fervour provided the means of sublimation. But her correspondence suggests that she was somewhat cynical about love and marriage, and was not strongly affected by sexual passion.

There is no hint of sadness about her single state, rather a sense of relief at not being married.[77]

Spinsterhood conferred definite benefits on Gwendolen. As the daughter of the Marquis of Salisbury, leader of the Conservative Party and Prime Minister for many years, she had unusual advantages, which she exploited to the full. Like Gladstone's daughter, Mary, she had the extraordinary experience, for a Victorian female, of becoming confidential private secretary to the Prime Minister. She was exceptionally well-informed about political affairs and could indulge her passion for politics in a family which included two prime ministers as well as several ministers and backbenchers. In a later generation she would probably have become an effective politician in her own right. When Lord Salisbury died in 1903 she gained more personal and intellectual freedom, moving into a small 'spinster house' on the Hatfield estate. The major interest in her life became the official biography of her father – an arduous task, given the voluminous material and Gwendolen's lack of methodical training. The *Life* was a considerable achievement, though she sacrificed one year of her own life for each year of her father's and never finished it. Her other passions were philanthropy and architecture, which were united in her plans for building comfortable homes for old people, better mental hospitals and cheerful sanatoria for consumptives.

The life of Helen, eldest of Gladstone's three daughters, also revolved around the towering figure of her Prime Minister father. Earnest, reserved and deeply religious, she seems to have been even more overwhelmed by their formidable parents than her sisters, with few friends, no formal education and little independent life outside the Gladstone family routine. The situation changed dramatically in 1877 when Helen was twenty-eight, because the more extrovert younger sister, Mary, conceived her 'startling plan' that Helen should go to Newnham College, Cambridge. The arguments used to obtain parental consent reveal the limitations of Helen's previous life. She felt a great need of 'stirring up' through disciplined courses, after the many aimless years in which her time had been largely wasted. Mary reported to the family that Helen was transformed by Cambridge: 'her intellectual life is stimulated, her moral life strengthened and encouraged'.[78] The plan was so successful that in 1880 Helen became assistant to Eleanor Sidgwick, Vice-Principal of

Newnham, and two years later succeeded her as Vice-Principal.

Cambridge provided personal fulfilment for Helen, but there was always a conflict with her view of her family duties. Mary accepted the full-time responsibility of caring for the 'Grand Old People' until her marriage in 1886, but she combined this with being her father's private secretary while he was Prime Minister. It was no great burden for Mary, who was a capable domestic manager and, like Gwendolen Cecil, was delighted to indulge her passion for politics. But Helen worried in her early years at Newnham 'whether I ought to stay so much away from home', and she reiterated in several letters that 'if Mary was to marry or I was in any special way needed at home, I would give it up *at once*'.[79] The crisis occurred in 1886, when Mary unexpectedly married at the age of thirty-nine. Helen inherited primary responsibility for their parents and this involved far greater sacrifice for her than Mary. Helen tried to respond unselfishly to Mary's marriage, but found the prospect of her own new family responsibilities 'rather grim'. 'Home duties' were 'so pressing' that she made arrangements with Newnham 'for being a great deal at home', with the possibility of full retirement if necessary. The conflict of interests was intensified a few months later when Helen was invited to become the first Principal of the newly established Royal Holloway College, London. Helen agonized over the dilemma of career versus domestic responsibilities, circulating a memorandum to friends and relatives giving both sides of the case and requesting their views.[80] Nora Sidgwick was the only person to question Helen's assumption that a woman's primary moral obligation was to her parents, and the outcome was a foregone conclusion. Even Mary commented that, if Helen accepted Royal Holloway, 'it would be simply impossible for her to be much at home – she would be far more tied and bound than by most marriages'.[81] So Helen refused the Royal Holloway offer, and temporarily stayed on at Newnham with time off for 'home duties'.

Helen Gladstone felt obliged to make the personal sacrifice, even though she was so much more effective and fulfilled at Newnham than in her filial capacity at Hawarden and Downing Street. Helen felt inadequate, especially by comparison with Mary: 'I am not of much use to my Father while he is in office – I am not of any immense use to my Mother at any time, but at least I am available'.[82] Helen was bored by Society functions, she found domestic duties tedious, and she lacked Mary's efficient organizing abilities on the home front. She tried to be a dutiful daughter, but she was temperamentally unable to transfer to her 'home duties' the independence and assurance she enjoyed at Newnham. She found the political responsibilities less of a strain, though she lacked Mary's natural flair and enthusiasm for politics. Helen took over Mary's work as personal secretary to the Liberal leader in 1886, and was 'a perfect tower of strength' in helping her elderly parents through the 1886 Home Rule crisis and the elections of 1886 and 1892. But her political role was almost entirely supportive and rarely gave her the fulfilment she found at Newnham.

The final sacrifice was required of Helen in the 1890s when her father became Prime Minister for the last time, and when she subsequently had to care for both parents through their last illnesses. Mary and Helen arranged to live alternately with their octogenarian parents in Downing Street during the 1893 session: 'Helen's having practically refused the Headship of Newnham privately before it was offered her, was done entirely to enable her to be of use to parents'. Helen left Cambridge forever in November 1896, 'to take my share regularly of home duties'. She even allowed her father to glimpse the pain it caused her to sever her last links with Newnham: 'You will not think I have done this lightly or easily'.[83] Unfortunately for Helen, her resignation coincided with the Drews' move away from the family home at Hawarden, where they had lived since their marriage. Helen wrote a letter of utter depression to Mary: 'the prospect of Hawarden with only me, is one to me so almost hopeless (seldom able to satisfy Mama and with no time to do any work for Father – except the letters – almost always inefficient in my own eyes and everybody else's)'. Helen took the usual spinster's role in caring for her father up to his death in 1898, and her mother until her death in 1900, but the declining health of both parents clearly depressed her intensely.[84] Helen's sense of filial obligation did not even end with their deaths, for subsequently she felt tied to Hawarden Castle to help John Morley with her father's biography. However, in 1901 she became Warden of the Women's University Settlement in Southwark and at last resumed her independent life. Though she was obliged to sacrifice a successful career at Cambridge, Helen

Gladstone was more fortunate and had more opportunities than most other Victorian spinsters. She gained a higher education at Cambridge and was able to enjoy ten years of Newnham life, since her family responsibilities did not begin until she was thirty-seven. It is also worth noting that Gladstone was far more tolerant and understanding in his attitude towards his daughters than towards his poor sister Helen.

Elizabeth Haldane was more emancipated than either Helen Gladstone or Gwendolen Cecil. She was a formidable woman with a powerful intellect, born in 1862 into a distinguished Scottish academic family. Her uncle and two brothers were Fellows of the Royal Society, while her eldest brother, Richard Burdon Haldane, was a distinguished philosopher and Liberal Minister. An equally important influence was her father's death when Elizabeth was only fifteen, which freed her mother 'to do many things that she could not do before and to give expression to faculties hitherto latent'. Elizabeth was brought up by her mother, assisted by two spinster aunts – three loving and independent women leading fairly full lives. This strong female influence in Elizabeth's life was in marked contrast to the male-dominated families of most other spinsters examined here. Elizabeth suffered the disadvantages common to her sex only in that she received no formal education. The family was not wealthy, 'the sons had to be set up in life', and 'for an only daughter to leave a widowed mother was indeed considered to be quite out of the question'.[85] But her mother and aunts supported the women's movement even in the 1880s and encouraged Elizabeth to be intellectually active and personally independent. She organized a rigorous process of self-education through correspondence classes, combined with frequent discussions on philosophy and scientific thought with her Aunt Jane. Elizabeth was also fortunate as a young girl in that she spent three months each year with her brothers in London, where she was exceptionally placed to meet interesting academics and politicians.

Against this supportive background, Elizabeth Haldane developed a strong sense of the potential for an independent female role in life. From an early age, she 'wanted to do for myself and not just to be the helper of others who were doing – a quite unbiblical ideal for any woman to have'. She was strong-minded and progressive in her opinions. There is no evidence that Elizabeth ever had any inclination to marry. She remarked later that she never knew the meaning of frustration, 'the disease which is supposed to attack unmarried women . . . life seemed brimming full and running over'.[86] Her mother commented in 1897 that marriage for Elizabeth 'would have been a hindrance. She has a self-sustaining nature'.[87] Even in politics she played more than a merely passive supporting role for her brother, Richard Haldane. She was not deeply interested in politics, but acted as his political hostess and kept house for him in London while parliament was sitting. Her fine mind and strong personality made her the equal of guests like Beatrice Webb, though some of their male visitors found her rather forbidding. But she also became more actively involved on Richard's behalf when necessary, canvassing and making speeches at election time. Indeed, in December 1909 she herself actually conducted the East Lothian campaign 'with great vigour' while Richard was ill.[88]

Elizabeth also led her own life in a highly successful manner. She was an accomplished philosopher and writer whose books included a *Life of Descartes,* a *Life of George Eliot* and *A History of Nursing,* as well as translations of the works of Hegel and Descartes. In 1906 she was awarded an honorary Doctor of Laws by St Andrews University – a remarkable achievement for a woman with no formal education. Elizabeth was also very fully involved in social work, nursing and philanthropy. She had endless energy and organizing ability, rushing around enlisting patronage and support for worthy causes. From 1892 she became a prominent fighter in the movement to revise the Scottish Poor Law and improve conditions in the workhouses and gave evidence to the Royal Commission on the Poor Laws in 1907. She was also a Manager of the Edinburgh Royal Infirmary from 1892, and campaigned for the registration of nurses and improvement in their hours and pay. By 1907 she was seen by the Local Government Board as an authority on the financing and organization of hospitals. She was a suffragist who saw her medical work as a breakthrough into the male sphere of nursing.[89]

She led an entirely independent and fulfilled life. She was a successful public figure in her own right, with no need or desire to live vicariously through her eminent brothers. She played a strong supportive role for her bachelor politician brother, but unlike Alice

Balfour or the Bryce sisters, she treated this as a secondary role in her life. She devoted much of her free time to her mother, aunts and brother, but there was no continual struggle between her own career and the obligations of 'home duties', as with Helen Gladstone. She was fortunate, in that her father died when she was fifteen while her mother lived to be over one hundred, so that she did not have to nurse elderly parents during her years of maturity and achievement.

The conventions of Victorian family life were founded on the primary values of social and moral duty combined with parental authority. Many spinsters in this study were talented, but the application of their abilities was severely restricted by their male-dominated environment and by Victorian assumptions regarding the obligations of unmarried daughters. When the fathers or brothers were famous politicians, accustomed to exercising power at Westminster, the domestic pressures were often substantially increased. One of Helen Gladstone's Newnham students commented that 'one of the things that kept her such a very "unmarried" person was her ingrained attitude of daughter'.[90] Many of these women were effectively conditioned to be spinsters from adolescence, especially if they were only daughters or their sisters seemed more likely to marry first on grounds of age or beauty. An assumption of spinsterhood was often reached by the mid-twenties and it was not easy to break that pattern, particularly when it was reinforced by family requirements. This is confirmed by the fact that two widows remarried for every spinster married in the age group over thirty during 1870 to 1872.[91]

The feminist, Rhoda Nunn, in George Gissing's *The Odd Women* contended that spinsters' lives were not 'useless, lost, futile'; rather 'the vast majority of women would lead a vain and miserable life because they *do* marry'. Elizabeth Haldane's aunt Jane Sanderson would have agreed with this up to a point. She knew that single women were often lonely, 'but it is far better to be single unless one is *truly* married'.[92] All upper-class spinsters were not necessarily more unhappy and frustrated than all married women. But the vast majority of spinsters found it hard to bear the crippling assumption that they were social and emotional failures because they did not marry and could not have children. Even worse than their own presumption of failure, they had to face the stigma of society – no easy matter in Victorian Britain. It is not surprising that one small group tried to escape the spinster role entirely, and that only a minority found fulfilment and independence as single women. This last group, which transcended the stereotypical spinster role, were often fortunate in their intellectual endowments, social opportunities and strength of character. They usually also had to be free from family responsibilities for a sufficient length of time to establish their own lives. Most upper-class spinsters were overwhelmed by family obligations, reinforced by parental authority and widely accepted social conventions. They also had to contend with the utter collapse of their lives which could so easily follow a father's death or a brother's marriage. Beatrice Potter believed that the best single women achieved a degree of nobility unattainable by their married sisters; but 'so few women have enough character to live an unmarried life, and not sink into a nobody, or still worse into a general nuisance'.[93]

Notes

I wish to thank Dee Cook for her excellent work as research assistant and for her helpful comments; Barbara Caine and John Hooper for their valuable suggestions; and the Australian Research Grants Committee for financial support. Place of publication is London, unless cited otherwise.

1. *Women in British Political Families, 1870-1914,* to be published by Oxford University Press.
2. S.R. Johansson, ' "Herstory" as History', in B.A. Carroll (ed.), *Liberating Women's History,* Urbana, 1976, p.404.
3. E.W. Monter, 'The Pedestal and the Stake', in R. Bridenthal and C. Koonz, eds., *Becoming Visible. Women in European History,* Boston, 1977, p.133.
4. L. Stone, *The Family, Sex and Marriage in England, 1500-1800,* 1977, p.380.
5. See e.g. W.R. Greg, 'Why are Women redundant?', *National Review,* April, 1862.
6. *Census of England and Wales, 1851,* General Report, vol.1, p.xIiii; *Census of England and Wales, 1911,* General Report, table xxxi, p.90; P. Hollis, *Women in Public: The Women's Movement, 1850-1900,* 1979, p.33.
7. *Census of England and Wales, 1881,* General Report, vol.4, pp.15-16;

B.R. Mitchell, *Abstract of British Historical Statistics,* Cambridge, 1962, p.6.

8.   *Ibid.*

9.   *Census of England and Wales, 1881,* General Report, vol.4, p.24; R.C. Ansell, *On the Rate of Mortality at Early Periods of Life – and other Statistics of Families in the Upper and Professional Classes,* 1874, pp.45, 83-5. See also J.A. Banks, *Prosperity and Parenthood,* 1954, *passim.*

10.   Richard Carlile, *Every Woman's Book or What is Love?,* 1838, pp.11, 35-6.

11.   William Acton, *Functions,* 1862, p.105.

12.   H. Spencer, *The Principles of Ethics,* 2 vols, 1892-3, I, 534.

13.   Miss E. Marion Ashton to fiance, James Bryce, 11 March 1899, M.S. Bryce, Adds. 21 (Bodleian Library, Oxford).

14.   Beatrice Potter to father, Richard Potter, 8 Nov. 1885, Passfield Papers, II 1 (i), 544-5 (London School of Economics).

15.   Beatrice Potter [Webb] diary, 10 Dec. 1886, Passfield Papers.

16.   Peter T. Cominos, 'Innocent Femina Sensualis in Unconscious Conflict', in M. Vicinus, ed., *Suffer and be Still,* Indiana, 1972, p.163 (citing Henry Maudsley, *The Pathology of Mind,* 1879, p.164.)

17.   David Roberts, 'The Paterfamilias of the Victorian Governing Classes', in A.S. Wohl, ed., *The Victorian Family,* 1978, pp.63-4.

18.   F.P. Cobbe, *The Duties of Women,* 1881.

19.   Beatrice Potter [Webb] diary, 5 Nov. 1883, Passfield Papers.

20.   Margot Peters, *Unquiet Soul. A Biography of Charlotte Bronte,* 1977, p.193.

21.   Vera Brittain, *Testament of Youth,* 1978, pp.401, 421-2, 536.

22.   Julia Wedgwood, 'Female Suffrage' in Josephine Butler, ed., *Woman's Work and Woman's Culture,* 1869, quoted in Hollis, *Women in Public,* pp.9-10.

23.   Quoted in Lawrence Stone, *The Family, Sex and Marriage in England 1500-1800,* 1977, p.386.

24.   S.A. Acland to father, Dr. Acland, 20 July 1879, MS. Acland d.105 f.56, (Bodleian Library, Oxford).

25.   'Memories in my 81st Year', MS. Eng. Misc. d.214,f.86.

26.   S.A. Acland to Dr. Acland, 28 July 1880, MS. Acland d.105, ff.60a-61b.

27.   Caroline [Gull] Acland to S.A. Acland, 20 Dec. N.D. [1880s], MS. Acland d. 143, ff.150-151.

28.   S.A. Acland to William A. Dyke Acland, 22 Oct. 1900, MS. Acland d.108, ff.64-5.

29.   S.A. Acland to W.A.D. Acland, 22 Oct. 1900, MS. Acland d. 108, ff.64-65.

30.   S.A. Acland to W.A.D. Acland, 18 Nov. 1900 and 6 June 1901, MS. Acland d.108, ff.67, 73-74, 99-100.

31. Mrs Elizabeth King to Mrs Margaret Gladstone, N.D. [c.1870] and reply 19 May 1870, Ramsay MacDonald Papers, P.R.O. 30/69/ 852-3.

32. Mrs E. King to J.H. Gladstone, 20 Dec. 1874, P.R.O. 30/69/861; M. Gladstone to sister Elizabeth King, 18 Feb. 1870, P.R.O. 30/69/852.

33. Agnes King to Mrs E. King, 18 April 1872, P.R.O. 30/69/970.

34. 'Prayers during the long struggle, AGK', 29 Feb. 1912, P.R.O. 30/69/970.

35. Mary to James Bryce, 30 Dec. 1887, MS. Bryce Adds. II, Bodleian Library, Oxford.

36. Katharine to James Bryce, 19 Dec. 1883, *ibid*.

37. Mary to James Bryce, 10 Jan. 1884, and 16 Nov. 1888, *ibid*.

38. Mary to James Bryce, 11 Jan. 1889, MS. Bryce Adds. 12.

39. Katharine to James Bryce, 12 April 1889, *ibid*.

40. Mary to James Bryce, 3 letters dated 4 and 6 Dec. and N.D. 1889, *ibid*.

41. Mary to James Bryce, 4 Dec. 1889 and 9 Aug. 1890, *ibid*.

42. Kenneth Young, *Arthur James Balfour,* 1963, pp.10-11.

43. Alice Balfour's diary, 18 Aug. 1898, Balfour (Whittingehame) MS.150.

44. Alice Balfour to Mary Gladstone, 31 Dec. 1885, Mary Gladstone Drew Papers, British Library, Add. MS. 46238, ff.89-90.

45. Frances Balfour to A.J. Balfour, N.D. [1897], Balfour (Whitt) MS. 159; Frances to Alice Balfour, March 1897, Balfour (Whitt) MS. 162.

46. Alice Balfour to A.J. Balfour, 11 June 1897, Balfour (Whitt) MS.159; A.J. Balfour to Frances Balfour (draft), 20 July 1897, Balfour (Whitt) MS. 159.

47. Betty to Gerald Balfour, two letters of Dec. 1905, Balfour (Whitt) MS. 273.

48. Alice Balfour to Mary Gladstone, 31 Dec. 1885, Mary Gladstone Drew Papers, British Library, Add. MS. 46238, ff. 89-90.

49. Frances to Gerald Balfour, 9 and 12 Oct. 1887, Balfour (Whitt) MS. 283; Frances to Arthur Balfour, 22 Oct. 1887, Balfour (Whitt) MS. 163.

50. Mary (Gladstone) Drew to A.J. Balfour, 5 Nov. 1899, Balfour (Whitt) MS. 164.

51. M. Cowell-Stepney to Mary Drew, 22 Sept. 1904, Mary Gladstone Drew Papers, B.L. Add. MS. 46250, ff. 28-29.

52. See e.g., A.J. Hammerton, *Emigrant Gentlewomen,* 1979.

53. See e.g., C. Smith Rosenberg, 'The Hysterical Woman', *Social Research,* Vol. 39, No. 4, 1972.

54. The section on Helen Gladstone is based on S.G. Checkland, *The Gladstones. A Family Biography 1764-1851,* 1971, and material in the Glynne-Gladstone MSS at Hawarden.

55. Louisa Duchess of Atholl to Dowager Duchess of Atholl, N.D. (1890); Dowager Duchess to Evelyn Murray, N.D. (1892), Atholl MS. 500 & 480 (Blair Castle).

56. Lorna Duffin, 'The Conspicuous Consumptive: Woman as an Invalid', in S. Delamont and L. Duffin, eds., *The Nineteenth Century Woman,* 1978, p.38.

57. Dowager Duchess of Atholl to Evelyn Murray, N.D. (1892); Duchess to Dowager Duchess, 28 May 1892, Atholl MSS. 480 and 501.

58. Duchess of Atholl to daughter, Evelyn Murray, 30 June 1892, Atholl MS. 501.

59. Evelyn Murray to Duke of Atholl, 10 Dec. 1891 and reply of 14 Dec. 1891, Atholl MS.63: Duchess to Dowager Duchess, 15 Dec. 1891, Atholl MS. 1663.

60. Dowager Duchess to Evelyn Murray, N.D. (1892), Atholl MS. 480.

61. Duchess to Dowager Duchess, 12 Nov. 1892, Atholl MS. 1663.

62. Evelyn Murray to cousin, Miss Emily Murray Macgregor, 3 Jan. 1896; Duchess to E.M. Macgregor, 17 Sept. 1896, Atholl MS. 482.

63. Evelyn Murray to Duke of Atholl, 28 Jan. 1904 and Oct. 1907, Atholl MS. 64.

64. Evelyn Murray to E.M. Macgregor, 14 March 1899, Atholl MS. 66.

65. Evelyn Murray to E.M. Macgregor, (1911) and 19 Dec. 1910, Atholl MS. 66; Evelyn to Kitty, Lady Tullibardine, 21 Sept. 1910, Atholl MS. 82/83/1.

66. Evelyn to Hamish Murray, 8 July 1900, Atholl MS. 489.

67. Notes by Lady Milner on Lord Milner's Life, N.D., MS. Milner dep. 674, f.2. (Bodleian Library, Oxford).

68. Alfred Milner to Marianne Malcolm, (c.1869), MS. Milner dep. 652, ff.17-18.

69. M. Malcolm to Milner, 25 Nov. 1872, MS. Milner dep. 652, f.136; Milner to M. Malcolm, 6 April 1875, dep. 653, f.93.

70. Notes by Lady Milner on Lord Milner's Life, 12 June 1926, MS. Milner dep. 674, f.27.

71. Milner to M. Malcolm, 20 Oct. 1883, MS. Milner dep. 654, ff.215-223.

72. M. Malcolm's diary, 25 May 1885, MS. Eng. Hist. e. 306, f.55.

73. *Ibid.,* 29 Sept. 1884, e. 305, f.95.

74. I am grateful to Barbara Caine for allowing me to see her valuable paper on Frances Cobbe, to be published shortly: 'Frances Cobbe and the English Women's Movement' (delivered at the Australasian Modern British History Association Conference, Melbourne, May, 1981).

75. See Hollis, *Women in Public,* pp.9-13, for useful extracts from the works of these women.

76. Lady Jeune *et.al., The Modern Marriage Market* (1898), pp.70-71; Stephen Gwynn, 'Bachelor Women', *Contemporary Review,* 1898, LXXIII, 867-8.

77. The material on Lady Gwendolen Cecil is based on Kenneth Rose, *The Later Cecils,* 1975, pp.309-320.

78. Helen to Henry Gladstone, 30 March and 30 Aug. 1877, and 5 July

1878, Glynne-Gladstone Mss. 44/3; Mary to Henry Gladstone, 9 and 11 May 1878, *Ibid.* 43/2 (St Deiniol's Library, Hawarden).

79. *Ibid.*

80. Helen Gladstone's memorandum, 12 July 1886, and her letter to Martin Holloway, 13 June 1886, Glynne-Gladstone Mss. 135/22.

81. Nora Sidgwick to Helen Gladstone, 9 July 1886, Glynne-Gladstone Mss. 135/22; Mary to Catherine Gladstone, N.D. [c.19 June 1886], Mary [Gladstone] Drew Papers, British Library, Add. MS. 46223, ff.335-6.

82. Helen Gladstone's Memorandum, 12 July 1886, Glynne-Gladstone Mss. 135/22.

83. Mary [Gladstone] Drew to Henry Gladstone, 12 June 1892, Glynne-Gladstone Mss. 43/3; Helen to W.E. Gladstone, 2 Nov. 1896, *Ibid.,* 23/11.

84. Helen Gladstone to Mary Drew, 8 March and 22 Dec. 1897, Mary [Gladstone] Drew Papers, B.L. Add. MS. 46231, ff.150-152, 155-7.

85. Elizabeth B. Haldane, *From One Century to Another,* 1937, pp.69-70, 72-73.

86. *Ibid.,* pp.15, 73.

87. Mary to R.B. Haldane, 24 April 1897, Haldane Ms. 6008, f.84 (National Library of Scotland).

88. R.B. Haldane, *An Autobiography,* 1929, p.263; see C. Addison, *Four and a Half Years,* 1934, I, 17.

89. Information obtained from the Haldane Papers in the National Library of Scotland.

90. *Newnham Letter,* Jan. 1926, 'Helen Gladstone: In Memoriam', p.72, Glynne-Gladstone Ms. 135/124.

91. Registrar-General's 35th Annual Report, pp. xii-xiii, cited in William Farr, *Vital Statistics,* 1885, p.80.

92. Gissing, *The Odd Women,* 1980, pp.37, 59; Jane C.B. Sanderson to Mary Haldane, 9 March 1881, Haldane Ms. 6091, ff. 143-5.

93. M. Harkness to B. Potter [c.1878], Passfield Papers, II 1 (ii) 128-31.

5

Raelene Davidson

'As good a bloody woman as any other bloody woman . . .' Prostitutes in Western Australia, 1895-1939

It is harder for historians to discover the realities of the lives of women in the past the further down the social scale one explores. The difficulty of writing the history of the poorer classes of women partially explains why it has been neglected for so long. It is possible to construct a believable picture of the lives of middle-class and aristocratic women using their own letters, diaries and other written evidence. It is a more daunting task to wade through masses of peripheral material in the hope of finding sufficient evidence to throw some light on the lives of women who could not or did not leave their own accounts. Prostitutes are one such group of women about whom the surviving records are scattered and difficult to use. The most useful sources of information in the case of the prostitutes in this study have been police records and the rare royal commission. Obviously, these records present an official view of prostitutes, but in both instances the voice of the prostitute can still be heard if one listens. Some bench clerks took verbatim notes on court proceedings in which prostitutes testified, as was the case with the evidence of royal commissions. Since many of the women in this study are still alive I was able to talk to them personally and so hear their voices directly. Historians of the twentieth century can thus 'create' sources by talking to people and so compensate for the lack of written material.

In the following essay I have explored which women were identified by the authorities as prostitutes and how they came to receive this label. To get a clearer picture of these women I have looked at their nationality and age and the reasons for their becoming prostitutes. Finally, I have examined the ways in which being a prostitute affected their lives and self-images. It would also be useful to be able to say where prostitutes fitted into the social structure, but this issue is beyond the scope of my research. If one rejects the notion that society is divided into two antagonistic classes by sex, there is still the problem of determining whether a woman under capitalism takes her class position from her own work or from that of her husband or father. Just as married women take their status and wealth from their husbands, prostitutes' status and wealth comes from their clients. But in a strictly materialist analysis brothel inmates would be in a different class from their madames. Nevertheless, their common membership of a 'deviant' sub-culture possibly overrides traditional notions of class interest. This is certainly the impression one gets from today's madames and prostitutes, who have a model of society made up of 'us' and 'them', where 'us' are the prostitutes and madames (or working girls, to use their terminology), and 'them' are the 'squares', or the rest of society excluding other 'deviants' such as criminals, drug addicts and homosexuals. Whether this was true of prostitutes in the past is not clear.

* * *

Although I use the term 'prostitution industry' it will be clear that even though prostitution was a viable economic alternative for working women in Western Australia, it was nevertheless different from other occupations such as domestic service and factory work. The essential difference was the very fact that prostitution was not a *respectable* alternative for women, so that those who did become prostitutes became 'deviant' in terms of the dominant values of that time. By 'deviant' I do not mean that their behaviour was disapproved of by the majority of the community. I mean that prostitutes did not conform to the notions of female chastity and womanliness held by those sections of the community who had the political and social power. These people were the law-makers and law-enforcers, the educators and the arbiters of taste and morals. Extra-marital sex of any kind on the part of women was frowned upon, and when it involved a number of different men it provoked punitive action. The women who are discussed in this chapter are therefore workers, but to the extent that they were ostracized and persecuted by the society in which they lived they were 'wayward workers'.

Prostitution itself was not illegal in Western Australia, but the laws were structured so that it was virtually impossible to carry on a legal prostitution business. Brothel-keeping was illegal, as was soliciting by 'common prostitutes' and loitering for the purposes of prostitution. As the law provided no definitions of 'soliciting' and 'common prostitute', it was difficult for women to defend themselves. Their interpretation was left in practice to the discretion of the police. Unfortunately there is no way of knowing which of the women labelled by the police as prostitutes were in fact prostitutes and which were merely called prostitutes because of other 'deviant' behaviour. Some of the 1567 women classified by the police as prostitutes never had a conviction for a specifically prositution-related offence, and others who were eventually convicted of soliciting or vagrancy had earlier been designated as prostitutes even though they were charged with being drunk or disorderly. Although it is probably reasonable to assume that the police sometimes labelled women inaccurately, there is no way the historian can resolve the problem. Just because the police or local government authorities harassed women only when they were drunk or disorderly does not mean that the women were not prostitutes anyway. The police were required to explain their labels only when the case was challenged in court. Such cases show that the police had a 'rule of thumb' which they used in deciding which women were prostitutes. Apart from the obvious fact of living in a brothel, women were classified as prostitutes if they were seen continually hanging about the streets and around hotels with a number of different men, were frequently drunk and did not have a regular legal source of income. The police assumption that prostitution was the most likely source of income for such women was probably reasonable. The historian has no alternative but to accept the police classification of women as prostitutes.

A more serious problem is the prostitutes who escaped official classification. Undoubtedly some prostitutes were so discreet they avoided police identification. There were prostitutes whose way of life was more acceptable to the authorities so they did not therefore invite interference. Aboriginal prostitutes must be included in this group. Only five of the 1567 prostitutes in this study were aborigines, yet aboriginal prostitution on the fringes of towns was reputedly much more extensive than these numbers indicate. Again, the extent of unreported prostitution is an insoluble problem for the historian.

Bearing these limitations in mind, I will discuss the results of my search for Western Australia's prostitutes between the goldrushes of the 1890s and the outbreak of the Second World War. This period has been singled out for study because it covers a period of great social change in Western Australia. It encompasses the exciting years of the 1890s gold boom, the unsettling period of the Great War and the traumatic economic depression of the 1930s. More specifically, these years saw a major transformation in the structure of the prostitution industry: in the years 1908-1918, Roe Street (Perth) and Hay Street (Kalgoorlie) were established as semi-tolerated 'red-light' districts into which all prostitutes were encouraged to move. This meant the gradual disappearance of the freelance streetwalker and her replacement by the brothel-prostitute.[1] This change was the result of attempts by the local police, magistrates, municipal councils and health authorities to control the 'social nuisances' associated with prostitution. These nuisances were of five types: disturbance to neighbours in the vicinity of brothels as a result of drunk and rowdy customers or excessive traffic in the street; the detrimental 'moral' effect on women and children in the community where prostitutes are visible; the decrease in the value of properties near brothels; the spread of venereal disease from prostitutes to clients; and the exploitation of prostitutes by landlords and 'bludgers' – the contemporary term for men who lived off the proceeds of a woman's prostitution.

Prostitution in Western Australia did not have any of the potent symbolism attached to it by other western societies at the time. In the United States and Imperial Germany in the period up to the end of the Great War, for example, prostitution was seen as a symbol of all that was decadent and corrupt in modern urban society.[2] It was used in this sense by all shades of the political spectrum. Neither did Western Australians share the concern of their contemporaries in Britain and Germany that prostitution was the 'gigantic trade that held the underworld together and nurtured all other forms of violence and criminality'.[3] But although the authorities in Western Australia did not argue so, they were still anxious to control the 'social evil'

174

in their midst.

The Western Australian community first regarded prostitution as a serious social problem in the late 1890s when large numbers of prostitutes arrived in the colony to take advantage of the ideal market conditions accompanying the goldrushes on the Eastern Goldfields. Prostitutes were clearly visible by night in the streets of Perth and Fremantle, and even by day in the goldfields towns. The police took action to remove any specific instances of annoyance caused to neighbours in these areas, but in general they regarded the presence of prostitutes as a 'necessary evil' in a society with such a marked imbalance between the numbers of men and women. It was assumed that men's sexual needs had to be met, and that since there were not enough marriageable women to go around, those men who did not have wives would either rape 'respectable' women, or use prostitutes. Consequently, many men saw prostitution as necessary to protect the chastity of their 'pure' womenfolk. As Margaret Anderson's chapter shows, the level of violence against women and children in nineteenth century Western Australia was high, so it is not surprising that people made this connection between the sex ratio and violence against women. The patriarchal ideology which dominated Western Australia prior to the goldrushes was also temporarily challenged by the sudden influx of outsiders, most of whom were men without families. This caused divisions of opinion, so that concern at a municipal and parliamentary level failed to result in any change in policy on prostitution. Prostitutes continued to operate with relatively little interference from the law.

This situation lasted until about 1905 when changes in the structure of the goldmining industry brought about changes in the social features of both the goldfields and the coast, and a corresponding change in attitudes to prostitution. The gold boom was over by 1903 when production declined and there was increased unemployment on the 'fields. After 1900 the balance of alluvial to company mining changed. Life on the fields was more comfortable after the opening of the water pipeline in 1903 and a drop in the cost of living caused by a reduction in rail freights and food tariffs. These changes encouraged miners on the 'fields to bring their wives and families to live with them permanently. Similarly, the passing of the gold boom reversed the population drift to the goldfields: some of those who had passed through the capital previously were, after 1904, returning to settle with their families on the coast.

This trend towards a more stable society affected the prostitution business. There was less demand for prostitution because men had their wives and daughters with them. Fewer men passed through the coastal towns. There was also increasing resistance to the operations of prostitution, especially on the goldfields. It was in Kalgoorlie over the period 1905-10 that the first segregated vice area was set up. Prior to 1905 moves to set up a red-light district foundered on the divisions within and between the Kalgoorlie Municipal Council, the police and the magistracy. After 1905 these three forces united to combat a problem which was increasingly unacceptable in a more family-oriented township. By 1910 Kalgoorlie's prostitute population was reduced by half and those remaining were forced to live and work in Hay Street.

In Perth in the years preceding the Great War moves which culminated in the establishment of Roe Street as the capital's red-light district began. The dispersal of prostitutes from the expanding commercial centre of Perth caused serious problems for the police in their efforts to supervise known brothels. With only bicycles and horses for transport, it was virtually impossible for the police to give adequate attention to the hundred or so brothels scattered over the inner suburban areas of North, East and West Perth. Their desire to localize the brothels was given added impetus by the concern to control the spread of venereal disease from prostitutes to their clients.

Attempts to deal with venereal disease by clauses in the Health Act of 1911 were abandoned in the face of strong opposition from women's groups, religious bodies and sections of the press, who saw this as another version of the notorious English Contagious Diseases Acts of the 1860s and 1870s. (These provided a pool of disease-free prostitutes for the use of troops in the garrison towns and were eventually repealed by the outcry of feminists, religious organizations and other concerned citizens.[4])

The lack of legislative authority did not deter some law enforcers in Western Australia from carrying out their own plans 'for the public good'. Throughout the period from 1905 to the outbreak of war the police acted in collusion with some magistrates to imprison prostitutes suspected of suffering from venereal disease. Prostitutes arrested on any grounds were brought before the Bench and remanded in custody for medical examination. If a woman showed signs of disease, a certificate testifying as much was handed to the magistrate, who then convicted the woman and sent her to Fremantle gaol for a period of up to six months.[5] Not all magistrates acted so before the War, and it was not until the problems of policing prostitution were exacerbated by the effects of the European war that far-reaching schemes to deal with the problem were adopted.

When several cases of venereal disease were reported amongst army recruits in Perth in October 1914, suspicion was immediately levelled at the town's prostitutes. In response to the concern of the military authorities the Perth police requested that the Government Medical Officer, Dr Blanchard, should examine prostitutes in Perth's brothels. After these initial examinations Blanchard arranged to visit a number of the brothels on a fortnightly basis, charging a guinea per visit. The Royal Commission which followed the public exposure of this practice revealed not only that the police and Blanchard were coercing prostitutes into accepting regular disease checks, but that the police had decided that Perth's brothels would be localized in Roe Street and they had already begun systematically to remove any brothels operating outside 'the street'. Any prostitutes or madames who were reluctant to co-operate were prosecuted under the Police Act. Despite a public outcry against this illegal procedure, and venereal disease provisions in the new Health Act of 1915, the police continued to use the Police Act to stop diseased prostitutes from doing business. By the end of the War they had also succeeded in localizing brothels in Roe Street. The number of streetwalkers gradually diminished over the following years, so that by the 1920s these were a rare sight outside of Roe Street.

Thus, by the end of the First World War prostitution in both Kalgoorlie and Perth was a closely regulated system. The increasing notoriety of Roe Street drew custom away from the port of Fremantle, so that by the mid-1920s only one brothel and numerous streetwalkers remained. This closer supervision of prostitutes which occurred in Western Australia during the War had its parallels in other countries, particularly the United States of America and Germany, but in neither of these countries did it survive the end of the War.[6] In contrast, the outlines of the system which were established in Western Australia during the War were consolidated during the 1920s and 1930s, with important consequences for the women involved. The following discussion must therefore be seen against this background of increasing control over the lives of prostitutes by the authorities.

Birthplaces of prostitutes and national differences

In terms of differentiating characteristics, the most striking feature of Western Australian prostitutes was the diversity of their ethnic origins. Information collected about 1567 prostitutes in this period shows 17 countries besides Australia as being birthplaces of prostitutes working in Western Australia. It is also clear that despite the strong contingents of French and Japanese women, especially in the earlier periods, Australian-born women at all times formed by far the greatest single group. By contrast, contemporaries received an entirely different picture of the relative prevalence of the various ethnic groups. For instance, in 1915 the Honourable R.H. Underwood (Member of the Legislative Assembly), proudly proclaimed that:

> We can take credit, and I think should take credit to ourselves in W.A. for our social conditions when we reflect that *the supply of prostitutes in this country has given out*. Most honourable members know that prostitutes in W.A. are supplied chiefly from France, Japan and Italy. As a matter of fact the Australian social system has kept the Australian women out of it.[7]

His confusion is understandable. In terms of the total Western Australian population the French and Japanese prostitutes were grossly over-represented. As percentages of the total Western Australian population at the turn of the century these nationalities were 0.1 and 0.5 per cent respectively. Italians were 0.7 per cent. However as percentages of the number of prostitutes whose birthplace was known in the same period they were 18.7, 9.6 and 1.5 per cent respectively. At the same time the Australian-born residents were nearly 70 per cent of the total Western Australian population,[8] compared with only one half of the total number of prostitutes. No marked discrepancy occurred in the representation of the different Australian colonies (States after 1901). Approximately 37 per cent of Australian-born prostitutes in the goldrush period were Western Australian born, with Victoria, New South Wales and South Australia being the other major contributors, which corresponds broadly to the figures for the Western Australian population as a whole. Given the over-representation of women from other countries in prostitution it is not surprising that local observers overlooked the native-born when faced with so much exotica.

The figures show that as time passed, Western Australians had even less cause to congratulate themselves on the 'purity' of their women. The proportion of Australian women steadily increased after the first decade of the twentieth century. By the period 1924-39 approximately three-quarters of the prostitutes were Australian-born, the rest being mainly British or French. This figure is much more closely related to that for the Western Australian population as a whole than in the earlier periods. In fact, the exact antithesis to Underwood's claim was provided by one of the Roe Street prostitutes in her evidence before the 1938 Royal Commission into the Administration of the Perth City Council. She stated that 'it was the social system of Australia that forced me to work for myself, and when I could not get a decent living wage anywhere else, I went there [i.e. to Roe Street]'.[9]

Thus the trend in Western Australia was for a more than proportionate number of prostitutes to be foreign-born, with this trend becoming less marked over the period up to World War II. Within this general trend it is possible to discern other differences in ethnic composition in the different regional centres. In the earlier years the French women were more heavily concentrated on the goldfields, with a significant number in Perth and only a handful in Fremantle. By World War I this had reversed with Perth showing the largest number of French women and only nominal representation in the other two centres. The Japanese were to be found primarily on the goldfields in the early years, with their numbers showing a sharp decrease after the 1901 Immigration Restriction Act. By the War there were only a few left in old established houses in Fremantle.

On the other hand British and Australian women tended to work in Perth and Fremantle rather than on the goldfields, especially in the earlier period.

The distribution of the different ethnic groups reflects a basic difference in their attitudes to their work as prostitutes. In general the French and Japanese had a more professional attitude to their work. They endured the inconvenience and hardship of life on the goldfields as long as the money was good. One reason for this was probably their greater involvement with 'bludgers' and organized syndicates. They had less freedom. In addition, the French and Japanese women working in Australia were usually in the prime of their working lives and returned to their homelands by the time old age, disease and/or alcoholism had caught up with them. In contrast, the British and Australian prostitutes in Western Australia tended to stay in the state throughout their old age so that proportionately more of them were old and dissolute.

The difference in attitude between the various national groups was widely commented upon at the time. The Japanese women were famous for their quietness, genteel manners and invisibility. This ensured minimum harassment from the police, who saw them as 'ideal prostitutes'.[10]

The French women adopted a different policy; they were certainly very visible, but could afford the fines for soliciting and brothel-keeping by maximizing their custom. They did this not only by soliciting but by offering the client a 'variety of vices' and reducing his fear of disease.[11] A French girl who hit a prospective client over the head with a bottle may have deterred some custom; but in the long run her action was good advertising as the man had become violent when she refused to do business with him because he was diseased.[12] On a less dramatic level, it was reported in the local press that some of the French women on the 'fields had weekly disease checks and displayed certificates of cleanliness in their bedrooms.[13] The *Sunday Times* also observed that 'it can at least be said in a general sense of the French, that they are free from filthy language and revolting drunkenness . . .[14] The police evidence bears out these observations: few French women were convicted of drunkenness or disorderliness and none came under police attention as carriers of venereal disease.

By contrast, the English prostitutes were regarded as the most damned of the damned. They were described as 'walking water-closets for Germans, Chinamen or anyone else who liked to get into them'[15], and 'sinks of moral and physical corruption . . . possessing no redeeming feature' who were hardly ever sober and consequently dangerously diseased.[16] Again, the police records support these comments. Similarly, other British and Australian women had many more arrests and convictions for drunkenness and petty larceny than for direct prostitution offences. There were numerous complaints about their general disorderliness and uncleanliness.

National differences observable between the prostitutes could be extended to include their associates and 'bludgers'. The Japanese tried to be inconspicuous and usually operated legitimate businesses such as laundries, or worked as cooks and waiters to avoid being charged as vagrants. The Frenchmen were less discreet: although many adopted a facade of legitimate employment they were con-spicuous about the streets and hotels of the goldfields and the city in their flash clothes and obvious affluence. Their covers ranged from tobacconists' shops, grocery stores, hairdressing salons, jewellery shops, and commission agencies to part ownership of a fishing vessel or market garden.[17]

Although it was rumoured that most of the French 'bludgers' were criminal escapees or ex-convicts from New Caledonia or French Guiana, no convincing evidence supports this claim. A man hung for the cold-blooded murder of a vigneron in 1903 was the only example discovered. His paramour, a prominent Fremantle madame for many years, was also from New Caledonia.[18] It seems likely that a few such flamboyant characters led people to exaggerated con-clusions about the French as a whole. Nevertheless, to say that French 'bludgers' were not all escaped convicts does not absolve them of the charges of criminality levelled at them. On the contrary, these men were not only trafficking in women but were also carrying on more orthodox criminal activities such as robbery.[19]

Nor were the French the only criminal elements mixed up in prostitution; some of the most notorious prostitutes working with thieves were Australian or British.[20] It was claimed that the English, 'if not as criminal in character as the French were certainly more degraded and abhorrent'.[21] Perhaps a fairer distinction is that the foreigners directed their criminal efforts toward the community at large, whereas the locals usually preferred the easy pickings of the prostitutes' customers.

Ages of prostitutes

In addition to the differences of background and behaviour, the prostitutes differed in age. One of the major trends from 1890 to 1939 was the way in which the average age of prostitutes increased. Around the turn of the century the heaviest concentration of prostitutes was in the age groups between twenty-six and thirty-five years, with large numbers in the groups twenty-one to twenty-five years and thirty-six to forty years. Over the decades from 1907 to the 1920s this pattern changed so that there were fewer and fewer prostitutes in the age group from twenty-one to thirty-five and relatively more in the over forty groups. The heaviest concentration of women in these years was in the groups from thirty-six to forty-five years, with significant numbers in the groups on either side, that is, thirty-one to thirty-five years and forty-six to fifty years. A similar trend was occurring in the general female population of Western Australia at the same time.

Furthermore, goldfields prostitutes tended to be younger than their counterparts on the coast. This was partly due to the number of foreign prostitutes involved. The European and Japanese women on the goldfields were younger than the locals and many of them returned home after the height of the gold boom had passed, around 1904. There was also a tendency for older prostitutes to predominate in Fremantle: older prostitutes who could not attract much custom elsewhere could still subsist on the patronage of drunken sailors in the port.

The women who stayed on after the boom were also ageing as a group. From the late 1890s to about 1906 there was a very high incidence of first offenders compared with the period between 1907 and World War II.[22] Thus, after the initial injection of large numbers of relatively young prostitutes to service the boom population, the situation became stable. The Great War period did show an increase in first offenders, as might be expected. Again, these women were in the younger age brackets, that is, twenty-six to thirty-five years. However their numbers were not large enough to have any significant impact on the general age trend over the following decades.

It is not immediately apparent that there was an increase in recruitment to prostitution in the early 1930s, as would be expected in a time of economic depression. This is probably because statistics for this period are generally deficient. Before 1926 most information was derived from police station occurrence books which give an account on a daily basis of prostitutes' encounters with the police. After 1926 the main source is the police file on Roe Street which contains a more general account of police policy and actions regarding prostitution in the form of reports. The lists of brothel inmates contained in these reports were not kept up-to-date on a daily or even monthly basis so that many women who stayed only briefly at Roe Street would not have been recorded in this file.[23]

Religion of prostitutes

The presence of so many prostitutes from overseas in Western Australia influenced the nominal religious affiliation of prostitutes generally. Compared with the figures for the total Western Australian population, Roman Catholics were grossly over-represented amongst prostitutes. Where the religion of prostitutes is known, Roman Catholics were at least twice as numerous amongst prostitutes as in the general Western Australian population. It is probable that the figure for Roman Catholics in the early period should be even higher than that given because so many in the 'not known' category were French, and therefore probably Catholics. The predominance of Catholics amongst prostitutes can be explained in part by reference to the large number of women from predominantly Catholic countries such as France, Italy and Spain. Since the trend continued and was in fact more noticeable even after the proportion of these women had decreased, it is more likely that prostitutes generally were drawn from poorer families either in Australia or Britain among whom Roman Catholics were more strongly represented than amongst the wealthier groups. The large number of people of Irish extraction among the poorer groups in Australia was the major reason for this trend.

It is one thing to talk about nominal religious adherance but quite another to ascertain how far religion meant anything to these women. The evidence either way is inconclusive. For instance, what is one to infer of religious belief from evidence given at a larceny trial stating that two prostitutes and two male acquaintances began a Sunday's outing by getting drunk at several hotels around the metropolitan area, stopped off in the Maylands bush to have sexual intercourse, then finished up with tea at an oyster saloon followed by attendance at the Salvation Army service?[24] It is hard to imagine that the four attended the religious service to worship, but not impossible. They may have gone just for the entertainment of the music and preaching, as the Salvation Army Citadel was only a few minutes walk from the oyster saloon.

Overall there is no evidence on church attendance of prostitutes, but a statement made in 1915 suggests another level of religious awareness. It was suggested that a Roe Street French prostitute was exaggerating the amount of the fee charged by the government doctor for venereal disease checks. The woman replied indignantly:

> I am kissing the Bible, and I am a Catholic woman, and I am here to tell the truth.[25]

If to this woman being a prostitute was not incompatible with being an honest and Catholic woman, perhaps there were others who felt the same way. Only about a dozen prostitutes indicated hostility to religion by having themselves registered as being of 'no religion', 'freethinker' or 'atheist'. Perhaps this indicates that prostitutes were neither more nor less religious than the general population.

Length of careers

The temporary presence of numbers of prostitutes from other countries in Western Australia also complicates any attempt to determine how long women remained as prostitutes. Some of these women, like the notorious Josie de Bray, spent up to thirty years in the state only to return to France in old age.[26] Others stayed only a few years before returning home to work as prostitutes or madames or to use their earnings to finance a more comfortable life outside prostitution. The same can be said of prostitutes coming from the eastern states on a seasonal basis: for particular racing meetings or celebrations such as the 1929 Centenary Celebrations. Thus, it is difficult to say definitely how long any woman worked as a prostitute. Heavy reliance on police records further complicates this picture. How many more women were there like the two sisters who earned their living as prostitutes and supported their children in Perth for thirteen years without attracting punitive attention from the police?[27] How many women worked from hotels and laneways for years before being identified by the police as prostitutes? All these factors make it obvious that any figure relating to the length of time women spent in prostitution will be an under-representation of the true situation. The table below represents the most conservative estimate possible.

Table 1. Number of years prostitutes in contact with police

Years:	1	1-2	3-5	6-10	11-20	21-30	31-40	41-50
Number of prostitutes	844	234	198	156	127	37	7	1

Although the numbers in all these categories are therefore under-estimates, this is particularly so in the first two groups. There were many overseas women in this group who only had one conviction during their stay in Western Australia but may have stayed for much longer than one or two years. This is particularly true in the case of the Japanese since it was a rare enough occurrence for them to have any convictions at all.

Given the limitation of these statistics, they still demonstrate some important points. At least ten per cent of these women worked in prostitution for more than ten years. For them it was a 'stage in their lives that they would pass through'[28] but only in the sense that any person's working life was a 'stage' of life. But one can deduce that spending such a long period of life in the business would permanently affect the woman's self-image and have irreversible consequences for her position in the local community if she remained in the area in which she had been a prostitute.

Career patterns

Table 1, used in conjunction with a survey of the police records of prostitutes suggests that there were different career patterns existing amongst prostitutes. Firstly, there were those women who went into prostitution for a very short period of time, a few months or years, but quickly left the business for marriage or a respectable job. Closely related to this group were the women who spent only a brief period of time as prostitutes in Western Australia but were prostitutes before and/or after leaving the State. Then there were the women who stayed in prostitution from three to ten years. These were probably the women who saw prostitution as a way to make fast money and/or have a good time, but not as a way of life. It would still have been possible for them to return to a respectable life in Western Australia, at least until the late 1920s. Finally, there were the women who spent more than ten years in the business. These were of two types: the upwardly mobile and the downwardly mobile.

The fate of prostitutes depended on how they coped with ageing. Since their ability to attract clients usually decreased as age made them less attractive to men, prostitutes had to become brothel-keepers to maintain their earnings. Success here depended on their business sense, and whether or not they were heavy drinkers. From the reconstruction of the lives of two women, we can see the two extremes.

Mary Ann Carter began her career as a prostitute in Fremantle in 1897 and was convicted in that year of vagrancy and sentenced to three months hard labour. It is not clear where she spent the early years of the century but in 1913 she was running a brothel in Essex Street, Fremantle, employing between two and four women. In 1917 she bought the property she was occupying in Bannister Street, Fremantle, and ran it as the main port brothel until 1923. By fair means or foul she obtained advance notice of the impending westward move of the Roe Street brothels and bought four houses west of Melbourne Road for £800 each. After leasing these to different madames, she retired to her house in Aberdeen Street from which she supervised her investments. A conservative valuation of her estate in 1938 was £10,000.[29]

The second woman, Lilly Lawton, began her career around the same time as Mary Ann. She appeared with a conviction for drunkenness in Perth in 1901; she was then aged thirty years. Between 1901 and 1932 she was convicted thirty-six times for drunkenness, twice for vagrancy, twice for loitering for the purposes of prostitution and once for theft. The last record of her was in 1932 when she was discharged from Fremantle Gaol at the age of sixty-two, having spent years of her life either in prison or in an inebriates' home. Although she was fifty when last convicted of soliciting, she was continually listed by the police as a prostitute.[30]

Between these two extremes there was some sort of continuum. Take, for example, Marie du Bois, a Belgian woman who first appeared in the police records in Kalgoorlie in 1907. She was then aged forty-three and had been a prostitute in France before coming to Australia.[31] Five years later she was convicted of keeping a brothel in Pier Street, Perth, which she shared with a younger woman.[32] After her conviction she took a house by herself in Roe Street and did all her own housework. She was not making a lot of money and explained that 'if things are bad I take a little work'. She also claimed that her medical expenses put her rent in arrears and made her pawn her goods.[33] She was obviously not improving her position. She disappeared from Roe Street shortly afterwards, so perhaps she saved enough money to return to Belgium.

Marie's case raises the question of part-time prostitution in relation to the time women spent as prostitutes. Part-time prostitution is usually discussed in the reverse context of prostitution being used to supplement wages, not wages being taken to supplement earnings in times of depression in the prostitution business. Marie was probably unusual, since it would appear that the common response to a drop in custom was to increase efforts at soliciting.[34] The more traditional type of part-timer did not leave much evidence of her activities. Jessie Holloway, a witness in a court case in 1918, admitted that she 'sometimes leads an immoral life', that is, she prostituted herself. Jessie was a widow on a military pension of £2/12/9- per fortnight and had five children, all in institutions. She lived in a Pier Street boarding house run by an ex-prostitute and frequented by prostitutes. The inference was that she only prostituted herself when her pension money had been used.[35] Obviously some prostitutes started their careers as part-timers then gave up their day-time jobs to concentrate on the more lucrative business of the streets. It would have been unusual for a woman to have held a respectable job for very long if she was also prostituting herself in places the size of Perth, Fremantle and the goldfields towns. By the 1930s the population of the metropolitan area had still not reached 150,000. Married women who engaged in prostitution were liable to have the police move against their husbands for living off the proceeds of prostitution, so that the widow and the temporary part-timer were therefore the more usual cases.

Motivations

Any discussion of the time women spent as prostitutes naturally invites a question about motivation. Why did women become prostitutes and why did they stop?

Contemporary opinions varied on the reasons for women becoming prostitutes. Most commentators argued that the 'economic motive' was the main cause of prostitution, but they disagreed about the meaning of the economic motive and the extent to which this made local girls become prostitutes. Some, like the Honourable R.H. Underwood, evaded the problem by denying the existence of locally-born prostitutes.[36] A writer in the February 1917 edition of *Western Women* did not deny that there were locally-born prostitutes, but discounted economic conditions in Australia as a motive:

> Low wages, poor food, and long hours of labour are all conditions which help to force women into this life; these conditions exist undoubtedly in Europe: in Western Australia this is hardly the case. Here the demand for workers is greater than the supply; hours of work, wages, and the standard of living can be to a great

extent laid down by the employed to the employer, so this is not . a salient cause.[37]

The writer thought that the desire for money for luxury goods and expensive amusements was more important in influencing Western Australia's 'thoughtless girls and women anxious for a "good time".' Others believed that low female wages led women into temptation in order to earn enough to live.[38] Even the women's groups changed their attitude after the depression of the 1930s. Their spokeswoman before the 1938 Royal Commission admitted that 'in many instances the economic position is responsible'.[39]

Motivations were clearly mixed in the actual Western Australian situation. There were always cases of the 'sin or starve' variety. One such case was a Kalgoorlie woman whose husband deserted her and her children at the end of 1915. She was receiving meagre government assistance and soon turned to prostitution. In March 1916 she was arrested on a vagrancy charge and was found to be suffering from venereal disease. Her children were charged as neglected children and committed to State institutions until eighteen years of age, while she was sent to Fremantle for treatment of her moral and physical ailments.[40] The position of deserted wives and widows was as precarious in early twentieth century Western Australia as it was in the mid-nineteenth century. Statistics on marital status of prostitutes do not show how many were deserted wives. Prostitutes living in de facto relatinships often registered themselves as 'married', as did women separated from their husbands, so that any figures would be misleading. Even though exact statistics are not available many prostitutes were in fact deserted or separated wives. For them, prostitution was a way out of desperate economic circumstances. Similarly, there would have been less cause for smugness amongst politicians and women's organizations had they been aware of cases like that of a young girl who came to the police desperate and threatening suicide after being unemployed for six weeks in 1904.[41]

On the other hand there were women and girls who could have existed on their small wages as domestics or factory-hands, but who preferred the freer life and better pay of prostitution. To these women, as to their English counterparts, prostitution represented a 'rational choice, given the set of unpleasant alternatives open to them'.[42] Susan Horan's study of South Australian prostitutes before 1914 supports such a conclusion regarding South Australian prostitutes as well.[43] Clearly, these women were choosing to take command of their own lives in defiance of the dominant ideology about woman's place in the family. We have noted other examples of women rejecting the accepted feminine role and choosing independent action. The *beguines* of the Middle Ages, the 'bad women' who appeared in the seventeenth century, the rebellious spinsters in nineteenth century Britain, and the 'over-assertive' wives of mid-nineteenth century Western Australia all fit into a pattern of women over the ages who have refused to conform to the stereotype of appropriate womanly behaviour.

We can see this attitude in the statements of the prostitutes themselves. Giving evidence to the 1938 Royal Commission, a Roe Street prostitute, Annie Jenkins, explained how and why she started her career:

> I have been all sorts of things. First of all, I worked in an office as a bookkeeper, then I had a business of my own, and I finished up as a barmaid. It was from the bar that I went to Roe Street. I found that at the occupation I was following I could not earn a decent wage to keep myself properly . . . I would willingly have taken anything I could have got, but not for fifteen shillings or one pound a week, because I could not keep myself on that.[44]

From her further evidence it is clear that the key words are 'keep myself properly'. She did not just want short-term comforts, but saw her stay on Roe Street as a way to finance independence in her old age. Annie's ambition in this regard would no doubt have been applauded by many who deplored her methods; she was hardly the vain and frivolous good-time girl envisaged by the writer in *Western Women* quoted above. Another woman who began working in a Roe Street brothel as a cook in 1938 also reached the same conclusions about her relative economic prospects. Her choice was obviously a very 'rational' one as she later became a prosperous owner of some of Perth's most notorious brothels.[45] Although not all prostitutes had such clearly thought out or articulated motives, those giving evidence to the 1938 Royal Commission indicated that they were doing 'this in preference to working for a few shillings a week'.[46]

Prostitution did pay more than traditional female jobs. At the time of the 1938 Royal Commission, a time of depression on Roe Street, women were making between one and five pounds a week and sometimes more. For this money they worked six days a week with one week off in four; their housework was done for them and their food provided.[47] In comparison, a waitress or a domestic servant worked upwards of forty-four hours a week for one or two pounds, did her own housework and cooking, and was lucky to have two weeks holiday a year.[48] During the earlier periods this contrast was even more striking, when some women in both Kalgoorlie and Perth brothels were earning more than fourteen pounds a week,[49] compared with between fifteen shillings and two pound ten at most female wage-earning jobs.[50] Admittedly these earnings were made during boom periods, but this does not detract from the point that throughout the period 1895 to 1939 it was more profitable for women to sell their sex than their labour.

It could be argued that the economic advantages of a life of prostitution were offset by its hazards and that therefore a woman's choice to become a prostitute was not so rational as the preceding discussion implies. It is unlikely that women considered the hazards of venereal disease, alcoholism, violence and unwanted pregnancies before deciding to become prostitutes. Wouldn't the young domestic servant be more inclined to contrast her lot with that of the brothel prostitute, well-dressed and with money to spare, than with the prostitute's companion, consumed by syphilis and gonorrhea and trying to conceal her occupation from her mother?[51] Would the widow, confronted with the prospect of years of drudgery with no certainty that her efforts would feed and clothe her children, seriously contemplate the possibility that she might end her days as a victim of pneumonia while spending the night in Fremantle lockup?[52] Or would she consider the success of Josie de Bray and Mary Ann Collins (alias Coates) with their properties and cars? When Annie Sherwood left her husband and three children to live as a prostitute, could she have anticipated that three years later she would be living in a tent and supporting a man who abused and beat her?[53] In any case, who can say she was worse off than if she had stayed with her family? Perhaps many women did reflect on these possibilities and their conclusions explain why there was no simple correlation between poverty and prostitution; most poor women faced the same alternatives but relatively few chose to become 'wayward workers'. Those who did choose to adopt what was regarded by society as a 'deviant' occupation were perhaps more concerned with short-term solutions to their problems than their respectable sisters. Other factors affecting an individual's personality and situation must also have played a part in this decision. Poor family life and 'lack of moral training' were seen by observers to make young women susceptible to the lure of the streets, and of course, the ever-present 'demon drink' was again regarded as a major culprit in this regard.[54]

There was certainly some truth in these claims. For instance, there were several families where prostitution was a kind of family tradition, with the daughters working in the 'family business' from an early age. Some may have tried the straight and narrow path but realized at an early stage the easier path to comfort. One such was Nellie Quinn, who married a timber worker and lived in a small mill settlement in the Darling Ranges. She quickly tired of the arduous and dull life and went home to her mother who ran a brothel in Fremantle, from which she started her career as a prostitute.[55]

What contemporary observers referred to as 'poor family life' describes the same process which modern sociologists label 'the lack of appropriate socialisation'. McConville's study of prostitution in Melbourne draws heavily on the theory that individual women became prostitutes because of their socialization into 'deviant' home backgrounds.[56] Finnegan noted factors such as ill-treatment by step-parents, bad parental example and alcoholic parents as adding to the generally impoverished home life of many girls who later became prostitutes in York (England).[57] No doubt such factors were important in some Western Australian cases as well. Unfortunately it has not been possible to obtain such information about most of the women in this study; while generalization from the fragments of evidence available would be inappropriate, these fragments do support such an idea.

Alcoholism led some women to prostitution. There were some striking instances of women who turned to drink and thus began a downward course that ended in destitution and illness. One of these unfortunate women, Rose Barlow, first appeared in the records in

1902 at Leonora when her husband had her placed on the prohibited list – a list compiled by the police and given to publicans giving them authority to refuse to serve alcohol to those named. The couple moved to Kalgoorlie where she began associating with prostitutes at hotels. In 1904 her husband left her, saying he could do nothing for her. She was convicted of vagrancy and sentenced to six months hard labour at Fremantle. On her return Rose renewed her association with the town's prostitutes but was eventually driven out of the more respectable brothels on account of her drunkenness. After a further six months in gaol in 1908 she stayed in Perth and Fremantle where she was regularly convicted of drunkenness, soliciting and vagrancy until she received an old age pension in 1939.[58] Nevertheless, cases such as this were in the minority. A study of all the case histories of prostitutes indicates that most who started drinking heavily did so after becoming prostitutes, not before. That they did so is not surprising. Quite apart from alcohol making their work more pleasant, there was a strong connection between prostitution and hotels, and the illicit sale of liquor was an important part of the profits at most brothels.

A more startling allegation was the one made about prostitutes being mentally deficient. In 1917 it was claimed that

> Observation, and the careful compilation of statistics, have proved that the great majority of girls and women, who become and remain prostitutes, are below the average in intelligence, and are wanting in moral sense and standards. They vary in degree from those who are inordinately vain and susceptible to flattery to those who are absolutely imbecile.[59]

Unfortunately the writer did not say where and by whom these statistics were 'carefully compiled'. As there is no evidence of any such survey ever having been undertaken in Western Australia, we must assume that the writer was generalizing from studies done elsewhere. In any case the comment was probably not referring to studies employing any reliable form of intelligence testing, since the Stanford-Binet Intelligence-Quotient was not used before 1916. It is unfortunate that the historian is not in a position to administer a class and culture-free I.Q. test to prostitutes long since dead to test these statements.

There were only three cases out of the 1567 prostitutes who were very obviously 'sub-normal' or 'weak-minded'. Of these, only one was considered unable to take care of herself. Of the remaining 1564 prostitutes there is no evidence to suggest that they were any less intelligent than the rest of the community. Only five were recorded as being unable to read or write, and these were old women who would have been children before the days of compulsory education.[60]

The charge that prostitutes were 'lacking in moral sense' is only the case if their behaviour is seen in terms of the dominant sexual ideology of the time: prostitutes and their juvenile counterparts were generally labelled 'abnormal' as opposed to 'subnormal', a distinction indicating a moral rather than an intellectual deficiency.[61] It is not surprising that such labels were applied to prostitutes since it was common for people who believed in the notion of woman as the 'good mother' to see those who did not conform as being in some way not normal. As with women in earlier times who murdered their children and were automatically defined as 'mad', prostitutes were often seen as sick, insane or stupid.

It does seem that what was referred to as 'abnormal' sexual behaviour was a factor in leading some young women into prostitution. Girls and women who became prostitutes were not usually innocent in a sexual sense. A Roe Street madame commented that most girls who came to work in the brothels were 'very hardened' and had been 'knocking around town'.[62] The inference was that these prostitutes began their careers as 'promiscuous amateurs' and eventually realized that they could get money while doing what they enjoyed. This was a more common phenomenon in times of war, when young girls were attracted by the romance and generosity of visiting soldiers, then gradually drifted into prostitution.[63] The line between accepting gifts and getting paid for sexual favours became blurred, so that girls may have found themselves on the road to prostitution before fully realizing it. A report filed by a Child Welfare Department Inspector in 1917 regarding six delinquent girls who escaped from the Salvation Army Home near Collie gives one example:

There is not the slighest doubt these girls are dangerous – they are also a source of contamination to other girls and in no institution would they be content for their main object is to get away amongst soldiers. They are boy mad. This could be easily seen by their manner when I brought them to Perth. The eldest Smith girl admits she was knocking about Perth for two years in soldiers' uniform.[64]

This was the beginning of a long career as a prostitute for this 'eldest Smith girl' which lasted at least until the end of the 1930s. What is apparent is that she was enjoying her way of life and if she got paid for doing it, so much the better. Some women who were divorced by their husbands on the grounds of adultery could also be included in the category of prostitutes who had 'deviant' sexual behaviour before becoming prostitutes. This applied to six of the sixteen cases traced in the divorce court records.[65]

Contemporaries saw cinemas and dance-halls as corrupting influences on young people and indirect causes of prostitution.[66] Although these entertainments may have contributed in individual cases, in general the proposition seems unlikely. The numbers of prostitutes in Western Australia actually decreased after the advent of the cinema, so that the cinemas may have operated in competition to the brothels.

More serious were the allegations that women were forced into prostitution by the violence of 'bludgers', the men who lived on the proceeds of prostitution. To some extent this belief was a product of the ideology which made women dependent: they could not take charge of their own lives and therefore they must be in a dependent relationship to a male. Many men were unwilling to admit that women might act on their own behalf, on their own choice. This may have led to an exaggeration of the extent of 'white slavery', but two sensational cases involving Europeans show that a certain number of women were unwilling prostitutes.[67] There were few other cases of a similar nature before the courts but although actual physical violence may have been the reason for only a few prostitutes entering the business, it cannot be discounted. It may have been more widespread than police records indicate, especially among Europeans and Asians, since many women could not speak English and would have been at the mercy of their captors in a strange land. There were also numerous suggestions that once established as prostitutes, women could be victimized out of their earnings by 'bludgers'. Violence was only one of the threats used, as other forms of blackmail were even more effective. These included the threat of the 'bludger' to act as police informer to convict prostitutes for sly-grog selling or to alert the authorities if the woman was diseased.

In summary, it is clear that most prostitutes in Western Australia were attracted to the profession by the relatively higher earnings and freer lifestyle. Still others found the work suited to their temperaments. Others became prostitutes to escape economic destitution or to support their drinking habits. Only a few were coerced into prostitution. Less measurable and more complex psychological and sociological factors no doubt played a part in the individual's decision to become a prostitute. Lack of information – partly because most prostitutes are now dead – makes it impossible for the historian to reach any firm conclusions about the causes of individual prostitution. As Finnegan has so aptly pointed out, 'however desperate her circumstances, the fact that an individual took to and continued in prostitution must, in the final resort, be seen as a complex mixture of influences on that individual's personality'.[68]

We can be more certain about the reasons for prostitutes giving up their occupation. Marriage was a fairly common outlet for prostitutes who preferred to be kept by one man than by many. Josephine Durant, a French prostitute working in Kalgoorlie, saw marriage as an escape from a life she had grown weary of. She explained her marriage to a wealthy middle-aged Afghan by saying, 'I am tired of this life – so tired'.[69] Marriage remained an option for some Roe Street women in the late 1930s.

The general consensus of contemporary opinion was that women were not accepted as respectable members of the community if their former careers were known. A spokeswoman for a voluntary rescue group in Kalgoorlie encountered this problem in 1900:

> We have sent girls to situations, but when it was discovered that they had 'once' been Magdalenes, they were dismissed and forced back in their former habits.[70]

Apparently public attitudes did not change much between 1900 and

1938 as a similar phenomenon was noted by a madame in a latter year. She claimed that 'the majority who go away to work are usually back in two or three weeks . . . I think they become known and if people find out what they have been, they do not care about employing them'.[71] The only difference was that by the 1920s and 1930s the number of prostitutes was smaller and their notoriety thus greater, so that it was very difficult for them to make a fresh start without leaving the state altogether. Given this impediment to finding respectable employment in Western Australia the prospects of the ex-prostitute were very circumscribed.

It is impossible to say how far employer attitudes were shared by the rest of the community, particularly at the lower levels of society. There was no neat division in Western Australia between a working-class supply of prostitutes and a middle-class demand, as there was in nineteenth century Britain and Germany.[72] The imbalance in sex ratios at all levels in Western Australian society meant that the clients of prostitutes were drawn from all strata, from thieves and labourers to clerks and businessmen.[73] It is also clear from complaints about prostitutes disturbing their neighbours that prostitution was regarded by rich and poor alike as a degrading business. But whether the poor were more sympathetic to the plight of the individual women is not clear, and it would require further research into the attitudes of working people before one could say whether or not ex-prostitutes could expect to be accepted by them.

Some women left prostitution in Western Australia but continued in the business in another state or country. A certain section of prostitutes moved around from town to town and state to state quite frequently which makes it hard to say exactly where they ended their careers; at least twenty per cent of prostitutes in Western Australia operated in more than one town in the state. Some used their savings from prostitution to finance legitimate businesses elsewhere, or simply retired and lived on their investments. Yet others never attempted to get out of prostitution and drifted along until they found themselves in the Fremantle Old Women's Home, or later, as old-age pensioners, or just died. Very few were actually 'rescued', despite visits to the Home of the Good Shepherd.

Generally speaking, prostitutes left the business when they were tired of it, had made enough money, married or were too old. Those who stayed did so because they were unable to work at respectable jobs, either through drunkenness or notoriety, or were still making enough money as madames or owners to keep them interested.

Attitudes and self-perceptions

Finally, I wish to consider the prostitutes' attitudes to themselves and their occupation and their perceptions of their place in society.

There is not much evidence to show whether prostitutes adopted society's notions about their being women of the 'unfortunate class' whose 'souls had been murdered'.[74] Kate King loudly proclaimed to Policewoman Dugdale that she was 'as good a bloody woman as any other bloody woman around here'.[75] She said this when being harassed by Dugdale for allegedly neglecting her children. Perhaps the point is that prostitutes did not see their work as having any particular relevance to their ability to carry on other relationships. A prostitute who was shot by her de facto husband was alleged to have asked her eleven year old son to tell her legal husband that she had 'always tried to be a good mother'.[76] Although there were a few exceptions, most prostitutes took their family responsibilities just as seriously as other women who had not 'fallen'.[77] The courts seem to have recognized this in dealing with cases of children living in brothels with their mothers. Strictly speaking, these children could have been deemed 'neglected' and sent to State institutions until eighteen years of age. When Perth police were investigating the circumstances of children living with their mothers in brothels in 1900 a note was attached to the report which reads:

> For your [i.e. Police Commissioner] information, Mr Roe [Police Magistrate] will not treat children in circumstances such as mentioned herein as neglected children unless very disgraceful conduct at the premises can be proved . . .[78]

No doubt part of the magistrate's concern was to avoid accumulating large numbers of State wards, but it was also a recognition that the children were not too badly off even with prostitutes as mothers.

The probability of prostitutes having children was much greater before the development of effective contraceptives and safe abortions. Prostitutes' clients used the condom as early as the First World War, both as a contraceptive and as a prophylactic against disease.[79] There were also devices available which did not require the co-operation of the customer. Various types of pessaries and syringes were available in Australia from the late 1880s so it is highly likely that prostitutes were among the heaviest patrons of these devices.[80] I was told by a woman who was a nursing sister during the inter-war period that it was common for Western Australian women to make their own dissoluble pessaries by mixing cocoa butter, glycerine, boric acid and fresh lemon juice together and setting the compound in small cake tins; the resultant tablet was then inserted before intercourse and ideally acted as both a spermicide and mechanical barrier.[81] The number of prostitutes described in the *Police Gazette* during the 1930s with 'a vertical scar on centre of stomach' suggests that it was not unusual for prostitutes to provide a more permanent solution to the contraceptive problem by hysterectomies.

If contraception failed, there was always the option of abortion. There is abundant evidence that abortion was common practice throughout this period.[82] Some chemists were associated with abortion throughout the entire period. A Perth doctor also blamed a 'certain class of horrible women', operating with flexible catheters, for the widespread practice of backyard abortions in Western Australia.[83] Margaret Anderson's chapter gives details on Holloway's Pills, which were still a popular abortifacient in the twentieth century.

The fact that women were prostitutes did not seem to affect their desire or ability to form long-term attachments to particular men. As mentioned earlier, statistics of conjugal condition, although available, are virtually meaningless in this context since they do not indicate if married women were living with their husbands or if single women were living in de facto relationships.[84] It was obviously an advantage to many prostitutes to have a man to protect her from the violence of other men (and women), but this does not exclude the probability that they were emotionally attached to their protectors as well. Women who worked on Roe Street had no real need to have a male protector since the police performed that function very effectively, but many had boyfriends whom they saw secretly. Again, the fact that there was often violence within these relationships did not mean they were abnormal. Violence was common within the marriages of other West Australians, as Anderson's study shows for the earlier period. Although there is no written record of any homosexual relationships between prostitutes, these apparently existed. A former Roe Street prostitute told me that despite the fact that lesbianism was not discussed even in the 1930s, there were a number of prostitutes in relationships which she recognizes in retrospect were homosexual. No doubt the contempt for men which often resulted from the prostitute/client interaction fostered attachments to other women rather than to men in some prostitutes.[85] Prostitution may also have attracted women who already felt this way.

One might expect prostitutes to have had different attitudes to the law and its enforcers from the rest of the community. Some had rather peculiar notions about the source of authority in the community. One maintained that she was not paying rent to the Perth City Council and was therefore not subject to its by-laws.[86] Another believed that because she owned her own house she could stand at the door and solicit if she so wished.[87] But in general prostitutes realized that in regard to their work they were at the mercy of the law and were thus usually receptive to police instructions on work matters. In particular, they recognized that if they did not conform to police directions regarding, for instance, venereal disease or the location of their houses, they would very promptly be prosecuted for vagrancy, brothel-keeping or sly-grog selling. Although some were more inclined than others to test out the police in this, eventually they were all brought into line. Apart from what was seen as legitimate influence on the part of the police, prostitutes do seem to have had some sense that their relationship with the police involved a notion of fair-play. For example, when given instructions to move house, they expected to be allowed a reasonable time in which to dispose of their property and find alternative accommodation. Similarly, if their relationship was abused by individual policemen, prostitutes were known to appeal to a superior police officer. One goldfields constable tried to force a prostitute to have sex with him. She complained to the Superintendent of Police and as a result the constable was transferred.[88] Another prostitute was assaulted by a constable during an argument in which he called her boyfriend a 'bludger'. The police were sent for and the offender was dismissed from the force.[89] Both these cases involved women of the 'lower class' of prostitute so that it was obviously not just the wealthy madames who received preferential treatment.

That prostitutes were not 'silent, defenceless and outcast victims of their society' is evident in their general attitude toward the law. They regarded the law and the police as being there for their protection and use. Police records contain dozens of cases of prostitutes prosecuting each other and other people for offences ranging from 'being the owner of a vicious dog', to disorderly conduct, assault and theft.

Furthermore, some prostitutes were more willing than others to involve the police in the settlement of disputes. This appears to have been related to the different cultural backgrounds of the women concerned. The cases referred to above involved French, Japanese, British and Australian women, but their attitudes were not shared by all. Maria Carlos, a new arrival on Brookman Street, Kalgoorlie, was subjected to name-calling and was beaten with sticks and stones by two French girls and an English woman. Maria did not report the incident to the police and explained that she was a Spaniard: 'We never go to the police in Spain'.[90]

Prostitutes in Perth, Fremantle and on the Eastern goldfields were not an homogeneous group over the period from 1895 to the Second World War. There were marked differences in ethnic composition, age structure, religious affiliation, motives and career patterns. A contemporary newspaper article referred to prostitutes as 'The Pariah Sisterhood of Shame',[91] but such terms seem inappropriate when applied to Western Australia's prostitutes. Prostitutes were women who believed they had the same rights as any other members of society except in matters directly relating to their work. Rather than accepting the prevailing ideology about themselves, most would have agreed with the prostitute who claimed to be 'as good a bloody woman as any other bloody woman . . .'

Notes

1. For a more detailed account of these developments see my chapter in K. Daniels (ed.) *A History of Prostitution in Australia,* to be published 1984 by Fontana, Australia.

2. R.F. Evans 'Prostitution, State and Society in Imperial Germany' *Past and Present,* no.70, 1976, p.127. R.E. Riegel 'Changing American Attitudes towards Prostitution (1800-1920)' *Journal of the History of Ideas,* no.24, 1968, pp.437-52. E. Feldman 'Prostitution, the Alien Woman and the Progressive Imagination, 1910-1915' *American Quarterly* 14, Summer 1967, pp.192-206. M.T. Connelly 'Fear, Anxiety and Hope: The Response to Prostitution in the United States, 1900-1920', Ph.D. thesis, Rutgers University, 1977.

3. Evans, *op. cit.,* p.119; J. & D. Walkowitz, ' "We are not beasts of the field": Prostitution and the Poor in Plymouth and Southampton under the Contagious Diseases Acts' in M. Hartman and L. Banner (eds.) *Clio's Consciousness Raised*, New York, 1974, p.192.

4. Walkowitz, *op.cit.;* F.B. Smith, 'Ethics and Disease in the Later Nineteenth Century: The Contagious Diseases Acts' *Historical Studies,* vol.15, no.57, October 1971, pp.118-135.

5. Evidence to Royal Commission on the Blanchard Affair, C.S.O. File 1083/1915; Perth Police Station Occurrence Books: 13 July 1904; 27 September 1904; 9 October 1912.

6. Connelly, *op.cit.;* Evans, *op.cit.;* Riegel, *op.cit.;* E. Shenehon, 'The Prevention and Repression of Prostitution in North America' *International Review of Criminal Policy* 13, 1958.

7. *West Australian Parliamentary Debates,* vol.51, 1915, p.637.

8. *Official Yearbook of the Commonwealth of Australia,* no.1, 1901-07.

9. Evidence to the Royal Commission into the Administration of the Perth City Council, 1938, p.843.

10. 'The Scarlet Stain' *Sun* [a Western Australian newspaper] 29 April 1900; 'About the Boulevard' *Coolgardie Pioneer,* 17 April 1897; Police File 3244/1905.

11. 'Scarlet Stain' *Sun,* 29 April 1900; 'The Social Evil' *Sunday Times,* 2 September 1900.

12. Kalgoorlie Police District Office Occurrence Book, 18 April 1902.

13. 'Scarlet Stain' *Sun,* 29 April 1900.

14. 'Voices of Babylon', *Sunday Times,* 31 March 1901, p.5.

15. This was a description applied to a reputed prostitute by her neighbour which led to an assault charge: Perth Police Court Minutes, 3 July 1919.

16. 'Scarlet Stain', *Sun,* 29 April 1900, p.5.

17. 'Voices of Babylon', *Sunday Times,* 17 March 1901, p.5; 'Social Evil', *ibid.,* p.2; 'Scarlet Stain' *Sun,* 15 April 1900, p.5; *ibid.,* 22 April 1900, p.3; 20 May 1900; Kalgoorlie Police Court Minutes, 19 May 1900,

18 May 1900, 23 February 1902; '8 Tried and 6 Sentenced to Death', *Mirror,* 7 September 1935.

18. *Ibid.*
19. e.g. Kalgoorlie Police District Office Occurrence Book, 21 November 1900; 'Charge of Detaining a Girl', *West Australian,* 13 September 1902; Kalgoorlie Police Court Minutes, 19 May 1900.
20. e.g. Perth Police Station Occurrence Books: 28 August 1901, 26 October 1901, 3 March 1905, 10 January 1911; Kalgoorlie Detective Office Occurrence Books: 26 May 1900, 31 January 1906.
21. 'Voices of Babylon', *Sunday Times,* 31 March 1901, p.5.
22. Absolute figures collected on first offenders must be seen as an indication of trends only, as women may have been working as prostitutes for months or even years before being noticed by police.
23. Police Department File No. 78/1938 – 'Roe Street, suppression of brothels in'.
24. 'Alleged Theft', *Daily News,* 9 December, 1910, p.5.
25. Evidence of Rose Simeon, 'Royal Commission enquiry into charges against Dr Blanchard' – C.S.O. file 1083/1915.
26. *Ibid.;* Perth Police Court Minute Book, 14 July 1917; Report 5 May 1940, Poice Department File 78/1938'.
27. However it is true that they were listed in annual police lists of prostitutes compiled for the information of the police. Police File 4389/1898; P.F. 3199/1900; 'Children in Brothels Evil', *Sunday Times,* 20 January 1901.
28. J. Walkowitz, 'The Making of an Outcast Group: Prostitutes and Working Women in Nineteenth Century Plymouth and Southampton', in M. Vicinus (ed.) *A Widening Sphere,,* London, 1977, p.193.
29. *W.A. Police Gazette,* 30 April 1897; Fremantle Municipal Council file 26/1913; Fremantle Municipal Council Ratebooks, 1913-23; *Mirror,* 30 August 1924; Perth City Council Ratebooks, 1923-24; Police File 78/1938; Evidence Franz Bergmeyer to Royal Commission on Perth City Council, pp.1144-7.
    With the exception of Josie de Bray and Mary Anne Collins/Coates, the names of women mentioned are fictitious.
30. Compiled from references too numerous to list individually in Perth Police Occurrence Books, 1901-20 and *W.A. Police Gazette.*
31. Kalgoorlie Plain Clothes Police Occurrence Book, 20 August, 1907.
32. Perth Police Station Occurrence Book, 25 June 1912.
33. Evidence Rose Simeon, 'Royal Commission into charges against Dr Blanchard', C.S.O. file 1083/1915.
34. e.g. Report 23 June 1932, Police File 78/1938.
35. Perth Police Court Minutes, 6 June 1918.
36. *West Australian Parliamentary Debates,* vol.51, p.637.
37. 'The Social Evil', *Western Women,* February 1917, p.5. This journal was produced by the W.A. women's groups.

38.   e.g. Rocke (M.L.A.), speech on 1918 Health Bill, *West Australian Parliamentary Debates,* vol.57, p.1246; also speech Jones (M.L.A.), *ibid.,* p.1257.

39.   Evidence by May Barron Vallance, State President Women's Christian Temperance Union, Minutes of Evidence of Royal Commission into Perth City Council, 1938, p.115.

40.   Police vs Pizer, Kalgoorlie Police Court Minutes, 22 March 1916.

41.   Perth Police Station Occurrence Book, 11 January 1904.

42.   Walkowitz, *op.cit.,* p.193. Eric Trudgill also supports this view on English working-class prostitution: 'A perhaps more important factor than squalor and destitution was the drabness of existence of many respectable working women'; Trudgill, 'Prostitutes and Paterfamilias', in H.J. Dyos and M. Wolff (eds.) *The Victorian City,* London, 1973, p.700.

43.   S. Horan, 'More Sinned Against than Sinning? Prostitution in South Australia, 1836-1914', B.A. Honours Dissertation, Flinders University, October, 1978.

44.   Minutes of Evidence of Royal Commission into Perth City Council, pp.844-5.

45.   Interview between Raelene Davidson and Mary Scrimgeour, Perth, October 1978.

46.   Minutes of Evidence to Royal Commission into Perth City Council, pp.860-5.

47.   *Ibid.,* p.827; Interview between Raelene Davidson and Mary Scrimgeour, Perth, October, 1978.

48.   *Pocket Yearbook of Western Australia,* 1935 (Perth, 1935), p.49-51.

49.   Police vs Loubens, Kalgoorlie Police Court Minutes, 18 May 1900; Police vs Wilsman, *ibid.,* 23 February 1902; Police vs Ah Young, Perth Police Court Minutes, 29 November 1918; Police vs Rowe, *ibid.,* 9 June 1919.

50.   *W.A. Pocket Yearbook for 1902-04* (Perth, 1906), p.1074; *W.A. Pocket Yearbook for 1922* (Perth, 1922), pp.44-7. Throughout this period barmaids were paid considerably more than most other female wage-earners, i.e. up to £4/15/- per week.

51.   Such a case came before the Perth courts in 1930. *Mirror,* 19 April 1930. This girl was only 19.

52.   Police File 369/1913 bears stark testimony to the fate of one such woman in 1913.

53.   *Daily News,* 26 April 1898. See also Police File 618/1904; By this date the couple had graduated to a 2-roomed weatherboard shed which, to P.C. Touhy's mind, 'was unfit for habitation'.

54.   e.g. 'Social Evil', *Western Women,* February 1917, p.5. *West Australian Parliamentary Debates,* vol.57, p.1245.

55.   Ryley vs Ryley, Divorce Court Records of the W.A. Supreme Court, 1895.

56. C. McConville, 'Outcast Melbourne: Social Deviance in the City 1880-1914', M.A. Thesis (University of Melbourne, 1974) Chapter IV.
57. F. Finnegan, *Poverty and Prostitution,* Cambridge, 1979, p.21.
58. *W.A. Police Gazette,* 26 February 1902; Police vs Roots, Kalgoorlie Police Court Minutes, 20 June 1903; Kalgoorlie District Office Occurrence Book, 20 June 1904; Police vs Roots, Kalgoorlie Police Court Minutes, 1 October 1908.
59. 'The Social Evil', *Western Women,* February 1917. Dr Roberta Jull also put forward this notion to the 1938 Royal Commission, *op.cit.,* p.559.
60. Police records.
61. Child Welfare Department files 849/1922 and 851/1922.
62. Minutes of Evidence to Royal Commission into Perth City Council, p.836.
63. This process was described by an ex-prostitute as the way in which she and others became prostitutes during the Vietnam War of the 1960s. Interview with Raelene Davidson and ex-prostitute, Kalgoorlie, September 1978.
64. Report H.B. Dugdale, 27 July 1917, in Child Welfare Department file 851/1922.
65. Divorce Court Records of the Western Australian Supreme Court. The remaining ten cases involved women who were already prostitutes by the time they were divorced by their husbands.
66. Report of the Child Welfare Department inspector of 3 March 1922 stated that the matron was of the opinion that picture shows were the principal cause of female juvenile delinquency. C.W.D. file 851/1922.
67. Police vs Loubens, Kalgoorlie Police Court Minutes, 18 May 1900; 'Capture of Cozzi', *Sunday Times,* 24 August 1902, p.5; 'Cossi and Guidothi', *ibid.,* 14 September 1902. Police vs Wilsman, Kalgoorlie Police Court Minutes, 23 February 1902 was a similar but less sensational case.
68. Finnegan, *op.cit.,* p.33.
69. *Sunday Times,* 31 March 1907.
70. 'The Scarlet Stain', *Sun,* 6 May 1900, p.5.
71. Minutes of Evidence of Royal Commission into Perth City Council, p.835.
72. Walkowitz, *op.cit.;* Evans, *op.cit.*
73. Police Station Occurrence Books contain numerous examples of prostitutes and clients being arrested for indecent behaviour in public. These arrests detail the occupation of clients. Clients also occasionally prosecuted prostitutes for theft.
74. R.H. Underwood, *West Australian Parliamentary Debates,* vol.51, p.637.

75. Police vs Francis, Perth Police Court Minutes, 3 April 1920.

76. 'Sordid Shooting Affair' *Sunday Times,* 27 September 1908.

77. Perth Police Station Occurrence Books: 23 June 1898; 20 March 1902; 25 May 1904; 10 February 1905; 19 December 1905; 8 June 1906.

78. Note from Inspector Drewry to Commissioner of Police, 6 October 1900, Police File 3199/1900. McConville, *op.cit.,* p.185, noted a similar policy on the part of Melbourne magistrates in the nineteenth century.

79. Police vs Rowe, Perth Police Court Minutes, 9 June 1919.

80. N. Hicks, *'This Sin and Scandal' Australia's Population Debate 1891-1911,* Canberra, 1978.

81. Information from Mrs I. Jackson, a nursing sister in W.A. between the wars.

82. Police Files 377/1899; 4112/1898; Detective Office Letterbooks: 14 April 1904, 7 May 1906; Kalgoorlie Detective Office Occurrence Books: 4 November 1898; 21 February 1900; 1 October 1901; 25 August 1905; 9 November 1906; 29 May 1908; *W.A. Police Gazette:* 10 March 1906; 15 March 1908; 13 May 1909; 7 June 1913.

83. *Sunday Times,* 30 May 1909.

84. Marital status was recorded by police when making arrests.

85. Interview Raelene Davidson and Mary Scrimgeour, October 1978. Police vs de Bray, Perth Police Court Minutes, 14 July 1917.

86. Letter from S. Graham to Town Clerk, 20 July 1898, Perth City Council file H11/7/.

87. Police vs Brown, Kalgoorlie Police Court Minutes, 6 July 1900.

88. Police File 2024/1899.

89. Police File 3987/1900.

90. Verne vs de Lacourte, Kalgoorlie Police Court Minutes, 17 July 1904.

91. 'The Scarlet Stain', *Sun,* 16 October 1898.

Suggestions for further reading

Theory and general

Ardener, S. (ed.), *Perceiving women* (Dent, London, 1975). Essay by E. Ardener has useful insights about the dangers of an exclusively male perspective.

Davis, N.Z., 'Women's history in transition: the European case', *Feminist Studies,* vol. 3 (1976), pp. 83-103. A good discussion by an early modern historian about problems and pitfalls of women's history.

Rowbotham, Sheila, *Hidden from History: 300 Years of Women's Oppression and the Fight Against It* (Pluto Press, London, 1973). Polemical, but should set thoughts in train.

Women in Society. Interdisciplinary Essays. The Cambridge Women's Studies Group (Virago, London, 1981). One of the useful general collections recently published.

Medieval and early modern

Baker, Derek (ed.), *Medieval Women. Studies in Church History* (Blackwell, Oxford, 1978).

Britton, E., *The Community of the Vill* (Macmillan, Toronto, 1977). A fascinating account of the lives of medieval people.

Bullough, V., *Sex, Society and History* (Science History, New York, 1976). Medieval theory and practice as it related to women.

Clark, Alice, *Working life of women in the seventeenth century* (London, 1919). Classic, and still very useful.

Laudrie, E. Le Roy, *Montaillou. Cathars and Catholics in a French Village 1294-1324* (Trans., Penguin, 1980).

Laslett, Peter, *The World We Have Lost* (Methuen, London, 1965). Family, not woman oriented, but designed for the general reader.

The Letters of Heloise and Abelard (Penguin, Harmondsworth, 1974). A fascinating primary source.

Maclean, Ian, *The Renaissance Notion of Woman* (Cambridge University Press, Cambridge, 1980). Scholarly and thorough, although not a feminist perspective.

Power, Eileen, *Medieval Women* (Cambridge University Press, Cambridge, 1973).

Thomas, Keith, 'Women in the Civil War Sects' in T. Aston (ed.), *Crisis in Europe 1560-1660* (Routledge and Kegan Paul, London, 1965). 'The Double Standard', *Journal of History of Ideas,* XX (1959). Both these articles by Thomas are exciting and important discussions by a good social historian.

Stone, Lawrence, *The Family, Sex and Marriage in England, 1500-1800*

(London, 1977; abridged, Penguin, 1979). Useful for an overview and should provoke critical thought about the roles of women and his views of social change.

Modern: Britain and Australia

Branca, Patricia, *Silent Sisterhood: middle class women in the Victorian home* (Croon Helm, London, 1975). Useful on middle-class women, if overly optimistic about modernization.

Davidoff, L., 'Mastered for life: servant and wife in Victorian and Edwardian England', *Journal of Social History,* 7 (1974), pp.406-28.

Delamont, Sara & Duffin, Lorna (ed.), *The Nineteenth-Century Woman: Her Cultural and Physical World* (Croon Helm, London, 1978). Includes some useful essays on the relationships between feminism and medical, social, and educational ideas in the nineteenth century.

Daniels, K., Murnane, M. (ed.), *Uphill all the Way: A Documentary History of Women in Australia* (University of Queensland Press, Brisbane, 1980). Useful collection of documents.

Daniels, K., Murnane, M. and Picot, A., *Women in Australia: an Annotated Guide to the Records,* 2 vols., (Australian Government Printing Service, Canberra, 1977). An essential starting point for students of women's historical experience in Australia.

Dixson, M., *The Real Matilda: Women & Identity in Australia, 1788-1975* (Pelican, Australia, 1976). An important argument linking women's status in Australia with our colonial experience.

Evans, R.J., *The Feminists: women's emancipation movements in Europe, America, and Australasia, 1840-1920* (Croon Helm, London, 1977).

Finnegan, F., *Poverty and Prostitution: a study of Victorian Prostitutes in York* (Cambridge University Press, Cambridge, 1979). Provides a useful British comparison with Raelene Davidson's chapter.

Grellier, M., 'The family: some aspects of its demography and ideology in mid-nineteenth century Western Australia', in C.T. Stannage (ed.), *A New History of Western Australia* (University of Western Australia Press, Perth, 1981).

Grieve, N. & Grimshaw, P. (eds.), *Australian Women. Feminist Perspectives* (Oxford University Press, Melbourne, 1981).

Grimshaw, P., 'Women & the Family in Australian History — a reply to *The Real Matilda', Historial Studies,* 18, No. 72 (April, 1979), pp. 412-21. Extends the historiographical argument about woman's role and identity in the past.

Hammerton, A. James, *Emigrant Gentlewomen* (Croon Helm, London, 1979). This provides a valuable revision of the traditional stereotype of the helpless 'distressed gentlewoman', by a study of emigration of single middle-class women from Britain to Australia (1830-1914).

It analyses the attempt to provide a link between the surplus women in Victorian Britain and the surplus males in colonial Australia.

Hartman, M. & Banner, L.W. (ed.), *Clio's Consciousness Raised: New Perspectives on the History of Women,* (Harper & Row, New York, 1974). An excellent collection of essays on a range of themes.

Holcombe, Lee, *Victorian Ladies at Work: Middle Class Working Women in England and Wales, 1850-1914* (David & Charles, Newton Abbot, 1973).

Hollis, Patricia, *Women in Public: The Women's Movement 1850-1900* (Allen & Unwin, London, 1979). Provides a useful collection of primary sources with good brief introductions to each question.

Kingston, B., *My Wife, My Daughter and Poor Mary Ann: Women and Work in Australia* (Thomas Nelson, Melbourne, 1975).

Kingston, Beverly, *The World Moves Slowly: a documentary history of Australian women* (Cassell, Australia, 1977). Covers a wide range of issues with useful introductions and commentaries.

Mackinolty, J. & Radi, H. (eds.), *In Pursuit of Justice: Australian Women and the Law 1788-1979* (Hale & Iremonger, Sydney, 1979). Essential introduction to the law as it has affected women.

Richards, Eric, 'Women in the British Economy since about 1700: an Interpretation', *History,* 59 (1974), pp.337-357. A helpful introduction to a highly controversial question.

Rosen, Andrew, *Rise Up, Women! the militant campaign of the Women's Social and Political Union 1903-1914* (Routledge, London, 1974).

Strachey, Ray, *The Cause: A Short History of the Women's Movement in Great Britain* (London, 1928). An old history of the Movement from within its ranks, but remains the only comprehensive study. A narrative which avoids examining the influence of ideology.

Summers, Anne, *Damned Whores and God's Police: The Colonization of Women in Australia* (Penguin, Australia, 1975). Useful introduction to ideas about women but reservations about the categories and chronology.

Tilly, L.A. & Scott, J.W., *Women's Work and the Family* (Holt, Rinehart & Winston, New York, 1978).

Tucker, M., 'Women in Australian History', *Historical Studies,* 17, no. 68 (1977), pp. 399-407.

Vicinus, Martha (ed.), *Suffer and Be Still. Women in the Victorian Age* (Indiana, 1972; Methuen paperback, 1980).
A Widening Sphere. Changing Roles of Victorian Women (Indiana, 1977; Methuen paperback, 1980). Very useful collections on women in Victorian England. Both contain helpful bibliographies by Barbara Kanner.

Welter, B., 'The Cult of True Womanhood, 1820-1860', *American Quarterly,* 18 (1976), pp. 151-174. Useful introduction to nineteenth-century attitudes to women.

Windschuttle, E. (ed.), *Women, Class and History. Feminist Perspectives on Australia 1788-1978* (Fontana, Melbourne, 1980). Quality of the papers varies, but overall, useful.

Index

Abelard, Peter 21, 32-3.
- *see* also Heloise
abnormality 196
Aboriginal prostitution 173-4
abortion 68-9, 199
abortifacients 68-9, 95, 114-15
Acland, Sarah Angelina (Angie) 136, 137-9
Aelred of Rievaulx 27
agriculture 38-41, 50, 54
alcoholism 156-7, 180, 192-3
amenorrhoea 66, 67, 69-70, 93
- *see* also menstruation
anorexia nervosa 152
aristocratic women (medieval) 33-8
artist 147
Ashton, Charlotte 91, 94
Ashton, Marian 133
Avery, Elizabeth 76

Balfour, Alice 144-8
- brother, Arthur J. 144-8
- sister-in-law, Frances (m. Eustace) 145-7
Baxter, Margaret 71
beguine movement 31
Benedict, St of Nursia 18, 20, 21
Bernard, St of Clairvaux 13, 14, 24-26, 29
Bible 57-8, 59, 65-6, 68, 109, 110, 163
- *see* also Eve
birth control
- *see* contraception
birth intervals 52, 92-4
Blanchard, Dr 179
Blanche of Castile 34
books 71
- reading 61
- writing 71, 76-7, 160, 164
Bourke, Mary Anne 94
Boyle, Mary 72
Brittain, Vera 135
Bronte, Charlotte 134-5, 136
brothels 173-201
Brown, Rev. J. 105
Brownmillar, Susan, historian 125
Brunswick, duchess of 36

Bryce, Katherine 141-4
- Mary 141-4
- brother Annan (m. Violet) 141-3
- brother James (m. Marian) 141-3
Bussell, Frances 107
Butler, Josephine 158

Carlile, Richard 132-3
Cecil, Lady Gwendoline 159-60
- father, Marquis of Salisbury 160
celibacy 11-15, 17, 59, 158
Channel, Eleanor 79-80
Charles II 57, 79
chastity 11, 12, 17, 59, 175
Chidley, Katherine 77
child-bearing 2, 74, 92, 99
childbirth 74, 96
- concealment of 98
- *see* also infanticide
- mortality rates in (W.A.) 96-7
children 50, 62
- assaults on 124
- attitudes 10, 75, 96, 198
- wanted 43-4, 73-4
Christian church
- ideologies about women 57-60, 79, 106-7, 118; *see* also Bible, ideologies
- medieval (Roman Catholic) 10-11
- medieval Eastern (Orthodox) 11, 12
- Church of England (Protestant) 56-7
- Roman Catholicism 56, 60, 151, 183-4
- sects 58
- *see* also Protestantism, Puritans, Quakers
Christina of Markyate 15, 31-2
Church, Mary Anne 123
Cistercians 24-26,
Clare, St 30-1
Clark, Alice, historian 54
class 2, 3-4, 67-8, 172, 197
clergy, secular 12, 17, 30, 59
- clergy, regular 17, 20
- *see* also Cistercians
Clifford, Lady Anne 61

ideologies about women
- *see* Christian church
- domestic
- patriarchal
- scientific
immigration, female 103-5
- Irish 104
industrialization 4, 54, 130
infanticide 61, 69, 97-8
invalidism 144, 148, 152, 156-7

James, Alice 148-9
- brothers, Henry, William 149
Jinner, Sarah 67, 77

King, Elizabeth 139-40
- Agnes 139-40

lactation 52, 65, 68, 75, 93, 108
Ladurie, Emmanuel le Roy, historian 69
Laslett, Peter 52
legal position of women 60, 61-2, 118
- of prostitutes 173
- *see* also wives
lesbian relationships 200
literature, as a source
- Jacobean drama 78
- Victorian fiction 135
London 53
Lund, Louisa 97-8
Luther, Martin 37, 65
Lytton, Lady Constance 135, 158

magical healing 67-8
Margaret, wife of Louis IX 34
marriage 11-13, 29-30, 37, 59, 60-61, 72, 89-90, 99, 196
- ages at 50, 91-2, 132
Marshal, William 19-20, 21, 38
Martineau, Harriet 158
Marxist interpretation of work 54
Mary of Guelders 43-4
Mary, Virgin 21, 57-8
- cult of 25
maternity 74-6, 90-100, 198

- *see* also child-bearing, domestic ideology, family
McConville, C., historian 192
medical ideology about women 63-70, 73, 113-15, 132
- *see* also scientific ideology
medical, practitioners, male 64
- theories of conception 64-5, 95
medicine 29
menstruation 32, 63-70, 95, 114
- *see* also amenorrhoea, dysmenorrhoea
midwives 55, 64
Millett, Janet 104-5
Milner, Marianne 156-7
- cousin, Alfred Milner 156-7
miscarriage 95
monasticism 15-33
- *see* also nuns
morality, women's greater 102
- *see* also domestic ideology, double standard
More, Sir Thomas 59
mortality 40
- in child-birth 96
- infant 40, 99-100
- rates 51, 99-100, 131
Murray, Lady Evelyn 148, 152-6
- father, Duke of Athol 152-6
- mother, Duchess of Athol 152-6
music 155

Newnham College, Cambridge 160-63
nunneries, dissolution of 57
nuns 1-2, 14, 15-33, 151
nursing 147, 164
- *History of* 164
- unpaid 138, 140, 144

old age 197
onanism 68
opium 150-52
Osborne, Dorothy 71-2

patriarchal ideology 56-63, 175
- *see* also ideologies about women
Paul, St 13

213